Grammar *of* Biblical Hebrew

STUDIES IN BIBLICAL HEBREW

Dennis R. Magary
General Editor

Vol. 1

This book is a volume in a Peter Lang monograph series.
Every volume is peer reviewed and meets
the highest quality standards for content and production.

PETER LANG
New York • Bern • Frankfurt • Berlin
Brussels • Vienna • Oxford • Warsaw

Wolfgang Schneider

Grammar *of* Biblical Hebrew

Translated and Revised by
Randall L. McKinion

PETER LANG
New York • Bern • Frankfurt • Berlin
Brussels • Vienna • Oxford • Warsaw

Library of Congress Cataloging-in-Publication Data

Names: Schneider, Wolfgang | McKinion, Randall L., translator.
Title: Grammar of biblical Hebrew / Wolfgang Schneider;
translated and revised by Randall L. McKinion.
Other titles: Grammatik des biblischen hebräisch. English
Description: New York: Peter Lang Publishing, [2015] |
Series: Studies in biblical Hebrew, ISSN 1081-0536; volume 1 |
Includes bibliographical references and index.
Identifiers: LCCN 2015003551 | ISBN 9781433125287 (hardcover: alk. paper) |
ISBN 9781453915721 (e-book)
Subjects: LCSH: Hebrew language—Grammar.
Classification: LCC PJ4567 .S3613 2015 | DDC 492.4/5—dc23
LC record available at http://lccn.loc.gov/2015003551

Bibliographic information published by **Die Deutsche Nationalbibliothek.**
Die Deutsche Nationalbibliothek lists this publication in the "Deutsche
Nationalbibliografie"; detailed bibliographic data are available
on the Internet at http://dnb.d-nb.de/.

This book is an English version of the German original edition,
Grammatik des biblischen Hebräisch: Ein Lehrbuch by Wolfgang Schneider,
published by Claudius Verlag, Munich, Germany © 2001.

The paper in this book meets the guidelines for permanence and durability
of the Committee on Production Guidelines for Book Longevity
of the Council of Library Resources.

© 2016 Peter Lang Publishing, Inc., New York
29 Broadway, 18th floor, New York, NY 10006
www.peterlang.com

Printed in Germany

Contents

Foreword. xiii
From the Foreword to the First Edition. xv

PART I ELEMENTS
SPEAKING—WRITING—READING 01–10

01 Consonants 2
    01.1 General Comments. 2
    01.2 Writing 2
    01.3 Groups of Sounds 4
02 Vowels 5
    02.1 Existence. 5
    02.2 Vowel Changes 5
03 Vowel Signs 7
    03.1 Vowel Letters. 7
    03.2 The Tiberian Punctuation 8
04 The Schwa-Sign 12
    04.1 Signs for Half-Vowels 12
    04.2 Signs for Vowellessness 12
    04.3 Differentiation of Schwa Mobile and Schwa Quiescens 13
05 Signs of Articulation 15
    05.1 Mappíq 15
    05.2 Dagesch. 15
06 Accent Signs 17
    06.1 Méteg 17
    06.2 Maqqéf 17
    06.3 Accents 18

07 Masoretic Notes on the Text of the Bible 20
   07.1 Ketíb and Qeré 20
   07.2 Qeré perpetuum 21
   07.3 Further Notes 21
08 Character and Vocalization of Syllables 23
   08.1 Basic Rules 23
   08.2 Open Syllables. 23
   08.3 Closed Syllables. 23
   08.4 On the Right Reading of the Qamets 24
09 Gutturals and Resch. 25
   09.1 Disappearance of Vowels 25
   09.2 Doubling. 25
   09.3 End of a Syllable 26
   09.4 Further Special Features. 27
10 Accent and Vocalization in Words with Changeable Vowels. 28
   10.1 Tone Syllable and Pre-Tone Syllable. 28
   10.2 Unaccented Syllable Before the Pre-Tone Syllable 29
   10.3 Construct State 30
   10.4 Rule of Thumb 30
   10.5 Special Places of Stress. 31

PART II FORMS

PARTICLES 11–15, NOMINALS 16–23, VERBS 24–43

11 Pronouns. 34
   11.1 Overview. 34
   11.2 Personal Pronouns. 34
   11.3 Suffixes 34
   11.4 Demonstrative Pronouns. 35
   11.5 The Personal Pronoun as Demonstrative
      Pronoun 36
12 Noun Companions 38
   12.1 Article. 38
   12.2 Prepositions with Regular Suffix Forms 39
   12.3 The Prepositions כ ל ב. 40
   12.4 Particles with Irregular Suffix Forms 41
   12.5 Prepositions with Apparent Plural Forms. .43
   12.6 Compound Prepositions 43

13 Clause Introducers 44
   13.1 The Conjunction וֹ (Waw copulativum) 44
   13.2 Relative Particle שֶׁ (Schin Prefix) 44
   13.3 Interrogative Particle הֲ (He interrogativum) 45
   13.4 Interrogative Pronouns 46
14 Clause-Forming Particles 47
   14.1 Existence 47
   14.2 Overview 47
15 Overview of the Proclitic Particles 48
   15.1 Prepositions and וֹ 48
   15.2 Article and He interrogativum 48
16 Forms of the Noun 49
   16.1 State 49
   16.2 Number and Gender 50
   16.3 He Locale and Relatives 52
17 Suffixes on Nominals 54
   17.1 Suffixes on the Singular 54
   17.2 Suffixes on Dual and Plural 55
18 Nominals with Helping Vowels (Segolata) 58
   18.1 Basic Form and Helping Vowels 58
   18.2 Formation of Forms 59
   18.3 Segolata with Waw or Jod as the 2nd Radical 60
   18.4 Segolata with Waw or Jod as the 3rd Radical 61
19 Nominals with Final ä 63
20 Nominals with Double End Consonants 64
21 Nominals Formed Irregularly 65
   21.1 Relationships 65
   21.2 Man and Woman 66
   21.3 Irregular Singular Forms 66
   21.4 Apparent Dual Forms 66
   21.5 Irregular Plural Forms 67
22 Numbers 68
   22.1 Cardinal Numbers from 1 to 20 68
   22.2 Tens, Hundreds, Thousands 69
   22.3 Ordinal Numbers from 1 to 10 69
23 Settled Rules for Nominal Forms 70
   23.1 Characteristics 70
   23.2 The Vowels of the Lexical Form 70

24 Verbs: General Comments on Formation. 72
   24.1 Terms 72
   24.2 Existence of Forms 72
   24.3 Strong and Weak Verbs 74
   24.4 Ways of Citing. 74
25 The Forms of the Preformative Conjugation 75
   25.1 Use 75
   25.2 Formation 75
   25.3 The Forms in the Base Stem (Qal) .76
   25.4 Imperfect Consecutive or Narrativ. 77
26 Further Personal Forms of the Imperfect Class. 78
   26.1 Imperative. 78
   26.2 Modi. 78
27 The Forms of the Afformative Conjugation 80
   27.1 Use 80
   27.2 Formation 80
   27.3 The Forms in the Basic Stem (Qal) 80
   27.4 The Perfect Consecutive 82
28 Nominal Forms of the Verb 83
   28.1 Infinitives 83
   28.2 Participles 84
29 The Derived Stems of the Verb. 85
   29.1 Function 85
   29.2 Overview. 85
   29.3 The Names of the Stems 85
   29.4 The Meanings of the Stems 86
30 The Forms of the Nifʻal 88
   30.1 Overview. 88
   30.2 Afformative Conjugation. 88
   30.3 Preformative Conjugation 88
   30.4 Nominal Forms. 89
31 The Forms of the Doubled Stems. 90
   31.1 Overview. 90
   31.2 Common Features. 90
   31.3 Piʻel 91
   31.4 Puʻal 91
   31.5 Hithpaʻel 92
32 The Forms of the Causative Stems 93
   32.1 Overview. 93
   32.2 Hifʻil 94

32.3 Hof'al 95
32.4 Analytical Features of All the Stems 95
33 Verb Forms with Suffixes 97
33.1 Use 97
33.2 Forms 97
33.3 Suffixes on Nominal Forms 99
34 Strong Verbs with Gutturals 100
34.1 General Comments 100
34.2 Verbs with a Guttural as the 1st Radical
(Verben primae gutturalis) 100
34.3 Verbs with a Guttural as the 2nd Radical
(Verben mediae gutturalis) 101
34.4 Verbs with a Guttural as the 3rd Radical
(Verben tertiae gutturalis) 101
35 Weak Verbs with Alef as the 1st Radical (פ״א verbs) 104
35.1 Existence 104
35.2 Forms 104
36 Weak Verbs with Nun as the 1st Radical (פ״נ Verbs) 105
36.1 Forms with Assimilation 105
36.2 Tables of the Qal PC 106
36.3 Weak Imperatives and Infinitives 106
36.4 The Verbs נתן, לקח and Doubly Weak Verbs 107
37 Weak Verbs with Jod as the 1st Radical (פ״י Verbs) 109
37.1 Weak Forms with i in the Preformative (Qal Imperfect) 109
37.2 Weak Forms with e in the Preformative (Hif'il) 109
38 Weak Verbs with Original Waw as the 1st Radical (פ״ו Verbs) 110
38.1 Qal Forms—Overview 110
38.2 Qal Forms 111
38.3 Forms with o or u in the Open Preformative Syllable
(Forms of the Nif'al, Hif'il, and Hof'al) and Forms
with Sharpened Preformative Syllable 112
38.4 Verbs with Special Features 113
39 Weak Verbs with Final Vowel (ל״ה Verbs) .114
39.1 General Comments 114
39.2 Weak Forms 114
39.3 Short Forms 115
39.4 Verbs with Gutturals 116
39.5 Tabular Overview of 39.2–4 117
39.6 Verbs with Special Characteristics 118
39.7 Doubly Weak Verbs 118

40 Weak Verbs with Final Vowel (ל״א Verbs) 120
  40.1 Weak Forms 120
  40.2 Tables of the ל״א Qal Forms 121
41 Two Radical Verbs with Long Vowel (Hollow Roots or ע״ו Verbs)......122
  41.1 General Comments......................................122
  41.2 Weak Forms Without Preformative (Qal) 123
  41.3 Weak Forms with Long a in the Open Preformative
       Syllable (Qal and Hif'il PC).............................124
  41.4 Weak Forms with Long e in the Open Preformative Syllable
       (Hif'il AC)...125
  41.5 Weak Forms with Open Preformative Syllable:
       Nif'al and Hof'al 125
  41.6 Weak Forms with Strengthened Preformative Syllable
       (Nif'al PC and Aramaized Forms) 126
  41.7 Doubled Stems 126
  41.8 Verbs with Special Characteristics 127
  41.9 Verbs with Gutturals 128
42 Two Radical Verbs with Short Vowel (So-Called ע״ע Verbs)..........129
  42.1 General Comments......................................129
  42.2 Features of the Weak Forms..............................129
  42.3 Weak Forms Without a Preformative (Qal Perfect and
       Imperative/Infinitive) 130
  42.4 Weak Forms with a in the Open Preformative
       Syllable (PC Qal and Hif'il, AC Nif'al) 131
  42.5 Weak Forms with e in the Open Preformative Syllable
       (PC Qal and AC Hif'il)..................................131
  42.6 Weak Forms with u in the Open Preformative Syllable (Hof'al)....132
  42.7 Weak Forms with Strengthened Preformative Syllable
       (PC Nif'al and Aramaized Forms) 132
  42.8 Doubled Stems 132
  42.9 Verbs with Gutturals 132
43 Features for the Analysis of Weak Verb Forms 134
  43.1 Forms with Strengthened Preformative Syllable...............134
  43.2 Forms with Preformative.................................135
  43.3 Forms without Preformative 136

PART III TEXTS
CLAUSES AND PARTS OF CLAUSES 44–51,
TEXT SYNTAX 52–54

44 Types of Clauses..138
  44.1 Classification 138

44.2 The Function of the Clause Types in the Text 140
44.3 Clause Construction in the Nominal Clause (NC) 143
44.4 Clause Construction in the Compound Nominal Clause (CNC) . . 145
44.5 Clause Construction in the Verbal Clause (VC). 146
44.6 Congruence. 147
45 Nominal Groups: Construct Connections 149
45.1 Function 149
45.2 Definiteness. 149
45.3 Extensions. 150
45.4 Possibilities of Translation 151
45.5 Construct Connections with Prepositions and Clauses 153
46 Nominal Groups—Appositions 154
46.1 Function 154
46.2 Concerning Translation. 154
46.3 Adjectival Attributes 155
47 Other Nominal Groups 157
47.1 Prepositional Attributes. 157
47.2 Nominal Groups with Numerals 158
48 The Verbal Part of the Clause—Tenses. 160
48.1 Existence and Distribution of Tense Forms 160
48.2 The Tenses in Narrative Texts. 161
48.3 The Tenses in Discourse Texts 163
48.4 Tense Transitions: Narrative to Dialogue 169
48.5 Tense Transitions: Foreign Tenses in Narratives 170
48.6 Tense Transitions: Discourse Story Telling. 172
48.7 Tense Transitions: Narrative Tense in Speech Context 175
48.8 The Imperative as Tense. 176
48.9 Overview 178
49 The Verbal Part of the Clause—Verbal Nominals. 179
49.1 Participles 179
49.2 Infinitive Absolute. 180
49.3 Infinitive (Infinitivus constructus) 181
50 Extensions of the Verbal Part of the Clause 184
50.1 Objects 184
50.2 Adverbial Substantives. 186
50.3 Prepositional Additions 186
50.4 Infinitive Absolute (Infinitivus absolutus) 188
50.5 Infinitive (construct) and Finitive Forms of Relative Verbs. 190
51 Description of the Statement of Intent (Mood) 193
51.1 Strengthening 193
51.2 Negation 193

51.3 Questions 195
51.4 Wish—Intent—Request 198
52 Orientation in the Meaning Structure of Texts—References in the Text. .203
52.1 References 203
52.2 The Levels of Meaning of a Text 204
52.3 Backward (Anaphoric) Referencing Elements 206
52.4 Elements Referenced (Deictically) on the Speech Situation 210
52.5 The Article as a Referencing Sign. 213
52.6 Forward (Kataphoric) Referencing Elements 219
52.7 Analysis of a Text. 221
53 Orientation in the Meaning Structure of Texts—Organizing Particles . . .223
53.1 The Conjunction וְ (Waw copulativum) .223
53.2 The Introductory Formulas וַיְהִי and וְהָיָה. 225
53.3 The Particle כִּי 227
53.4 The Particle אֲשֶׁר 229
53.5 The Particle אִם 231
54 Orientation in the Meaning Structure of
Texts—Macrosyntactical Signals 234
54.1 Opening Signals and Transition Signals in Dialogue 234
54.2 Beginnings of Narratives 237
54.3 Transition Signals in Narratives 239
54.4 Conclusion Signals 241

Topical Index 243
Index of Hebrew Letters and Words 257
Index of Scripture Passages 267

Foreword

Hebrew is nothing special. Even though an amazing and miraculous history was told by it, Hebrew is a normal language of **normal humans**. To study and describe their grammar means to get on the trail of the regularity upon which humans have settled when they communicate with one another in their native tongue. And in Hebrew these are hardly different than in other languages.

I have studied this for many years as a Hebrew teacher, and I have tried to orient my textbook from 1973 logically with a view to this.

The morphology has thus been adjusted for only those things that serve for instructions regarding the independent shape of forms. Features of form and syntax, which help with **analysis**, stand in the foreground. Likewise, the grammar now contains more detailed tables of forms, but not for learning by heart, rather as visual aids and material for comparison. Many "exceptions" remain unmentioned or are marked (in footnotes) as rarities.

I have preserved the text-grammatical approach in the syntax. It should not fall victim to the **polemic**. On the contrary, I have only been confirmed through a serious **discussion** that started approximately 10 years after the writing of the grammar. Above all, Alviero Niccacci, as well as Ecp Talstra and members of the Societas Hebraica Amstelodamensis, have picked up and continued my proposals so that I can present this today much better, simpler, and clearer.

In principle (ignoring minor details) it was not changed in **structure** and paragraph enumeration; at the same time one can use the book in the future with the book of exercises, *Debarim*.

Mönchengladback, February 2001

From the Foreword to the First Edition

This grammar is a textbook. This does not mean that one can use it for **teaching Hebrew** continuously from § 1 to § 54 or that it should in general be regarded as the sole object of instruction. It only means, on the one hand, that the presentation strives for less than completeness, on the other hand, it is intent on the greatest possible comprehensibility and clarity. …

As a textbook, the grammar is oriented toward that which the learner brings to grammatical insight in order to be able to understand Hebrew texts. … The one who would understand a word form or a syntactical construction **in a text** asks not about the regularity of the linguistic historical development of sound. That one must know the relatively few formal and syntactical **features** which help with understanding, and he has consulted the grammar about them. In its structure, the grammar attempts to comply with this direction of question. To a large extent, linguistic historical discussions are avoided or relegated to the footnotes.

Because the goal of Hebrew instruction is not the active mastery of the Hebrew language, all rules can lapse that are necessary for a back translation from German into Hebrew, thus for all instructions concerning the independent formation of verb forms and nominal forms. For that reason, this grammar also contains no complete conjugation-tables, because the information in the text and the special tables in the individual paragraphs of the grammar are enough for the **analysis** of verb forms.

Naturally the presentation is based on reliable, detailed scientific grammar as e.g. … that of Gesenius/Kautzsch. I have gone separate ways where analogy to Latin grammar books appears to me to obscure the particular nature of Hebrew rather than to clarify it. In the syntax, I have taken up suggestions of newer **linguistics** and tried to present the Hebrew tenses according to a simple and coherent theory (§ 48) and to grasp the regularity in the constitution of texts (§§ 52 and 54).

Wuppertal, September 1973

PART I
Elements

Speaking—Writing—Reading 01-10

01 Consonants

01.1 General Comments

In principle only the consonants are written. Vowel signs have only been invented relatively late (→ § 03).

In print, above all in the Bible, the so-called **square script** is customary (→ table in § 01.2). In addition, in modern Hebrew, i.e. the "Ivrit," a **cursive script** (writing script) is also used (→ table in § 01.2).

Numerals

The use of Hebrew consonants as signs of numbers (→ table) does not occur in the text of *Biblia Hebraica*, only in the Masora (→ § 07.3). **Compound numbers** have the order hundred-tens-ones from right to left, e.g.: יא equals 11; קיא equals 111. Hundreds from 500–900 are denoted through the final consonants ך through ץ or through combination with ת, which equals 400.

In order to avoid the group of letters יה (an abbreviation of the name of God יהוה), טו (9 + 6) is written for the number 15.

01.2 Writing

Writing is done from right to left. In the square script, the individual letters are not connected. A space the size of a square letter appears between two words. There is no word division.

Summary of Consonant Signs (Alef-Bet)

Name	Square Script		Cursive	Transli-	Comments on	Number
		final		teration	Pronunciation	Value
Álef		א	ĸ	ʾ	lighter voiced beginning, as in "ʾanʾordnen," "ʾerʾerben"	1
Bet		ב	ב	b	b or v as in "bravo" (BeGaDKeFaT → § 01.3)	2
Gímel		ג	c	g	g	3
Dálet		ד	ʒ	d	d	4

Name	Square Script		Cursive	Transli-teration	Comments on Pronunciation	Number Value
		final				
He		ה	ה	h	h	5
Waw		ו	/	w	as in English: "way"; in modern Hebrew as in German: "Weg"	6
Sáyin		ז	כ	z	voiced s	7
Chet		ח	ח	ḥ	guttural sound, between h ("Hof") and ch ("ach"), today it is no different than Kaf as ch in "Koch"	8
Tet		ט	ט	ṭ	not very different than t (Taw)	9
Jod		י	'	j	j as in "ja"	10
Kaf	ך	כ	כ כ	k	k or ch as in Koch (BeGaDKeFaT → § 01.3)	20 (500)
Lámed		ל	ל	l	l	30
Mem	ם	מ	מ נ	m	m	40 (600)
Nun	ן	נ	נ נ	n	n	50 (700)
Sámech		ס	ס	s	voiceless s as in English "Sir", not very different from Sin (ś)	60
Áyin		ע	ע	ʻ	very hard throat sound, in Western languages there is no cxample (today mostly like Alef)	70
Pe	ף	פ	פ פ	p	p or f as in "Potifar" (BeGaDKeFaT → § 01.3)	80 (800)
Sadé	ץ	צ	פ 3	ṣ	as z in "Zion"	90 (900)
Qof		ק	ק	q	k	100
Resch		ר	ר	r	r	200
Sin		שׂ	ė	ś	voiceless s, = Sámech	300

Name	Square Script		Cursive	Transli-teration	Comments on Pronunciation	Number Value
		final				
Schin		שׁ	ℓ	š	sch as in "schön"	
Taw		ת	ת	t	t	400

01.3 Groups of Sounds

BeGaDKeFaT

Stops and **Fricatives** (Mnemonic Word: "BeGaDKeFaT": בְּגַדְכְּפַת):

The consonants Bet, Gímel, Dálet, Kaf, Pe and Taw are pronounced **hard** (as stops) when they carry a diacritical point (**Dagesch** → § 05.2):

תּ	פּ	כּ	דּ	גּ	בּ[1]
t	p	k	d	g	b

They are pronounced **soft** (as fricatives) when they carry **no such point**. Most of the time today, it is still common to follow this distinction only with Bet, Kaf, and Pe:

פ	כ	ב
f	ch	v

Bumaf

Labials (Mnemonic Word: "Bumaf" בּוּמַף):

פ	מ	ו	ב

Gutturals

The **guttural sounds** (gutturals[2]) have particularly special vocalization (→ § 09):

	ע	ח	ה	א
ר has some special fea-tures in common with the gutturals.	ר			

1   Tables in which the order of Hebrew linguistic signs plays a role are aligned from right to left.
2   The guttural sounds are always called "Gutturals" in this grammar, even though this is not entirely correct linguistically. Other grammars also call them "Laryngals."

02 Vowels

02.1 Existence

There are full vowels and half vowels.

Full Vowels

In masoretic Hebrew, seven **full vowels** have been distinguished. Each one has a separate sign (→ § 03.2).

short	i			ä	a	å			u
long	i		e	ä	a			o	u

å is pronounced as a short, open o as in the English: "not."

e and o are always regarded as long (→ § 03.2).

Half Vowels

Half vowels occur under changing conditions of accent.[1] In Hebrew they can appear only in a syllable before a full vowel (anacrusis/upbeat). In biblical Hebrew, two kinds of half vowels are differentiated by character:

Half vowels with German echoes to the vowels a, ä, and å (→ **Chatéf vowels** § 04)

and an entirely disappearing sound as e.g. e in English "the" (→ **Schwa** § 04).

Double Sounds

Hebrew has probably known the **double sounds** (diphthongs) **au**, **ai** and **oi**.

However, those who pointed the text have not recognized and, as a result, pointed the double sounds, so that they are always **vowel + consonant**. Thus they should be read aw, ay, oy. We follow this rule with two exceptions: aj = ai (אֲדֹנָי ᵃdonai); and we read ajw (יָו) as aw in particular suffix forms (→ § 17.2).

02.2 Vowel Changes

In general, historical-linguistic processes are not referred to for explanation in this grammar, because they are complicated and its research is not undisputed. For

---

1 Cf. e.g. in German the vowel e in the syllable "ge" in the cases of "**gé**ben" and "Ge**bét**."

particular regularity of formation of verb and noun forms, however, historical-linguistic considerations are helpful. For that reason, here some vowel changes are indicated:

From the "pre-semitic" vowels that were in existence—namely **i—a—u (short)** and **î—â—û (long)**—new vowels originate through change of sound, contraction, lengthening, and reduction.

Sound Change

Examples for **change of sound**:

â > ô		רָאשִׁים	râšim	רֹאשׁ rôš
i > ä	e.g. with gutturals	tiḥkam > täḥkam:		תֶּחְכַּם
u > å		huqṭal > håqṭal:		הָקְטַל

Contraction

Examples for **contraction**:

ay > ê	bajtu > bajt > bêt	בֵּית
aw > ô	mawtu > mawt > môt	מוֹת
iy > î	tijṭab > tîṭab	תִּיטַב
uw > û	huwšab > hûšab	הוּשַׁב

In general, vowels that are originally long are unchangeable by contraction.

Lengthening

Example for **lengthening**:

i > ê	kabid > kâbêd	כָּבֵד
a > â	jammím > jâm	יָם
u > ô	qaṭun > qâṭôn	קָטוֹן

Vowels arising through lengthening are changeable.

Reduction

Examples for **reduction**: ê > ä, â > a, ô > å. In unstressed, closed syllables a > i.

03 Vowel Signs

Various systems have been developed that also represent the vowels and therefore can fix the pronunciation of the sacred texts. The system of vowel letters is old (9th century b.c.): Individual consonant signs stand for vowels. Systems of punctuation that could determine the pronunciation precisely were invented later (5th–9th century a.d.).

03.1 Vowel Letters

Jod and Waw

The half-vowels **Jod** (י) and **Waw** (ו) as consonants can be made **silent** after vowels. They continue in Scripture, appearing now to mark the vowel standing there.

E.g.:	תיטב	*tijṭab (j is silent) →	tîṭab:	תיטב	(Jod for *i*)
	הושב	*huwšab (w is silent) →	hûšab:	הושב	(Waw for *u*)

Alef and He

The end sounds Alef (א) and He (ה) as consonants can be cancelled out and appear now to mark the **final vowel**.

Finally, vowel letters are also written in cases where no consonant was dropped.

The Individual Vowel Letters

Waw (ו) stands for the **deep** vowels o and u.	לוט	lōṭ
	רות	rūt
Jod (י) stands for the **light** vowels i, e or ä.	דויד	dawid
	היטיב	heṭib
	אלהיך	ʾᵃloḥäka
He (ה) stands in the **final sound of a word** for **all** long vowels other than i.	עשה	ʿaśa - ᶜśe - ʿośä
	פה	po

If a He (ה) at the end of the word should be pronounced as a consonant, then it has a diacritical point called a Mappíq: הּ (→ § 05.1).

Alef (א) stands in the **final sound of a syllable** for **every** long vowel.	עזרא	äz ra
	לא	lo

Technical Terms

Mater lectionis	= vowel letters (lat.: "mother of reading")
a consonant **quiesces**	= it stands for a vowel (lat.: "rests")
plene writing	= a vowel is written with a vowel letter (lat: "full")
defective writing	= a vowel is written without a vowel letter (lat: "defective")
homogeneous vowels	= vowels for which a vowel letter can stand at any time. For example, u and o are homogeneous for Waw, other vowels are not.

Vowel letters were **not** set in the consonantal text—i.e., the text which has produced the Masoretic and which they have not altered—**according to logical rules**. No distinction in articulation or meaning exists between plene and defectively written vowels. Many words are handed down both in plene writing as well as in the defective writing. This is important to know e.g. when using a **lexicon**.

03.2 The Tiberian Punctuation

From the 5ᵗʰ century a.d. on, various systems of additional signs were developed, through which was attempted the fixing of the canonical pronunciation of the biblical text. The system of the masoretic school¹ of Tiberius, which was worked out in the 8ᵗʰ through 10ᵗʰ century a.d., has clearly gained acceptance.

In the Tiberian system of punctuation, each one of the seven vowel sounds (→ § 02.1) is represented through a separate sign. But, in principle, length or brevity of the vowel has not been taken into account.

Ambiguous Qámes

The Tiberians pronounced the **long a-sound as long å** (as in Danish, "Århus").[2] Thus, they set the same sign for short and long å. In comparison in biblical studies another tradition[3] is followed that reads the same signs (Qámes: ָ see below) either as long a or as short å.

---

1 The scribes are called "Masoretes" because they protected the tradition (from Hebrew: מָסוֹרָה "tradition").
2 This "Ashkenazic" (= German) pronunciation was normal in Germany and Eastern Europe.
3 This is the Sephardic (= Spanish) pronunciation, normal in Babylon and on the Iberian peninsula and since Johannes Reuchlin (1455–1522) in European biblical research, on the basis of the pronunciation in modern Hebrew.

Overview

i	ê	ä	a	â	å	ô	u
לִ	לֵ	לֶ	לַ	לָ	לָ	לֹ	לֻ
short and long	long	short and long	short	long	short	long	short and long
Chíreq[4]	Seré	Segól	Pátach	Qámes	Qámes chatúf	Chólem	Qibbús

Seré and Chólem Long; Pátach Short

Seré and **Chólem** are regarded in the grammatical tradition as **always long**, **Pátach as short**. Even though this is doubted by some researchers, this grammar still retains that arrangement as a matter of simplicity.

Length and shortness of other vowels arises from the rules of word and syllable lengthening (→ § 08).

Other than the Chólem-point, the vowel sign stands **under** the sign of the consonant, after which the vowel is spoken.

לִ	li
לֻ	lu

Chólem stands **above** the sign of the consonant:

חֹשֶׁךְ	ḥóšäk

The Qámes-sign is inscribed inside final-kaf and final-nun:

ךָ	-ka
ןָ	-na

Pátach Furtivum [Furtive Pátach]

Only the Pátach furtivum (→ § 09.4) is spoken before the consonant under which—slightly moved—the sign stands:

מִזְבֵּחַ	miz be^aḥ

The vowel signs were also placed where a vowel letter already stood. In this case, the vowel sign stands with the consonant that precedes the vowel.

---

4   In this book, Hebrew grammatical terms are not technically written in correct transliteration, thus e.g. חִירֶק is not ḥîräq but rather "Chíreq."

Combination: Vowel Letters and Punctation

e.g.:	**plene** (with Seré magnum):	חֵיל	ḥêl
	in contrast to **defective** (with Seré parvum):	חֵל	ḥêl
Vowel *u*, combined with Waw, resulting in וּ (**Schúreq**):		מוּת	mût
The vowel letters **Alef** (א) and **Waw** (ו) draw the		צֹאן	ṣôn
Chólem-dot on themselves:		מֹות	môt
With **Sin** (שׂ) and **Schin** (שׁ) are always put in this grammar,		מֹשֶׁה	môšä
as in Biblia Hebraica, both the Chólem-dot as well		שֹׂכֹה	śôkô
as the diacritical dot of the שׁ:			
In other printings, Chólem-dot and diacritical dot can		מֹשֶׁה	
combine:		שֹׂכֹה	

Whether Alef (א), He (ה), Waw (ו), and Jod (י) are used as **consonants** or as **vowel letters** can be recognized through the **punctuation**.

Waw and Jod

ו and י are vowel letters when a homogeneous vowel precedes them and no further vowel sign (or Schwa → § 04) stands under them.

He and Alef

At the end of a word, ה is always a vowel letter when it stands without any sign (thus has also not been marked by a Mappíq as a consonant → § 05.1).

א is a vowel letter when no vowel sign or Schwa immediately follows.

Examples

סוּסִי	susi	Jod is a vowel letter.
סוּסַי	susaj	Jod is a consonant.
לַיְלָה	lajla	Jod is a consonant; He is a vowel letter.
עָוֹן	ʻawón	Waw is a consonant.[5]
עוֹד	ʻod	Waw is a vowel letter.[6]

---

5   The Chólem-dot stands as well somewhat left of the Waw.
6   The Chólem-dot stands as well above the shaft of the Waw.

מַלְכָּה	malká	He is a vowel letter.
מַלְכָּה	malkáh	He is a consonant.
סוּסֶיהָ	susäha	He is a consonant; Waw and Jod are vowel letters.
יָבֹא	jabó	Alef is a vowel letter.
יָבֹאוּ	jabó'u	Alef is a consonant; Waw a vowel letter.

04 The Schwa-Sign

04.1 Signs for Half-Vowels

Schwa Mobile

The "Schwa"[1] sign, a **double dot** under the preceding consonant sign, indicates the vowel reduced at its strongest.

e.g.:   לְ   lᵉ

In contrast to the Schwa quiescens ("silent Schwa"[2] → below § 04.2) the sign of the Schwa is called in this function Schwa mobile ("movable schwa"[3]).

In contrast to the Schwa compositum (→ below) it is called "Schwa simplex" (simple Schwa).

Chatéf Vowels

The Schwa sign, combined with a vowel sign for a, ä, or å, denotes a half vowel, which is reminiscent of German a, ä, or å. These vowels are called Chatéf vowels (→ § 9.1).

e.g.:   אֲנִי   ᵃní   Chatéf-Pátach

                  אֱלֹהִים   ᵉlohim   Chatéf-Segól

                  חֳלִי   ḥᵒlí   Chatéf-Qámes

In contrast to the simple Schwa (→ above) the signs for the Chatéf vowels are called "Schwa compositum" (composite Schwa).

04.2 Signs for Vowellessness

Schwa Quiescens

The Schwa-sign has one other function: Inside of the word, it stands with consonants where no vowel follows the consonant. The Schwa in this function is called "Schwa quiescens" (resting Schwa).

e.g.:   אַבְרָהָם   ʾab ra ham

---

1 Aramaic: שְׁוָא "nothing."
2 Hebraic: שְׁוָא נָח.
3 Hebraic: שְׁוָא נָע.

Details

Vowel letters do not receive Schwa quiescens.

At the end of a word, Schwa quiescens appears only in the **final-Kaf** ך so that it can be distinguished better from the final-Nun. When a word is closed by two consonants, both receive a Schwa (e.g.: כָּתַבְתְּ katabt), if the last of the two consonants is not an Alef (א) (e.g.: וַיִּרְא wajjar).

04.3 Differentiation of Schwa Mobile and Schwa Quiescens

In principle, the following rules, which arise from the rule of the structure of syllables (→ § 08), are valid. A Schwa is mobile:

1. at the **beginning** of the word (because every syllable begins with a consonant[4]):	יְהִי	jᵉ hí
2. the **second** of two (when two Schwas stand next to one another in the word, the second is Schwa mobile, the first quiescens):	יִרְמְיָהוּ	jir mᵉ já hu
3. with a consonant with **Dagesch**[5] (→ § 05):	עַל־פְּנֵי	'al - pᵉ né
	הַגְּדֹלִים	haggᵉ do lím
4. after a **long vowel**: With the vowels Chíreq or Qámes, a Méteg (→ § 06.1) indicates whether the vowel is long.	שֹׁמְרוֹן	šo mᵉ rón
	חָכְמָה	ḥåk má
	חָכְמָה	ḥâ kᵉ má
	יִרְאוּ	jir 'u
	יִרְאוּ	jî rᵉ 'u

In Biblia Hebraica,[6] the Méteg is not placed in every case. If it is missing, then one must know the word and its formation in order to read the Schwa correctly.[7]

---

4 Single exception: שְׁתַּיִם štajim (= two) begins with a double consonant.
5 Exceptions only at the end of words with a few verbal forms with double final syllable.
6 Actually "Biblia Hebraica" is a plural, a Greek-Latin mixture: "the Hebrew books." It has however become customary to use the title of the book as a singular.
7 In the Biblia Hebraica (BHK) published by Kittel, a missing Méteg was added by the editor and appears to the right of the vowel sign. In the Biblia Hebraica Stuttgartensia (BHS), the spelling

When (rarely) the syllable before the Schwa-sign is stressed, a Schwa quiescens can also stand after a long vowel:

לַ֫יְלָה	lªj lâ

On Méteg after a short vowel before Schwa quiescens → § 06.1.

---

of the manuscript is reproduced exactly. Therefore, it should be taken into account that now and then a Méteg drops out.

05 Signs of Articulation

05.1 Mappíq

A Mappíq (מַפִּיק "emphasizing") stands in the He (ה) at the end of a word when it should be a consonant and not a vowel letter.

05.2 Dagesch

A diacritical mark can stand in some consonants other than Alef (א), Chet (ח), Ajin (ע) and Resch (ר). It is called a **Dagesch** (דָּגֵשׁ "sharpen") and indicates a strengthening of the consonant in question. The Dagesch has **two functions**:

Dagesch Lene

Dagesch lene[1] denotes the **hard pronunciation** of the six consonants "BeGaD-KeFaT": Bet (ב), Gimel (ג), Dalet (ד), Kaf (כ), Pe (פ) and Taw (ת). These consonants have the hard pronunciation (with Dagesch lene) when no vowel or half vowel immediately precedes them.

Often after a **consonantal final syllable**, the Dagesch lene is missing in the "BeGaD-KeFaT" consonant that follows. This is explained most of the time by the supposition that the **lack of a vowel** at this place is not original; thus a vowel has fallen out.[2]

A "BeGaDKeFaT" consonant in the initial sound of a syllable has Dagesch lene after a **pause in speech** or after a consonant in final position.

A "BeGaDKeFaT" consonant at the **end of a word** has Dagesch lene when it is the second consonant of a **doubly-closed syllable** (→ § 08.3, Examples in the table for § 27.3).

Also the prepositions בְּ and כְּ **often** have a Dagesch lene when the preceding word ends in a **vowel**.

Dagesch Forte

Dagesch forte[3] indicates that a consonant is **doubled**[4]: Such a consonant **closes one syllable** and **simultaneously begins the next** (→ § 08.3). For this reason,

---

1 Hebr.: דָּגֵשׁ קַל "light Dagesch."
2 E.g. מַלְכֵי from מְלָכִים compared with מַלְכִּי → § 18.2. Many a grammar explains such a Schwa as "Schwa medium," thus, so to speak, half audible.
3 Hebr.: דָּגֵשׁ חָזָק or דָּגֵשׁ כָּבֵד "strong" or "heavy Dagesch."
4 The doubling of a consonant is also called "lengthening" or "sharpening" or "gemination."

Dagesch forte does not stand at the end of a word.[5] With "BeGaDKeFaT" consonants, both Dagesches denote the **hard pronunciation**.

Dropping Out

A Dagesch forte can **drop out** when the consonant in which it should stand does not belong to the group "BeGaDKeFaT" and has with it a **Schwa**.

Euphonicum

Dagesch forte can be placed for grammatical reasons (lat.: necessarium "necessary") or **for tone reasons** (lat.: euphonicum "melodious"). Fairly frequent is the Dagesch forte **coniunctivum**[6] (lat.: "conjunctive"), which stands in the first vowel of the following word after final a or ä, occasionally also after u, in order to draw the two words closely together for tone.

Dagesch forte and Dagesch lene are for this reason easy to distinguish, in that a consonant with **Dagesch forte** must **always precede a vowel**.

For that reason one cannot confuse e.g. a Waw with a Dagesch forte (וּ) with the vowel sign Schureq (וּ): e.g. עִוֵּר ʾiwwer, עוּר ʿur.

Rafé

The Rafé (רָפֶה "soft"), a horizontal stroke above the consonant, which denotes in contrast to the Dagesch the **soft pronunciation** of the "BeGaDKeFaT," **does not occur** in the newer editions of the text of Biblia Hebraica.

5　Two exceptions: אַתְּ "you" (f) → § 11.1 and נָתַתְּ "you (f) have given" → § 36.4.
6　Examples of a Dagesch forte coniunctivum are in § 51.4, text example j: לֵאמֹר אֶל־מֹשֶׁה.

06 Accent Signs

06.1 Méteg

Words of three or more syllables frequently have a **secondary tone syllable**, which can be marked by a Méteg (מֶתֶג "bridle").

Méteg is a short, vertical stroke under the consonant that begins the secondary tone syllable. If a **vowel sign** stands there, then a Méteg stands to the **left** of it.

In the manuscript to which Biblia Hebraica returns, **no consistent rule** is used for the placing of a Méteg. In general, accented and unaccented syllables alternate.

A Méteg, which stands in an open syllable with long vowel before **Schwa mobile**, often helps to distinguish between a long Qámes (â) and Qámes chatuf (å).

Méteg after a Short Vowel

However, a Méteg can also stand reversed next to a short vowel before **Schwa quiescens**.

Examples:			
	a)	הַמְדַבְּרִים	hàm dab bᵉ rím
	b)	וַיְהִי־אֹור	wàj hi - 'ór
	c)	הַלְלוּ יָהּ	hàl lu jáh
	d)	יִהְיֶה	jìh jä

Examples a) through c) show syllables that should have been sharpened, in which however the Dagesch forte (→ § 5.2) has dropped out.

a)   Article הַ with following Dagesch forte (→ § 12.1),
b)   Tense-sign וַ with following Dagesch forte (→ § 25.4),
c)   Pi'el with Dagesch forte in the 2nd radical (→ § 31.2).
d)   In some **verb forms** of היה and היח (→ § 39.6), a Méteg stands in the closed preformative syllable.

06.2 Maqqéf

Connector

Through the Maqqéf (מַקֵּף "connector"), a horizontal stroke on the upper line of writing, two words are put together for a **single accent**.

Maqqéf frequently stands with a monosyllabic particle, e.g.: עַל־הָאָרֶץ,

often also between sections of a **construct connection**, e.g.: בֶּן־אָדָם.

De-Accented

The syllable before the Maqqéf **loses its accent** and changeable long vowels in closed syllables are often **shortened**. If the vowel before the Maqqéf should remain long, it receives a **secondary stress** through a Méteg or through a weak accent.

06.3 Accents

Functions

The Masoretes have provided **every word** in the biblical text with an accent.[1] These signs have **three functions**: They serve as a kind of note for the liturgical recitation, they give clues for the **structuring of the Bible verses**, and (most of the time) they indicate the **primary stressed syllable** of a word. Only words that are de-accented through a Maqqéf have no accent.

Position

The accent generally stands above or below the **consonant** that **begins** the stressed **syllable**. Underneath the consonant, the accents stand to the left of a possible **vowel sign**, while above they stand to the right of a possible **Chólem dot**.

A few accents always stand at the beginning of a word ("prepositive"), some always at the end ("postpositive"), thus not denoting the **tone syllable**.

Structure

Instead of **punctuation**, disjunctive ("domini" or "distinctivi") and conjunctive ("servi" or "conjunctivi") accents serve to **structure** the verse.

Disjunctive accents mark first the end of the verse, then the middle of the verse and then always divide further the individual parts of the verse.

In contrast, words that belong closely together inside of the parts of the verse are connected through **conjunctive** accents.

Two Systems

In the Hebrew Bible, we find **two** different **systems of accents**: the **poetic** system in the books of Psalms, Job, and Proverbs (Sayings) and the **prose** system for the

---

1   The sign ό, which is used in this grammar as a sign for the stress, is not a masoretic accent.

other books. A summary of all accents is enclosed with Biblia Hebraica. Here should only be pointed out some important signs.

Disjunctive

The important **disjunctive** accents of the prose systems:

	e.g.
Sillúq (סִלּוּק) stands before the **end of the verse** (sof pasúq סוֹף פָּסוּק), which is denoted on its part by a thick double dot.	דָּבָר׃
Athnách (אַתְנָח) divides the verse in half.	דָּבָר
Zaqéf qatón (זָקֵף קָטֹן) often indicates the quarter of the verse.	דָּבָּר
Paštá (פַּשְׁטָה), a postpositive, has before itself a "twin" on the tone syllable, when the word is accented on the next-to-last syllable.	מֶלֶךְ

Conjunctive

The important conjunctive accents of both systems:

Munách (מוּנָח) often stands in construct chains.	דָּבָר
Mehuppák (מְהֻפָּךְ)	דָּבָר
Meraká (מֵירְכָא)	דָּבָר

Citations

When one cites parts of Bible verses, the half of the verse before the Atnách is denoted with "a," the part after the Atnách with "b." The quarters are called "α" and "β." For example, "Gen 1:2bβ" denotes the part of the verse from the last Zaqéf qatón up to the Sof pasúq: מְרַחֶפֶת עַל־פְּנֵי הַמָּיִם׃.

One other possibility is to count the individual clauses of a verse with "a, b, c" etc.; then the clause example above would only be a part of the clause "Gen 1:2c."

07 Masoretic Notes on the Text of the Bible

07.1 Ketíb and Qeré

Variants

In a great deal of places, the ancient scribes, the Soferim (סֹפְרִים "writers," actually "numbers"), who took care of a unified consonantal text until a.d. 100, already proposed some **other variants** alongside the consonantal text fixed by them. There they distinguished the "written" (Aramaic כְּתִיב) from the "read" (Aramaic קְרֵי), which they themselves proposed. In the course of time, the number of such places grew to 1,314.

The Masoretes, who arranged the pronunciation of the biblical text in the 8ᵗʰ–10ᵗʰ centuries a.d., received the traditional changes, consciously placed the different variants as a choice, and noted them **in the margin** (Masora, → § 07.3). They did not intervene in the canonical consonantal text.

In the masoretic text, as it stands today in Biblia Hebraica, we find in the current text the **consonants of the "Ketib"** (thus the variant rejected by the Masoretes) with the **vowels of the "Qeré"** (thus the variant proposed by the Masoretes). A small circle over the word refers to the marginal note.

Marginal Notes

The consonants of the Qeré stand in the margin, beside the indication קרי or ק.

e.g.: (Genesis 39:20)

מְקוֹם אֲשֶׁר־אֲסוֹרֵי הַמֶּלֶךְ אֲסוּרִים	אסירי ק

This means: Qeré demands אֲסִירֵי (ᵃsiré) instead of the Ketíb אֲסוּרֵי (ᵃsuré).

Where a word that is **not in the text** should be read, only the vowel signs are found along with the consonants in the margin with the note: כתיב ולא קרי (Aramaic: qeré welâ ketib): "to be read, although not written."

Where a word that is in the text should **not** be **read**, it appears unpunctuated, and in the margin appears only the note: קרי ולא כתיב (ketib welâ qeré): "written, but not to be read."

07.2 Qeré perpetuum

Permanent Qeré

With some words that appear frequently and that should **always** be read **differently**, the Masoretes have put the vowel sign of the Qeré for the Ketib, but have **not noted** the Qeré **in the margin** (Qeré perpetuum, "permanent" Qeré).

The Name of God

The name of God (probably "**Yahweh**": יַהְוֶה) was avoided, and אֲדֹנָי ("**Adonai**" = "Lord") was read in its place.[1] This reading is regarded as a Qeré perpetuum. The Ketib יהוה[2] received the vowel signs of אֲדֹנָי, somewhat simplified, and thus יְהֹוָה[3] stands in the text. In the Biblia Hebraica since the 3rd edition most of the time יְהוָה appears. When the name of God יהוה stands beside the word אֲדֹנָי, it is vocalized according to the Qeré אֱלֹהִים, i.e., אֲדֹנָי יְהוִה.[4]

There is also acceptance of the Qeré for יהוה being vocalized according to the Aramaic word שְׁמָא "**the name**," and one reads Hebrew הַשֵּׁם, which in German is "der Name."

The other three cases of Qeré perpetuum are:

a) הוּא (Qeré הִיא) for the feminine instead of the masculine pronoun of the 3rd person, singular: הוּא in the 5 books of Moses (Pentateuch),
b) יְרוּשָׁלַם (Qeré יְרוּשָׁלַיִם: **Jeruschalayim**) for the name יְרוּשָׁלֵם Jerusalem,
c) יִשָּׂשכָר (Qeré יִשָּׂכָר) for the name **Jissachar**.

07.3 Further Notes

Of all the masoretic notes that appear in Biblial Hebraica, only the most important are mentioned here:[5]

---

1 Long Qámes distinguishes this form from אֲדֹנִי "my Lord." In older editions of the Luther translation, "der HErr" appeared.
2 The mark יהוה is also called the "Tetragramm" (four-letters).
3 Since the Middle Ages, the Ketib has been read falsely with the vowels of the Qeré (in ignorance of the facts) as "Jehovah."
4 Luther Bible: "der Herr HErr."
5 For details, thorough presentations can be be compared, e.g. E. Würthwein, *Der Text des Alten Testaments, Eine Einführung in die Biblia Hebraica*, Stuttgart 1988, 5th Edition, or: E. Tov, *Der Text der Hebräischen Bibel. Handbuch der Textkritik*, Stuttgart/Berlin/Köln 1997.

Deletion Dots

Deletion dots (puncta extraordinaria) stand above some words, e.g. in Gen 33:4: וַיִּשָּׁקֵהוּ ("and he kissed him"), which the Soferim would have known already as deleted and which also the Greek translators (Septuagint) have **not read** here.

Masora

The Masora consists of detailed **marginal notes** that are published only in part in Biblia Hebraica. There the Masoretes have given information about the frequency of words or groups of words. This information is cited in part in **Aramaic and most of the time is abbreviated**.

Sections

Section points in the text are marked through gaps and standing in them ס (סְתוּמָה "closed") or פ (פְּתוּחָה "open").

Large ס (סֵדֶר "**Seder**") or פרש (פָּרָשׁ "**Parasch**") in the margin denotes sections for liturgical reading.

08 Character and Vocalization of Syllables

08.1 Basic Rules

Every syllable begins with **a single consonant**. There is no syllable beginning with a vowel,[1] in the same way that two consonants are not at the beginning of a syllable.[2]

Two vowels do **not** stand immediately next to one another inside of a syllable.[3]

08.2 Open Syllables

Open syllables **end with a vowel**. With this counts also the syllable where a vowel letter stands at the end, e.g.: לֹא or בָּרָא.

Long Vowel

As a rule, open syllables have a **long vowel**, e.g.: תֹהוּ וָבֹהוּ. The large number of open syllables with short vowels are almost always **originally closed syllables** that have only been opened secondarily and at the same time have kept their short vowel (→ e.g. § 06.1, § 09: Virtual Doubling and Broken Syllables, § 18: Segolates).

Open syllables with a half vowel (Schwa mobile or Chatéf-vowel) are **suggestive syllables**.

08.3 Closed Syllables

Closed syllables **end** with an **audible consonant**.

Short Vowel

Unaccented, closed syllables have a **short** vowel. Most of the time, accented, closed syllables have a long vowel, rarely a short vowel.

e.g.:   מַלְאָךְ   st.c. מַלְאַךְ

---

1   A single exception: The conjunction וּ in the form וּ (→ § 13.1).
2   A single exception: The numeral for "two": שְׁתַּיִם štájim.
3   Pátach furtivum (§ 09.4) is the only apparent exception.

Doubly Closed Syllables

Doubly closed syllables, which thus end with **two consonants** (→ § 04.2), are rare and appear almost exclusively at the end of some verb forms.

Sharpened Syllables

Closed syllables, which close with **the same consonant** with which the following syllable begins (→ above § 05.2 Dagesch forte), are also called **sharpened** syllables.

08.4 On the Right Reading of the Qamets

Qámes denotes long â in open or in accented, closed syllables.

Qámes denotes **short å** (Qámes chatúf) in **unaccented, closed** syllables.

e.g.:

חָכָם	ḥâkâm
חָכְמָה	ḥåkmâ

09 Gutturals and Resch

The gutturals—Alef (א), He (ה), Chet (ח) and Ajin (ע)—were hardly still pronounced as guttural sounds at the time of the Masoretes. The Masoretes have tried to preserve them as consonants and for that reason used special rules of vocalization with them and in part also with Resch (ר).

09.1 Disappearance of Vowels

Chatéf Vowels

With gutturals, the **Chatéf vowels** stand instead of Schwa mobile:

e.g.

אֲנִי	אֱלֹהִים	חֳלִי
ʾªni	ʾªlohim	hªli

09.2 Doubling

Gutturals and Resch have **no Dagesch forte.**[1] Instead of doubling, **compensatory lengthening** or **virtual doubling** occurs.

Compensatory Lengthening

"Compensatory lengthening" means: The original short vowel turns into an open syllable before the guttural and is lengthened.[2] In the process it is **i to ê, a to â, and u to ô.**

e.g. (→ § 34.3) normal:

with guttural (Resch)

יְכָתַב	יְכָתֵּב	כָּתַב
יְבֹרַךְ	יְבָרֵךְ	בֵּרַךְ

Virtual Doubling

"Virtual doubling"[3] means: The short vowel is preserved before the guttural, although it stands now in (seemingly) an open syllable. The syllable is so formed **as if** the guttural were **doubled.**[4]

---

1   Leaving aside very few exceptions, e.g. Hab 3:13: ראֹשׁ.
2   Compensatory lengthening almost always occurs with ר and א, frequently with ע, rarely with ה and ח.
3   Virtual doubling occurs mainly with ה and ח, rarely with ע, hardly with א and ר.
4   One speaks also of a "Dagesch forte implicitum."

e.g. (→ § 34.3):

יִכָּתֵב	יְכֻתַּב	כֻּתַּב
יִנָּחֵל	יְנֻחַל	נֻחַל

09.3 End of a Syllable

Broken Syllables

Gutturals can close a syllable, thus have with them a Schwa quiescens. Often however this "**hard syllable ending**" is avoided: the syllable is "**broken open.**" In particular, the short vowel of the closed syllable is **repeated** after the guttural **as a Chatéf vowel**. A Méteg can stand with the first vowel in the broken syllable.

e.g. (→ § 34.2):

	hard closed syllable	broken syllable
	יַעְבֹד	יַעֲבֹד
	יֶחְזַק	יֶחֱזַק
	יַעְבָד	יַעֲבָד

If in a corresponding removal of the tone syllable (→ § 10.2) the vowel that follows a broken syllable **disappears**, then the guttural begins an unaccented, closed syllable with short, **full** vowel **instead of** the Chatéf vowel.

יַעַבְדוּ	←	יַעֲבְדוּ*	←	יַעֲבֹד
יַעַבְדוּ⁵	←	יַעֲבְדוּ*	←	יַעֲבָד

Prefix Before Chatéf

When one of the **prepositions** בְּ, כְּ, and לְ or the conjunction וּ stands before a word what begins with a Chatéf vowel, then an **open** syllable is always vocalized instead of a closed syllable. The short vowel with the prefix has the tone quality of the Chatéf vowel (→ §§ 12.3 and 15.1).

לַאֲנָשִׁים	<	לְ	+	אֲנָשִׁים
בֶּאֱמֶת	<	בְּ	+	אֱמֶת

---

5   Here two Qámes chatuf stand next to one another.

09.4 Further Special Features

For the most part, the vowel **a** stands with gutturals; with Alef (**א**) often **ä**.

Pátach furtivum

At the **end** of a word, a guttural (He with Mappíq, Ḥet and Ajin) must be **preceded** by an **a-sound**. Any other vowel is **replaced** by a; or there is inserted after it a quick, unaccented a-sound, which one calls "**Pátach furtivum**."[6] It is denoted by a Pátach written a little to the right under the guttural, but pronounced before it.

e.g.

ruᵃḥ	רוּחַ

---

6   Lat.: "surreptitious [or furtive] Pátach".

10 Accent and Vocalization in Words with Changeable Vowels

The long vowels â, ê, and ô can be changeable. When they have been lengthened from the short vowels a, i, or u, the lengthening or even the entire vowel also falls out again under particular conditions of accent.

10.1 Tone Syllable and Pre-Tone Syllable

Tone Syllable

The **changeable long vowels** â, ê, and ô, which are lengthened from a, i, and u, stand in the **tone syllable**. Most of the time, the tone syllable is the last syllable of a word.[1]

a		e		o	
Primary stress		Primary stress		Primary stress	
בָר	דָ	< dabar	קֵן	זָ	< zaqin	טל	תְק	< taqtul
דָם		< dam	שֵׁם		< šim			

Pre-Tone Syllable

The variable vowels can also stand in the **pre-tone syllable**. The pre-tone syllable is the open syllable **before the tone syllable**. A variably longer vowel in the syllable before the stress is called a **pre-tone-vowel**.

Tone	Pre-Tone	Tone	Pre-Tone	Tone	Pre-Tone
בָר	דָ	בָב	לְ	לוֹן	טְ	תְק
מִים	דָ					

Instead of long ê and long ô, a **Schwa** often already stands in the pre-tone syllable.

מוֹ	שְׁ		לוֹ	טְ	תֶק

---

1   On conditions of stress in words with helping vowels (segolates) → § 18.

10.2 Unaccented Syllable Before the Pre-Tone Syllable

Antepenultimate Syllable

In principle, **changeable** long vowels do **not** stand in antepenultimate positions, thus in syllables that are separated from the tone syllable by a full syllable.[2]

Schwa or Short Vowel

The antepenultimate syllable is a **suggestive syllable** with Schwa (e.g. דְּ/בָ/רִים), when it is formed from *one* consonant, with which a variable vowel stands in other forms of the same word (e.g. דְּ/בָר).

The antepenultimate syllable is an **unaccented closed syllable** with a short vowel, when it is formed from *two* consonants (e.g. דִּבְ/רֵי/הֶם). **Most of the time**, the short vowel is an *i* (from time to time, before some with gutturals, also ä or a).

The unaccented closed syllable in the antepenultimate place can also be formed by the first consonant of a word plus a proclitic **preposition** (לְדְ/בָ/רִים → § 12.3).

Syllable before the Antepenultimate Syllable

Before such an unaccented closed syllable can appear in the fourth-to-last place either a leading-in syllable or a full syllable.

(a)			(e)		
Primary Stress	Pre-stress	Antepenultimate Syllable	Primary Stress	Pre-stress	Antepenultimate Syllable
רִים	בָ	דְ	בוֹ	בָ	לְ
הֶם	רֵי	דְּבַ			
רִים	בָ	לְדְ	בוֹ	בָ	בְּל
הֶם	רֵי	לְדְּבַ			
			דְּ	שְׁמָ	

---

2 As an exception with verb forms and before the suffix ךָ, the long vowel can be withheld in the antepenultimate syllable through a secondary stress (Méteg) (→ § 27.3).

Words **with long ê** often already have in the syllable before the primary stressed syllable—thus instead of a pre-stressed syllable—an unaccented closed syllable with a short vowel.

10.3 Construct State

No Primary Stress

When a word stands in the construct state, its **tone syllable** is **not** regarded as a **primary stress**. The long vowel â in the tone syllable of a nominal in the construct state can be shortened to a; ê can be ablauted to a.

The syllable before the tone syllable with a nominal in the construct state can **not** be a **pre-tone syllable**. In it, the variably long vowels do not stand. Rather, the penultimate syllable is thus formed **as the antepenultimate one** in other words.

st abs	st c		st abs	st c	
Primary Stress		antepenultimate syllable	Primary Stress		antepenultimate syllable
הַבְּרִית	דַם		הַבַּיִת	קַן	זִ
דָּוִד	בַּר	דְּ	הָאִישׁ	בַב	לְ
דָּוִד	רֵי	דְּבַ			

10.4 Rule of Thumb

Further-Moved Stress

The lexical form of a word is taken as the starting point; then one imagines thus the occurrence of the building of the form, as would be the word in a steady process of growth always for some time, and with this would move the **place of accent** always **further away from the beginning of the word** (what is actually not even the case). Then one can also express this as follows:

The long vowel in the pre-tone syllable has **disappeared with the further moving of the accent.**

דָּבָר ⟶ ׀ דְּבָרִים

Two Leading-In Syllables

When in the progress of this process two Schwas meet at the beginning of a word, the **vowel with the second consonant** is thus **cancelled out**, and further

the original **short vowel** occurs with the **first** consonant, most of the time reduced to i:

דְּבָרִים ← *דִּבְרֵיהֶם ← דִּבְרֵיהֶם

In a **construct chain**, the nominal in the absolute state carries the primary stress,
and the preceding one goes accordingly:

דָּבָר ← דְּבַר דָּוִד
דְּבָרִים ← דִּבְרֵי דָּוִד

Most of the time, original **short a** is **reduced** in an unaccented, closed syllable **to i**.

10.5 Special Places of Stress

Pause

In pause[3]—i.e., at a place with a particularly **strong accented clause**—accent and
vocalization frequently deviate from the norm. Pause forms are found regularly
before the **Sof pasúq** and with the **Atnách**, often also with other strong accent
divisions (→ 06.3).

The vowel of the tone syllable can be **lengthened** in pause.

Instead of the last syllable, the next-to-last syllable can be **accented** and have a
long vowel.

Instead of other vowels, **often long a** appears in pause; also short a appears instead
of e.

Maqqéf-Connection

In closed syllables, which are de-accented through a Maqqéf (→ § 06.2), generally
the corresponding **short vowels** stand instead of the variably long vowels:

for ê: ä,
for â: a,
for ô: å.

Nesiga

So that two primary-stressed syllables do not push on one another, the **stress** can
be **withdrawn** from the final syllable of the preceding word. This occurrence is

---

3   Abbreviated: "i.P."—opposite: "in context"—"i.C."

called "Nesiga."[4] For example, instead of נָתַן לוֹ stands נָֽתַן לוֹ. In the closed, unaccented final syllable that results, the shortened vowel stands instead of the variably long vowel,

e.g.: לָתֵת לִי « לָֽתֶת לִי.

PART II

Forms

Particles 11-15

Nominals 16-23

Verbs 24-43

11 Pronouns

11.1 Overview

	Singular			Plural	
	Pronoun	Suffix		Pronoun	Suffix
1st—"I"	אֲנִי or אָנֹכִי	◌ִי [נִי]	1st—"we"	אֲנַחְנוּ[1]	נוּ
2nd—"you" (m)	אַתָּה	ךָ	2nd—"you" (m)	אַתֶּם	כֶם
2nd—"you" (f)	אַתְּ[2]	ךְ	2nd—"you" (f)	אַתֵּן[3]	כֶן
3rd—"he"	הוּא	הוּ [וֹ, ו]	3rd—"they" (m)	הֵם or הֵמָּה	הֶם [ם]
3rd—"she"	הִיא	הָ [◌ָה]	3rd—"they" (f)	הֵם or הֵנָּה	הֶן [ן]

11.2 Personal Pronouns

Most of the time, the individual personal pronoun appears as the subject or in apposition to the subject (details → §§ 44, 47 and 52).

The pronoun of the 1st person has one common form for both genders. Forms are different in the 2nd and 3rd person masculine and feminine. There is not a neuter form. In cases where we would put a neuter in German, a feminine form is often used (→ § 11.4).

11.3 Suffixes

Suffixes are personal pronouns that have been connected to form an ending with the preceding word. They appear on particles, nouns, and verbs. (Forms → § 11.1)

Forms

The forms of suffixes are basically always the same. However, in cases of additions on particles, nominals, and verbs, some distinctive features arise → §§ 12.1–12.5, § 14.2, § 17 and § 33.

---

1   Or—only 6 times—also נַחְנוּ.
2   The form originally was read אַתִּי.
3   Only once as אַתֶּן and 4x as אַתֵּנָה.

Use: Nouns

Suffixes on nouns indicate possession (German: possessive pronoun "mein/dein" etc.) → § 17.

סוּס	horse
סוּסִי	my horse

Use: Verbs

Suffixes on verb forms (→ § 33) and on the sign of the accusative אֵת (→ §§ 12.4; 50.1) indicate the (accusative) object.

וַיִּקְרָא	then he called
וַיִּקְרָאֵהוּ	then he called him
or: וַיִּקְרָא אֹתוֹ	

Translation

Hebrew prepositions with suffixes correspond to German prepositions with case forms of the personal pronoun or reflexive pronouns (für mich/bei mir/mit sich).

לָהֶם	for them
בָּהֶם	in/with them

11.4 Demonstrative Pronouns

Forms

The demonstrative pronoun זֶה (or זֹאת and אֵלֶּה) is deictic,[4] which means that it refers to the speech situation ("this/these here present").

Singular		Plural	
זֶה	this here (m)	אֵלֶּה	these (m. or f.)
זֹאת	this (f)		

---

4 "Deictic" from Greek: δείκνυμι (point) = reference to the speech situation → § 52.

Adjectival

The pronoun זֶה can stand as an adjectival attribute: In this case it follows the word referred to and receives the article (→ § 46.3).

הָאִישׁ הַזֶּה	this man	הַדְּבָרִים הָאֵלֶּה	these things/words
הָאִשָּׁה הַזֹּאת	this woman		

After Construct State

The substantive pronoun זֶה can stand after a nominal in the construct state.

Accusative and after a Preposition

It appears after the sign of the accusative זֶה and after a preposition.

דְּבַר זֶה	the word of this (one)
וַיַּרְא אֶת־זֶה	he saw this
וַיְהִי בָזֹאת קֶצֶף עַל־יִשְׂרָאֵל (1Chr 27:24)	As a result (= durch dies[5] [on account of this]), there was an anger over Israel.

On זֶה in the interrogative clause → §§ 51.3 and 52.4.

11.5 The Personal Pronoun as Demonstrative Pronoun

As a demonstrative pronoun הוּא (הִיא/etc) refers inside of the text ("this/those/ the aforementioned").[6]

Substantively

It can be used substantively and, in that case, is the subject of a nominal clause most of the time (→ §§ 44.3 and 52.3).

	Singular	Plural	
הוּא	that one [jener[7]]/ the one (from which the speech came)	הֵם/הֵמָּה	those
הִיא	that one/the same		

---

5   Feminine for neuter (→ above § 11.2).
6   Technical term: "anaphoric" from Greek: αναφερειν "take up" → § 52.
7   The translation "jener" is used here only to contrast it from the translation "dieser" for זֶה. In terms of the text, the right German translation of the pronoun depends on the context (in detail in § 52); "jener" is hardly common in German.

Adjectivally

Adjectivally the pronoun can follow a word. In that case, it receives the article
(→ § 46.3).

Singular		Plural	
הָאִישׁ הַהוּא	that man	הַדְּבָרִים הָהֵמָּה	those things/words
הָאִשָּׁה הַהִיא	that woman		

12 Noun Companions

12.1 Article

*The article is **proclitic**: It connects with the following word to form a unit.*[1]

Normal Form

The normal form of the article is: He with Patach and following **Dagesch forte**: ⊙ הַ.

הַשָּׁמַיִם

With words that begin with the prefix יְ or מְ, most of the time the Dagesch forte is missing in the first consonant (→ § 5.2).

הַיְלָדִים

Before Gutturals

If the word begins with a **guttural** or **Resch**, compensatory lengthening (to הָ or הֶ) or virtual doubling (to הַ) occurs instead of doubling the first consonant (→ § 9).

הָ:

Compensatory lengthening before Resch (ר) and Alef (א) and most of the time before ʿAjin (ע).

הָרְקִיעַ
הָאָדָם
הָעֶרֶב

הֶ:

Compensatory lengthening before ʿAjin (ע) and He (ה) with unstressed *a* and before Chet (ח) with Qámes or Chatéf-Qámes.

הֶעָרִים
הֶהָמוֹן
הֶחָזָק

הַ:

Virtual doubling before He (ה)[2] and Chet (ח).

הַהוּא
הַחֹשֶׁךְ

Theoretically, He (ה) before a word at the beginning of a clause can also be He interrogativum (**interrogative particle** → § 13.3). In practice, however, no confusion is likely.

---

1   On the combination of the article with other prefixes → §§ 12.3 and 13.1.
2   Exceptions: הָהָר "the mountain/hill" and הָהֵמָּה "those."

Prepositions—Overview of 12.2 and 12.3

	נֶֽגֶד	אַחֲרֵי	בֵּין	בְּ	לְ	כְּ
Singular						
1st	נֶגְדִּי	אַחֲרַי	בֵּינִי	בִּי	לִי	כָּמֹונִי
2nd m.	נֶגְדְּךָ	אַחֲרֶ֫יךָ	בֵּינְךָ	בְּךָ	לְךָ	כָּמֹוךָ
			(i.P. בֵּינֶ֫ךָ)	(i.P. בָּךְ)	(i.P. לָךְ)	
2nd f.	–	אַחֲרַ֫יִךְ	בֵּינֵךְ	בָּךְ	לָךְ	–
3rd m.	נֶגְדֹּו	אַחֲרָיו	בֵּינֹו בֵּינָיו	בֹּו	לֹו	כָּמֹוהוּ
3rd f.	נֶגְדָּהּ	אַחֲרֶ֫יהָ	–	בָּהּ	לָהּ	כָּמֹוהָ
Plural						
1st	–	אַחֲרֵ֫ינוּ	בֵּינֵ֫ינוּ בֵּינֹותֵ֫ינוּ	בָּ֫נוּ	לָ֫נוּ	כָּמֹונוּ
2nd m.	נֶגְדְּכֶם	אַחֲרֵיכֶם	בֵּינֵיכֶם	בָּכֶם	לָכֶם	כָּכֶם כְּמֹוכֶם
2nd f.	–	–	–	בָּכֵן	–	–
3rd m.	נֶגְדָּם	אַחֲרֵיהֶם	בֵּינֵיהֶם	בָּהֵ֫מָּה	לָהֵ֫מָּה	כָּהֵ֫מָּה
3rd f.	–	אַחֲרֵיהֶן	בֵּינֹתָם	בָּהֶם בָּם בָּהֵ֫נָּה בָּהֵן	לָהֶם לָהֵ֫נָּה לָהֵן	כָּהֶם כְּמֹוהֶם כָּהֵ֫נָּה

12.2 Prepositions with Regular Suffix Forms

Many prepositions are **originally nominals** and form their suffix forms regularly according to the pattern of the **nominal** in the singular or in the plural (→ §§ 17 and 18).

Singular Forms

The following examples have singular forms:

נֶ֫גֶד	"before/opposite,"
בְּעַד	"for, through,"
לְמַ֫עַן	"for the sake of."

Plural Forms

The following examples have plural forms:

אַחַר   "behind": אַחֲרֵי,

סָבִיב   "all about": סְבִיבוֹת,

תַּחַת   "under/instead of."

בֵּין "space/between" sometimes has singular forms, sometimes plural forms, in particular in addition to בֵּינֵי also בֵּינוֹת.

See above for a series of forms.

12.3 The Prepositions בּ ל כּ

Connection with the Following Word

בּ (preposition of contact: "in/on/by/with"), ל (preposition of unspecified attention: "to/for/concerning"), and כּ (preposition of comparison: "as/in accordance with/accordingly") are **proclitic** particles. They connect with the following word to form a unit.

Normal form: upbeat syllable with **Schwa mobile:**	יִשְׂרָאֵל	+	ב	> בְּיִשְׂרָאֵל
Before a word that begins with Schwa mobile, these prepositions have a short i: the **Schwa is quiescent** (→ §§ 10.2, 10.4):	דְּבָרִים	+	ל	> לִדְבָרִים
Before a nominal with an article, the preposition has the **vocalization of the article** (with or without following Dagesch forte → § 12.1). The He (ה) of the article drops out.	הַשָּׁמַיִם	+	ב	> בַּשָּׁמַיִם
	הַחֹשֶׁךְ	+	ל	> לַחֹשֶׁךְ
Before initial יְ, a **long i** occurs through contraction:	יְהוּדָה	+	ל	> לִיהוּדָה
Before a **Chatéf-vowel** the preposition has the corresponding **full vowel:**	אֱמֶת	+	ב	> בֶּאֱמֶת
Before אֱלֹהִים the preposition has long e, the Alef is silent:	אֱלֹהִים	+	ל	> לֵאלֹהִים
Similarly, a short a stands before אֲדֹנָי:	אֲדֹנָי	+	ל	> לַאדֹנָי
Before the Tetragrammaton יהוה, these prepositions are vocalized just like **the Qeré** אֲדֹנָי:				בַּיהוָה לַיהוָה

If one wants to pronounce the name of God, though, "**b^{e}yahwäh**," etc., must be read.

Before words that begin with the primary-stressed syllable, these prepositions are frequently vocalized with **initial-Qámes** ($\to$ § 10.1):	בְּזֹאת לָבוֹא

Suffix Forms

The two prepositions בְ and לְ have in common that the connecting vowel *a* also stands before the 1st and 2nd person. The suffix forms for כְ are developed in part from the core כְּמוֹ. Series of forms $\to$ above (summary table).

12.4 Particles with Irregular Suffix Forms

Prefixed מִן

מִן (preposition of separation: "from/about/more than") stands in the **normal form** מִן־ before the article:	מִן־הַשָּׁמַיִם
Before a noun without an article most of the time the **Nun** (ן) has **assimilated** to the following consonant (**Dagesch forte**):	עֶרֶב עַד מִבֹּקֶר
Before a guttural or Resch **compensatory lengthening** occurs most of the time: i > e ($\to$ § 9.2).[3]	בֹּקֶר עַד מֵעֶרֶב
Before י is **contracted** iyy^e to long i:	מִיהוּדָה > מִן + יְהוּדָה
Before the **Tetragrammaton** מִן is vocalized as before the Qeré אֲדֹנָי, thus with compensatory lengthening:	מֵאֲדֹנָי : מֵיְהֹוָה

If one wants to pronounce the name of God, "**miyyahwäh**" must be read.

Suffix Forms

Before the suffixes of the singular and the 1st plural, the מִן is **reduplicated** (stands twice), the Nun (ן) is assimilated. In the form with the suffix of the 3rd singular, the He (ה) is assimilated to the ending like the Nun.

---

3 Virtual doubling occurs (מֵחוּץ), also compensatory lengthening before the article (מֵהָאֱלֹהִים).

Overview of 12.4 and 12.5

	מִן	עִם	אֵת (prep.)	אֵת (acc.)	אֶל־	עַל
Singular						
1st	מִמֶּנִּי	עִמִּי / עִמָּדִי	אִתִּי	אֹתִי	אֵלַי	עָלַי
2nd m.	מִמְּךָ / מִמֶּךָּ	עִמְּךָ	אִתְּךָ / אִתָּךְ	אֹתְךָ / אֹתָךְ	אֵלֶיךָ	עָלֶ֫יךָ
2nd f.	מִמֵּךְ	עִמָּךְ	אִתָּךְ	אֹתָךְ	אֵלַיִךְ	עָלַיִךְ
3rd m.	מִמֶּ֫נּוּ	עִמּוֹ	אִתּוֹ	אֹתוֹ	אֵלָיו	עָלָיו
3rd f.	מִמֶּ֫נָּה	עִמָּהּ	אִתָּהּ	אֹתָהּ	אֵלֶיהָ	עָלֶ֫יהָ
Plural						
1st	מִמֶּ֫נּוּ	עִמָּ֫נוּ	אִתָּ֫נוּ	אֹתָ֫נוּ	אֵלֵינוּ	עָלֵ֫ינוּ
2nd m.	מִכֶּם	עִמָּכֶם	אִתְּכֶם	אֶתְכֶם	אֲלֵיכֶם	עֲלֵיכֶם
2nd f.	מִכֶּן	–	–	–	אֲלֵיכֶן	עֲלֵיכֶן
3rd m.	מֵהֶם	עִמָּם / עִמָּהֶם	אִתָּם	אֹתָם / אֶתְהֶם	אֲלֵיהֶם	עֲלֵיהֶם
3rd f.	מֵהֵ֫נָּה	–	–	אֹתָן / אֶתְהֶן	אֲלֵיהֶן	עֲלֵיהֶן

Suffix Forms of עִם and אֵת

עִם and אֵת, the prepositions of commonality ("with/by"), both appear to **double** the **second consonants**. The connecting vowel *a* appears irregular, with עִם also before a suffix of the **2mp**.

The variant form עִמָּדִי is probably derived from the root עמד.

אֵת, the sign of the accusative, has the form אֹת before suffixes. אֵת can also stand before the accented suffixes of the 2nd and 3rd plural. The connecting vowel *a* appears irregular before suffixes of the 1st and 2nd person.

12.5 Prepositions with Apparent Plural Forms

Signs of the Plural

Before suffixes, the prepositions אֶל־ (goal: "to/for"), עַד (limit: "until")[4] and עַל ("on/over/for the sake of/against") have **forms as if they** were nominals that stand in the **plural** (→ § 17.2).[5]

12.6 Compound Prepositions

Words occur that are put together from two prepositions. Frequently they are combinations with place and direction information.

By combinations with מִן (e.g. מֵאֵת מֵעַל מִתַּחַת) the meaning "from" predominates most of the time. The lexicon should be referred to for details.

---

4 עַד with suffix is extremely rare: The word appears ca. 1250 times, but of them only 14 times with suffix and only in poetic texts.

5 With עַל certainly and with אֶל־ and עַל probably, a Lamed-Jod root is used as a basis, → § 39.1.

13 Clause Introducers

13.1 *The Conjunction* וּ *(Waw copulativum)*

Normal Form as Prefix

The conjunction וּ ("and/but/that") is combined to form a unit with the following word (**proclitic**). Normal form: **upbeat syllable** with **Schwa mobile**:

רוּחַ אֱלֹהִים	the Spirit of God
וְרוּחַ אֱלֹהִים	and the Spirit of God

The connection with the following word is partly the same as with the prepositions בְּ, לְ and כְּ (→ § 12.3).

Before יְ contraction to long i	יְהוּדָה	+ וּ >	וִיהוּדָה
Before Chatéf-vowel of the corresponding full-vowel	אֱמֶת	+ וּ >	וֶאֱמֶת
Before אֱלֹהִים long e	אֱלֹהִים	+ וּ >	וֵאלֹהִים
Before אֲדֹנָי	אֲדֹנָי	+ וּ >	וַאדֹנָי
Before יהוה as before אֲדֹנָי	יְהוָה	+ וּ >	וַיהוָה
Before the stressed syllable with preceding Qámes			וָבֹהוּ תֹהוּ

Different than with בְּ, לְ, כְּ

Before article unchanged	הָאָרֶץ	+ וּ >	וְהָאָרֶץ
Before the consonants Bet (בּ), Waw (וּ), Mem (מ) and Pe (פּ) (Mnemonic word: BUMAF) and	בֹּקֶר	+ וּ >	וּבֹקֶר
Before Schwa mobile is וּ to וּ.	שְׁמוּאֵל	+ וּ >	וּשְׁמוּאֵל

13.2 *Relative Particle* שֶׁ *(Schin Prefix)*

Above all in poetry and later prose, Schin prefix occurs with the same meaning as אֲשֶׁר:

In the first letter of the following word stands **Dagesch forte**.

(Eccl 4:10)	הָאֶחָד שֶׁיִּפֹּל	the one who falls

Before gutturals stands a or ä:

(Ps 135:2)	שֶׁעֹמְדִים בְּבֵית יְהוָה	who stands in the house of Yhwh
(Judg 6:13)	וְעָשִׂיתָ לִּי אוֹת שָׁאַתָּה מְדַבֵּר עִמִּי	... thus give to me a sign that you are the one (it is you) who speaks with me.

13.3 Interrogative Particle הֲ (He interrogativum)[1]

Normal Form

The proclitic particle הֲ before the first word introduces an interrogative clause. Normal form: He with Chatéf-Patach: הֲ

	שֹׁמֵר אָחִי אָנֹכִי	I am the guardian of my brother.
(Gen 4:9)	הֲשֹׁמֵר אָחִי אָנֹכִי	Am I the guardian of my brother?

Before Schwa

Before non-gutturals with half vowel stands הַ, sometimes with and sometimes without a following Dagesch forte.

(Gen 17:17)	הַלְּבֶן מֵאָה שָׁנָה יִוָּלֵד	Should (a child) be born to a hundred-year-old man?
(Gen 29:5)	הַיְדַעְתֶּם אֶת־לָבָן	Do you know Laban?

Before Gutturals

Before gutturals stands הַ or הֶ:[2]

(Judg 12:5)	הַאֶפְרָתִי אַתָּה	Are you an Ephraimite?
(Num 13:18)	וּרְאִיתֶם ... אֶת־הָעָם ... הֶחָזָק הוּא	And you will find out whether the people are strong.

---

1   Word of note for the proclitic particle: מֹשֶׁה וְכָלֵב "Moses and Caleb," though מֹשֶׁה contains the particle with the vowel, וְכָלֵב the particle with Schwa.

2   In the case of He with following Dagesch forte or also before gutturals, theoretically a confusion of He interrogativum with the article may be possible. Practically the context of the text always excludes a mistake.

13.4 *Interrogative Pronouns*

מִי ("who?")

The substantival pronoun, which asks about a person, only has the one form: מִי.

It occurs after a nominal in the **construct state**:	בֶּן־מִי	whose son?
after prepositions:	לְמִי	for whom?
and after **the accusative sign** אֶת	אֶת־מִי	whom?

מַה־ ("what?")

The substantival pronoun, which asks about a thing, has the form מַה־ with **Dagesch forte** in the first consonant of the following word.

	מַה־זֹּאת	What is this?
Before gutturals and Resch **compensatory lengthening** or **virtual doubling** occurs (according to the same rule as with the article, but not used as consistently):	מֶה־אֱנוֹשׁ	What is a man?
	מֶה־עָשִׂיתָ	What have you done?
	הֲזֶה מַה־הַדָּבָר	What is this thing?

In combination with לְ ("for what?/why?") the forms לָמָּה and לָמָה appear.

14 Clause-Forming Particles

14.1 Existence

Some particles as original nominals can take **suffixes** and thus form **nominal clauses**:

the interrogative word	אַיֵּה	"where?",
the negation	אֵין	"non-existence,"
the position	יֵשׁ	"existence,"
the pointing word	הִנֵּה	"look,"
the adverb	עוֹד	"still/always."

In these nominal clauses, the **suffix** has **the role of subject**, e.g.:

אַיֶּכָּה	"where are you?"
הִנְנִי	"here I am"

14.2 Overview

Clause Forming Particles with Suffixes

	אֵין	יֵשׁ	אַיֵּה	הִנֵּה	עוֹד
with suffix	I am not … etc.	you are there … etc.	where are you? … etc.	here I am … etc.	I am still … etc.
1st sing.	אֵינֶ֫נִּי			הִנְנִי הִנֵּ֫נִי	עוֹדִי עוֹדֶ֫נִּי
2nd m. 2nd f.	אֵינְךָ אֵינֵךְ	יֶשְׁךָ	אַיֶּכָּה	הִנְּךָ הִנָּךְ	עוֹדְךָ עוֹדָךְ
3rd m. 3rd f.	אֵינֶ֫נּוּ אֵינֶ֫נָּה	יֶשְׁנוֹ	אַיּוֹ	הִנּוֹ	עוֹדֶ֫נּוּ עוֹדֶ֫נָּה עוֹדָהּ
1st pl.				הִנְנוּ הִנֶּ֫נּוּ	
2nd m.pl.	אֵינְכֶם	יֶשְׁכֶם		הִנְּכֶם	
3rd m.pl.	אֵינָם		אַיָּם	הִנָּם	עוֹדָם

Feminine forms in the plural are not found.

15 Overview of the Proclitic Particles

15.1 Prepositions and ו

	כ ,ל ,ב	ו	מִן
before Schewa mobile:	צְדָקָה　בִּצְדָקָה	וּצְדָקָה	מִצְּדָקָה
before "je":	יְהוּדָה　לִיהוּדָה	וִיהוּדָה	מִיהוּדָה
before Chatéf-vowel	אֲנָשִׁים　כַּאֲנָשִׁים	וַאֲנָשִׁים	מֵאֲנָשִׁים
before article:	הַמֶּלֶךְ　לַמֶּלֶךְ	וְהַמֶּלֶךְ	מִן־הַמֶּלֶךְ　מֵהַמֶּלֶךְ
with "Älohim":	אֱלֹהִים　לֵאלֹהִים	וֵאלֹהִים	מֵאֱלֹהִים
with "Adonai":	אֲדֹנָי　כַּאדֹנָי	וַאדֹנָי	מֵאֲדֹנָי
with YHWH:	יהוה　בַּיהוָה	וַיהוָה	מֵיְהוָה

15.2 Article and He interrogativum

	Normal Form	Before Schewa	Before Resch	Before Guttural
Article	הַמֶּלֶךְ	הַבְּרִית הַיְלָדִים	הֶרֶכֶב הָרְכָבִים	הָאִישׁ הַהוּא הֶחָזָק
He interrogativum	הֲמֶלֶךְ	הַבְּרִית הַבְּרִית	הֲרֶכֶב הַרְכָבִים	הָאִישׁ הַהוּא הֶחָזָק

16 Forms of the Noun

*Substantives, adjectives, and numbers are described as nominals in this grammar.
There is fundamentally no distinction in their form and use.*[1]

16.1 State

No Case

There are no case endings in Old Testament Hebrew (→ however below § 16.3).
The construct state (status constructus) is not a case form, rather a **variation of
accent** with a syntactical function:

Two or more nominals are moved so closely to one another that they form a
linguistic unit and at the same time also express a **unit of meaning**. This word
connection is called a "construct chain." Only the last nominal has the full tone; it
stands in the "status absolutus,"[2] i.e. just as it would appear alone. The preceding
nominals have a reduced tone; they stand in the "status constructus,"[3] i.e. belonging to the last word.

דָּוִד	בֶּן		Son	of David
absolute state	construct state		definite word	determining word

Genitive

Most of the time we can **translate** such a construct chain into German by connecting the last nominal in the **genitive** to what precedes. For more on the function and translation of the construct chain → § 45.

A nominal can therefore appear in every number and every gender in **two forms**:
the fully accented form, which is the **status absolutus** (st a), and the leaning
slightly against a following word, weakly accented form, which is the **status constructus** (st c).

---

1   On the use of nominals that we express with adjectives in German, → § 46.3.
2   Lat.: "detached, single," hebr.: נִפְרָד "single."
3   Lat.: "fitted together," hebr.: נִסְמָךְ "leaning." One such connection is called in Hebrew סְמִיכוּת
    "dependence."

Changeable vowels change when a nominal in the construct state is accented weakly. No rule needs to be drawn up about the kind and degree of vowel changes. The principles presented in § 10 are valid.

דָּבָר		Word	
דְּבַר דָּוִד		David's Word	
st a	st c	determining word	
accented	unaccented	accented	unaccented

16.2 Number and Gender

With Hebrew nominals, three numbers are distinguished:

Singular   for the singular,

Dual   for two,

Plural   for plural.

Gender

With nominals, as with verbs, there are two genders distinguished:

masculine (male) and **feminine** (female)[4]; there is not a neuter.

Feminine Singular

Only feminine nominals have an **ending** in the singular; masculine nominals do not. The **ending** הָ stands in the absolute state.

In the construct state and before suffixes, the original feminine **ending** תֹ is preserved.

תּוֹרָה	instruction
תּוֹרַת אֱלֹהִים	the instruction of God
תּוֹרָתִי	my instruction

---

4   The greater differentiation of gender is in Hebrew the result of a multi-layered process of development: Originally the endings a/t and ot denoted probably "Nomina unitatis," thus single things in contrast to collective terms (e.g. שֵׂעָר "hair/covering of hair," שַׂעֲרָה "individual hair"); this function is with some numerals still clear (→ § 22, § 47.2). In addition, a system is found that uses the endings for the number of classes: "things/little ones/weak/minor" in contrast to the unmarked classes: "persons/large/strong/important." From here the endings would adopt "feminine" for the labeling of natural gender (sexuality). (→ Diethelm Michel, *Grundlegung einer Hebräischen Syntax*, pp. 25ff., Neukirchen 1977.)

Special Features

The feminine sign ת can be added without a vowel to a word ending in a consonant. Then the double consonant is picked up through a **helping vowel** (a or ä → § 18).	אֹמֵר one speaking אֹמֶרֶת one speaking (f) שֹׁלֵחַ one sending שֹׁלַחַת one sending (f)
Most of the time with feminine forms made this way, **absolute** state and **construct** state are the **same**.	
With some nominals, the feminine ending הָ◌ (st a) changes to a consonantal ת (st c):	(st a) ruler מֶמְשָׁלָה (st c) מֶמְשֶׁלֶת
Rarely feminine endings are ית◌ and וּת.	שְׁבִית captivity מַלְכוּת kingdom

Dual

Dual forms are still used in biblical Hebrew only with **terms of number** and **measurement** and with the names for things occurring in pairs, mostly **parts of the body**. Otherwise the number for "two" with the plural of a nominal is used.[5]

The dual ending for both genders are:	יוֹם a day
in st a תַיִם◌	יוֹמַיִם two days
and in st c יֵ◌	*יוֹמֵי two days of …
With nominals with feminine endings, a ת is preserved before the dual ending.	שָׂפָה lip שְׂפָתַיִם lips

Plural

Masculine plural endings are:	סוּס a horse
in st a יִם◌ and	סוּסִים horses
in st c יֵ◌	סוּסֵי horses of …
The **feminine** plural ending in both states is וֹת.	סוּסָה mare סוּסוֹת mares

---

Often nominals that are labeled in the **singular** as **feminine** have a **masculine** ending in the **plural** and vice versa.

שָׁנָה	year/years
שָׁנִים	
מָאוֹר	lamp/lamps
מְאֹרֹת	

Overview of Noun Endings

	masculine		feminine	
	st a	st c	st a	st c
Singular	–	–	הָ ◌	תְ◌
			תָ◌ ◌	
			תֶ◌ ◌	
Dual	◌ִים	◌ַי	◌ָתַיִם	תַי
Plural	◌ִים	◌ַי	וֹת	

16.3 He Locale and Relatives

Only remnants of case endings are preserved in biblical Hebrew. Outside of the He locale, these endings **no** longer have **meaning**. On the syntax → § 50.2.

He Locale

The He locale goes back to an old **accusative** ending. It marks an adverbial qualification, above all of the place, and consists of the addition of an unaccented long a.

צָפוֹן	north
צָפוֹנָה	toward/in the north
אֶרֶץ	land
אַרְצָה	to the land
רָמָה	Ramah
רָמָתָה	in/to Ramah

With **segolates** (→ § 18) the He locale is added on the **basic form**.

With nominals with a **feminine** sign a ת stands before the He locale.

Chíreq Compaginis

The "Chíreq compaginis" or "Chíreq paragogicum" is probably an old **genitive** ending, which as a rule is an additional accented **long i** (◌ִי) added at times on the construct state of a nominal.

(Gen 49:11)   בְּנִי אֲתֹנוֹ   the foal of his donkey

Chólem Paragogicum

The "Chólem paragogicum" probably goes back to an old nominative ending, an additional accented **long o** (וֹ).

(Gen 1:24)   חַיְתוֹ־אֶרֶץ   the animals of the land

17 Suffixes on Nominals

Most of the time, suffixes on nominals denote possession (German: possessive pronoun "mein/dein/sei" etc.). Their forms are basically like those cited in § 11. Differences arise from the form of the nominal onto which the suffixes are put.

17.1 Suffixes on the Singular

Overview

	סוס	סוסה	דָּבָר	שֵׁם	צְדָקָה
Suffixes in the Singular	horse	mare	word	name	righteousness
1ˢᵗ	סוּסִי	סוּסָתִי	דְּבָרִי	שְׁמִי	צִדְקָתִי
2ⁿᵈ m.	סוּסְךָ	סוּסָתְךָ	דְּבָרְךָ	שִׁמְךָ	צִדְקָתְךָ
2ⁿᵈ m. in pause	סוּסֶךָ	סוּסָתֶךָ	דְּבָרֶךָ	שְׁמֶךָ	צִדְקָתֶךָ
2ⁿᵈ f.	סוּסֵךְ	סוּסָתֵךְ	דְּבָרֵךְ	שְׁמֵךְ	צִדְקָתֵךְ
3ʳᵈ m.	סוּסוֹ	סוּסָתוֹ	דְּבָרוֹ	שְׁמוֹ	צִדְקָתוֹ
3ʳᵈ f.	סוּסָה	סוּסָתָה	דְּבָרָהּ	שְׁמָהּ	צִדְקָתָהּ
Suffixes in the Plural					
1ˢᵗ	סוּסֵנוּ	סוּסָתֵנוּ	דְּבָרֵנוּ	שְׁמֵנוּ	צִדְקָתֵנוּ
2ⁿᵈ m.	סוּסְכֶם	סוּסַתְכֶם	דְּבַרְכֶם	שִׁמְכֶם	צִדְקַתְכֶם
2ⁿᵈ f.	סוּסְכֶן	סוּסַתְכֶן	דְּבַרְכֶן	שִׁמְכֶן	צִדְקַתְכֶן
3ʳᵈ m.	סוּסָם	סוּסָתָם	דְּבָרָם	שְׁמָם	צִדְקָתָם
3ʳᵈ f.	סוּסָן	סוּסָתָן	דְּבָרָן	שְׁמָן	צִדְקָתָן

Suffixes on nominals with **unchangeable** vowels and without the sign of the feminine:	Example: סוס "horse"

Connecting Vowels

Connecting vowels stand before suffixes that end in a consonant, in particular e or ä and (only before suffixes of the 3ʳᵈ person) a.

Accent

In principle, the vowel **before** the **suffix** is accented, other than כֶם and כֶן, which are always accented (heavy suffixes), and ךָ, which is accented in context. Before these three suffixes, the **connecting vowel** has **elided or disappeared** (Schwa).

Contraction

The suffixes of the 3rd person singular, הוּ and הָ, in context are **contracted** with the preceding connecting vowel to וֹ or הֹ.

Rarely a suffix מוֹ appears for the 3rd person masculine plural in **poetic** texts.

Suffixes on nominals with **unchangeable** vowels and a **sign of the feminine**:	Example: סוּסָה "mare"

Feminine Sign ת

The feminine sign ת is **preserved** before suffixes. In the remaining, the forms are thus formed as the forms of words without a feminine sign.

Suffixes on nominals with **changeable** vowels:	Examples: דְּבָר "word" שֵׁם "name" צְדָקָה "righteousness"

The vowels a and e change with different **accents**. The principles presented in § 10 apply for these changes.

On nominals with helping vowels (**Segolata**) → § 18.

17.2 Suffixes on Dual and Plural

Plural Sign Jod

A Jod (י) stands before suffixes that are placed on the dual or plural of a nominal.[1] Nominals with a feminine sign show a Taw (ת) before the Jod. Through the joining of the connecting vowel with the helping vowel Jod, characteristic suffix forms arise that are different from those of the singular.

---

1   Occasionally suffix forms occur without Jod, e.g. אֲנָשׁוֹ "his men" (1Sam 23:5).

Overview

	סוּס	סוּסָה	צְדָקָה	דָּבָר	יָד	שָׂפָה
	horse	mare	righteousness	word	hand	lip
Plural	סוּסִים	סוּסוֹת	צְדָקוֹת	דְּבָרִים		
Dual					יָדַיִם	שְׂפָתַיִם
st c	סוּסֵי	סוּסוֹת	צְדָקוֹת	דִּבְרֵי	יְדֵי	שִׂפְתֵי
w. Suffix						
1ˢᵗ sing.	סוּסִי	סוּסוֹתַי	צִדְקוֹתַי	דְּבָרַי	יָדַי	שְׂפָתַי
2ⁿᵈ m	סוּסֶיךָ	סוּסוֹתֶיךָ	צִדְקוֹתֶיךָ	דְּבָרֶיךָ	יָדֶיךָ	שְׂפָתֶיךָ
2ⁿᵈ f	סוּסַיִךְ	סוּסוֹתַיִךְ	צִדְקוֹתַיִךְ	דְּבָרַיִךְ	יָדַיִךְ	שְׂפָתַיִךְ
3ʳᵈ m	סוּסָיו	סוּסוֹתָיו	צִדְקוֹתָיו	דְּבָרָיו	יָדָיו	שְׂפָתָיו
3ʳᵈ f	סוּסֶיהָ	סוּסוֹתֶיהָ	צִדְקוֹתֶיהָ	דְּבָרֶיהָ	יָדֶיהָ	שְׂפָתֶיהָ
1ˢᵗ pl	סוּסֵינוּ	סוּסוֹתֵינוּ	צִדְקוֹתֵינוּ	דְּבָרֵינוּ	יָדֵינוּ	שְׂפָתֵינוּ
2ⁿᵈ m	סוּסֵיכֶם	סוּסוֹתֵיכֶם	צִדְקוֹתֵיכֶם	דִּבְרֵיכֶם	יְדֵיכֶם	שְׂפָתֵיכֶם
2ⁿᵈ f	סוּסֵיכֶן	סוּסוֹתֵיכֶן	צִדְקוֹתֵיכֶן	דִּבְרֵיכֶן	יְדֵיכֶן	שְׂפָתֵיכֶן
3ʳᵈ m	סוּסֵיהֶם	סוּסוֹתֵיהֶם or סוּסוֹתָם	צִדְקוֹתֵיהֶם	דִּבְרֵיהֶם	יְדֵיהֶם	שְׂפָתֵיהֶם
3ʳᵈ f	סוּסֵיהֶן	סוּסוֹתֵיהֶן or סוּסוֹתָן	צִדְקוֹתֵיהֶן	דִּבְרֵיהֶן	יְדֵיהֶן	שְׂפָתֵיהֶן

Particularly conspicuous are (1) the form ◌ַי (pronounced ai) in the suffix of the 1ˢᵗ person singular, (2) the form ◌ַיִךְ in the suffix of the 2ⁿᵈ person feminine singular, and (3) the form ◌ָיו (pronounced aw) in the suffix of the 3ʳᵈ person masculine singular.

In the **dual**, only nominals with a feminine sign (and some Segolata → § 18.2) have different suffix forms before the plural. (→ table, columns יָד and שָׂפָה)

Nominals with Changeable Vowels

Suffixes in the plural of nominals with **changeable** vowels:

Changeable vowels react, even at a distance from the tone syllable, as presented in **§ 10** (→ also § 23.2).

> Examples: דָּבָר "word"
>
> יָד "hand"
>
> צְדָקָה "righteousness"

In the **dual** and with plurals with "**-im**" (◌ים), the forms with light suffixes have the same vocalization as the status **absolutus** plural; the form with the heavy suffixes כֶם, בֶן, הֶם and הֶן have the same vocalization as the status constructus plural. With plurals with "**-ot**" (וֹת), all suffix forms have the same vocalization as the status **constructus** plural.

18 Nominals with Helping Vowels (Segolata)

A large group of nominals are described as "Segolata" which in the singular (status absolutus and status constructus) are accented like מֶ֫לֶךְ on the next to last syllable and show a short ä[1]—sometimes also a (as with נַ֫עַר)—in the last syllable.

18.1 Basic Form and Helping Vowels

Overview

When such Segolata take **endings**, in particular for all suffixes, a form is visible that is called the **basic form**: If the ending is taken away, a word with **doubled final syllable** remains.

In the lost-ending form, a whole short **helping vowel**, denoted with Segol or Patach, fits in between the two ending consonants.[2]

The form expanded through a helping vowel remains **accented** on the **first syllable**, which is now open.

Singular with Suffix	מַלְכּוֹ	סִפְרוֹ	בְּקָרוֹ
Basic Form	* ma<u>lk</u>	* si<u>pr</u>	* bu<u>qr</u>
Helping Vowel	ä	ä	ä
Singular without Ending	מֶ֫לֶךְ	סֵ֫פֶר	בֹּ֫קֶר

Vowels of the 1st Syllable

Very often the short vowels in the first syllable appear **lengthened**: i to long **e** (סֵ֫פֶר), u or å to long **o** (בֹּ֫קֶר), a (in pause) to long **a** (מָ֫לֶךְ). In the first syllable, **ä** also appears very often (מֶ֫לֶךְ), which nowadays is pronounced most of the time as **short**, even though it stands in an open syllable (→ § 8.2).

1　The sign "Segol," so the latinized form "segolatum" = to provide with Segol.
2　Linguistically one can thus imagine the process such that an original nominative ending "u" fell out and as a result the one-syllable form has occurred.

18.2 Formation of Forms

Basic Form and Endings

From the basic form are formed as a rule:

the singular form with added **suffixes**,	Suffix	אַרְצוֹ	נַעֲרוֹ	לַחְמוֹ	אַלְפּוֹ
the singular form with added **He locale** and	He loc	אַרְצָה			
the **dual** form.	Dual				אַלְפַּ֫יִם
	Basic Form	'ars	na'r	lahm	*'alp
Most of the time the helping vowel is a before and after **gutturals**. In these cases the short a also can be preserved in the first syllable.	Helping Vowel	ä	a	ä	ä
	Singular	אֶ֫רֶץ	נַ֫עַר	לֶ֫חֶם	אֶ֫לֶף

Plural Forms

The plural forms are like the plural form of nominals with two changeable vowels (**pattern** דָּבָר). The monosyllabic basic form is **expanded** through the **vowel a** (*malk - *malak - *malakim):

		*malk	*sipr	*buqr
	*dabar	*malak	*sipar	*buqar
	דָּבָר			
st a	דְּבָרִים	מְלָכִים	סְפָרִים	בְּקָרִים
st c	דִּבְרֵי	מַלְכֵי³	סִפְרֵי	בָּקְרֵי

Plural with Suffixes

Appropriately, the suffix forms are the same:

דְּבָרָיו	מְלָכָיו	סְפָרָיו	בְּקָרָיו
דִּבְרֵיהֶם	מַלְכֵיהֶם	סִפְרֵיהֶם	בָּקְרֵיהֶם

The **status constructus of the dual** is different than that of the plural only when the 2nd radical belongs to the group "BeGaDKeFaT." In the plural, a vowel has dropped out; thus there is **no Dagesch lene** (→ § 5.2).

---

3   Without Dagesch lene, because the loss of vowel is not original, rather a vowel has dropped out.

	אֶ֫לֶף	thousand
אַלְפֵּי	אַלְפַּ֫יִם	two thousand
אַלְפֵי	אֲלָפִים	thousands
	אַלְפֵיהֶם	their thousands

Special Features

The relationships between the **vowel** in the **basic form** and the vowel in the **first syllable** of the Segolatum are not always quite fixed. From the same word, forms with **different basic vowels** can appear.

e.g.:   נֵ֫דֶר "vow" compared to נֶ֫דֶר

בֶּ֫רֶךְ "knee" compared to dual: בִּרְכַּ֫יִם.

Instead of the basic vowel *i*, *ä* can also appear.

e.g.:   נֶ֫גֶד "before," suffix form נֶגְדִּי,

חֵ֫פֶץ "delight," with suffix חֶפְצִי (because of the guttural).

With **gutturals** as the 2nd radical, **broken syllables** appear (→ § 9.3):

e.g.:   נַעֲרוֹ—נַ֫עַר "his servant,"

אָהֳלִי—אֹ֫הֶל "my tent"

Irregular Plural Forms

Irregular **plural forms** with the basic vowel *u* appear in some Segolata:

אֹ֫הֶל	"tent":	אֹהָלִים	o not changed
קֹ֫דֶשׁ	"sanctuary":	קָדָשִׁים	with Qames Chatuf in the 1st, open syllable
שֹׁ֫רֶשׁ	"root":	שָׁרָשִׁים	

Feminine Ending

In the singular, a feminine ending is added to the basic form: מַלְכָּה > מֶ֫לֶךְ.

Feminine plural has **stem expansion** like the masculine: מְלָכוֹת, st. c.: מַלְכוֹת.

18.3 Segolata with Waw or Jod as the 2nd Radical

As Segolata are also valid some words with **Waw** or **Jod** as radicals,[4] with which the Masoretes have fashioned **helping vowels**. The Segolata with Waw or Jod

---

4   On the term "radical" → § 24.1.

as the 2ⁿᵈ radical (in the status absolutus singular) are recognized by their **accent**.

Segolata in the Status Absolutus Singular

Segolata of the type מָוֶת or בַּיִת had a double vowel before the Masoretes' time. The Masoretes recognized double vowels, thus read at the time a **doubly closed syllable**.

These were preserved through **helping vowels**. The newly-formed Segolate form was fixed for the **singular absolute state**.

Contracted Forms

In the other forms, aw or ay **simplified** (**contracted**) to long vowels.

*maut	*bait
*mawt	*bayt
Helping vowel ä: מָוֶת	Helping vowel i: בַּיִת
aw > o: מות	ay > e: בֵית

Examples[5]:

	st c	m. Suffix	Dual	Plural	st c with He loc.
עַיִן (eye)	עֵין	עֵינוֹ	עֵינַיִם		
אָוֶן (wrong)	אוֹן			אוֹנִים	
בַּיִת (house)	בֵּית				בֵּיתָה

Incidentally, **not all** nominals with Waw in the middle are Segolata; קוֹל (voice) and יוֹם (day), for example, are not. Only מָוֶת (death) and תָּוֶךְ (middle) are somewhat frequent.

18.4. Segolata with Waw or Jod as the 3rd Radical

Some "Segolata" have Waw or Jod[6] as the 3ʳᵈ radical, which has an effect on the helping vowel used: Before Waw u is used as a helping vowel, before Jod i:

*piry (fruit)	*tuhw (wasteland)
*pirʲy	*tuhᵘw
*píri	*túhu

---

5   There are a number of "exceptions," mostly secondary forms, e.g. pl. עֲיָנוֹת "springs," בַּיִת pl. בָּתִּים → § 21.5, He locale frequently in the basic form, e.g. הָעַיְנָה, הַבַּיְתָה.

6   Also "Segolata Lamed-Waw-Jod (ל״וי)" → § 24.3.

iy is **contracted** to long i, uw to long u:	פְּרִי
Long i Accented	
The long i has pulled the tone to itself,	
the final u is unaccented and the stem vowel lengthens	תֹּהוּ[7]
to o.	
Suffixes	e.g.: פִּרְיוֹ
Suffixes are added to the **basic form** as with other Segolata.	
To be sure, both plural as well as dual have a stem expanding, unchangeably long e.	פְּרָיִים פְּרָיֵ

---

7   The example is established because of "Tohu wa Bohu," which appear 20 and 3 times, respectively.

19 Nominals with Final ä

מִקְנֶה	possession of cattle
שָׂדֶה	field

Roots

Nominals, which in the singular **absolute** state look for -ä (הֶ◌) and in the **construct** state for -e (הֶ◌), can be traced back to roots, whose original 3ʳᵈ radical **Waw or Jod has dropped out** (like Lamed-He (ל״ה) verbs → § 39.1).

The **He** is a **vowel letter** for the final long vowel and is missing before an ending.

שָׂדִים	fields
שָׂדְךָ	your field

Jod before a Suffix

In the **singular form** with suffix, the original **Jod** can appear. Then forms appear which are like those of the plural:

1ˢᵗ sing.	מִקְנִי	compared to	שָׂדִי
2ⁿᵈ masc. sing.	מִקְנֶיךָ		
or	מִקְנְךָ	compared to	שָׂדְךָ
3ʳᵈ masc. sing.	מִקְנָיו	compared to	שָׂדוֹ
or	מִקְנֵיהוּ		
2ⁿᵈ masc. pl.	מִקְנֵיכֶם	compared to	שָׂדֵיכֶם

With feminine forms, the **ending** הֶ◌ stands instead of the final הֶ◌.

יָפֶה	beautiful
יָפָה/יְפַת	a beautiful one

20 Nominals with Double End Consonants

Examples:	עַם	עֵת	חֹק
	(people)	(time)	(statute)

Dagesch Forte

With single-syllable nominals, most of the time with long vowels, the 2ⁿᵈ radical can appear to double.[1] The doubling appears before the ending as a Dagesch forte. The corresponding short vowel stands before the doubled consonant.

עַמִּים	עִתּוֹ	חֻקּוֹת

Gutturals

Words with gutturals or ר as the last consonant have compensatory lengthening; often virtual doubling with ח.

פַּח - פְּחִים	שַׂר - שָׂרִים	רַע - רָעִים

Occasionally, the 2ⁿᵈ radical is repeated:

לֵבָב	compared to	לֵב
לְבָבוֹ		לִבּוֹ

---

1   Most of the time these are Ajin-Ajin roots → § 42.1. There are also roots with assimilated Nun, e.g.: עֵז "goat" from עֵנז.

21 Nominals Formed Irregularly

21.1 Relationships

	st c sing.	sing. + suffix	st a st c Plural	Plural + Suffix
אָב father	אֲבִי	אָבִי אָבִיו אֲבִיהֶם	אָבוֹת אֲבוֹת	אֲבוֹתֵינוּ
חָא brother	Singular as אָב		אַחִים אֲחֵי	אַחִי אֶחָי אָחִיו אֲחֵיכֶם
אָחוֹת sister	אֲחוֹת	אֲחוֹתִי		אֲחוֹתַיִךְ אַחְיוֹתָיו
בֵּן son	בֶּן־ בֶּן	בְּנִי בִּנְךָ	בָּנִים בְּנֵי	
בַּת daughter		בִּתִּי	בָּנוֹת בְּנוֹת	

אָב "**father**": In the singular, the element ׳ׅ appears, which is probably an old genitive ending. Thus, here the ׳ is **not a sign of the plural**. The suffix (הו) of the 3ms is contracted with the preceding *i* to יׄ; the plural ending is וֹת.[1]

אָח "**brother**": The **singular forms** are formed **just like אָב**. In the plural the first syllable is virtually doubled in part. Before Chet (ח) with Qames there is compensatory lengthening to Segol.

אָחוֹת "**sister**": וֹת is here not a sign of the plural. For the plural there is only a suffix form, in 5 cases from the expanded form אַחְיוֹת*.

בֵּן "**son**": In the plural, **long a** stands as a pre-tone vowel (thus changeable → § 10).

בַּת "**daughter**": with ending ת the **feminine of** בֵּן. The נ appears assimilated in the doubled suffix form of the singular (*bin > *bint > *binti > *bitti).

---

1   This is obviously not a sign of the feminine → § 16.2, note.

21.2 Man and Woman

	st c singular	sing. + suffix	st a st c plural
אִישׁ man			אֲנָשִׁים אַנְשֵׁי
אִשָּׁה woman	אֵשֶׁת	אִשְׁתִּי	נָשִׁים נְשֵׁי

אִישׁ "**man**": Regular singular form, **plural** from the root אנשׁ* (→ אֱנוֹשׁ "mankind").

אִשָּׁה "**woman**": In the singular form (other than st abs) a consonantal, additional ת stands as a sign of the feminine (with half-vowel → § 18). The **plural** shows the ending ‎ים‎.

21.3 Irregular Singular Forms

	st c singular	sing. + suffix	plural
פֶּה mouth	פִּי	פִּי פִּיו	פִּיוֹת
שֶׂה sheep	שֶׂה	שֵׂיוֹ	

פֶּה "mouth": One-radical stem **in i**; the st.a.-form has become like nominals in ä (ה‎); i-hu (3ms) is contracted to יו‎.

שֶׂה "sheep": Suffix forms with consonantal Jod (י) do not follow the example of nominals in -ä (ה‎).

21.4 Apparent Dual Forms

	st c	+ suffix	
מַיִם water	מֵי מֵימֵי	מֵימָיו	
שָׁמַיִם heavens	שְׁמֵי	שָׁמֶיךָ	

מַ֫יִם "water" and שָׁמַ֫יִם "heavens" are formed as **Segolata** (→ בַּ֫יִת), but sound **like duals** (◌ַ֫יִם). Formation and construction correspond to this. The st.c. מֵימֵי is formed through reduplication.

21.5 Irregular Plural Forms

	st c sing.	sing. + suffix	st a st c Plural	Plural + Suffix
בַּ֫יִת house			בָּתִּים בָּתֵּי	בָּתָּיו
כְּלִי vessel			כֵּלִים כְּלֵי	כֵּלָיו
יוֹם day	יוֹם	יוֹמוֹ	יָמִים יְמֵי	
עִיר city			עָרִים עָרֵי	עָרָיו עָרֵיהֶם
רֹאשׁ head			רָאשִׁים רָאשֵׁי	רָאשָׁיו

בַּ֫יִת "**house**": The **plural** has an unchangeable **long a**. The Dagesch in the Taw (תּ) shows the irregular, hard pronunciation of the Taw.

כְּלִי "**vessel**": Originally a **Segolatum** (→ § 18.4), singular with suffix e.g. כֶּלְיְךָ. It forms the **plural** differently than other Segolata not with expansion of the stem, rather thus as if it were read in the singular כֵּל.

יוֹם "**day**": In the singular and dual it has an unchangeable **o**, in the **plural** a changeable **a** (pre-tone Qames).

רֹאשׁ "**head**": In the singular o undergoes ablaut from a; the **a of the plural** is original and unchangeable.

The (unique) plural form רָאשִׁים (Josh 15:2) is newly formed according to the pattern of the singular.

22 Numbers

22.1 Cardinal Numbers from 1 to 20

	1 to 10					11 to 20	
	masculine form[1]		feminine form			masculine	feminine
		st c[2]		st c			
1	אֶחָד	אַחַד	אַחַת		11	אַחַד עָשָׂר עַשְׁתֵּי עָשָׂר	אַחַת עֶשְׂרֵה עַשְׁתֵּי עֶשְׂרֵה
2	שְׁנַיִם	שְׁנֵי	שְׁתַּיִם	שְׁתֵּי	12	שְׁנֵי עָשָׂר שְׁנֵים עָשָׂר	שְׁתֵּי עֶשְׂרֵה שְׁתֵּים עֶשְׂרֵה
3	שָׁלֹשׁ	שְׁלֹשׁ	שְׁלֹשָׁה	שְׁלֹשֶׁת	13	שְׁלֹשׁ עֶשְׂרֵה	שְׁלֹשָׁה עָשָׂר
4	אַרְבַּע		אַרְבָּעָה	אַרְבַּעַת	14	אַרְבַּע עֶשְׂרֵה	אַרְבָּעָה עָשָׂר
5	חָמֵשׁ	חֲמֵשׁ	חֲמִשָּׁה	חֲמֵשֶׁת	15	חֲמֵשׁ עֶשְׂרֵה	etc.
6	שֵׁשׁ		שִׁשָּׁה	שֵׁשֶׁת	16	שֵׁשׁ עֶשְׂרֵה	
7	שֶׁבַע	שְׁבַע	שִׁבְעָה		17	שְׁבַע עֶשְׂרֵה	
8	שְׁמֹנֶה		שְׁמֹנָה		18	שְׁמֹנֶה עֶשְׂרֵה	
9	תֵּשַׁע	תְּשַׁע	תִּשְׁעָה		19	תְּשַׁע עֶשְׂרֵה	
10	עֶשֶׂר		עֲשָׂרָה	עֲשֶׂרֶת	20	עֶשְׂרִים	

---

1   On the gender of numbers in conjunction with counting → § 47.2.
2   Numbers, whose st c is the same as its st a, are not cited twice, also not the normal feminine st c form with "at."

22.2 Tens, Hundreds, Thousands

10 to 90		Hundreds		Thousands	
10	עֶשֶׂר	100	מֵאָה (מְאַת st c)	1,000	אֶלֶף
20	עֶשְׂרִים	200	מָאתַיִם	2,000	אַלְפַּיִם
30	שְׁלשִׁים	300	שְׁלֹשׁ מֵאוֹת	3,000	שְׁלֹשֶׁת אֲלָפִים
40	אַרְבָּעִים	400	אַרְבַּע מֵאוֹת	4,000	אַרְבַּעַת אֲלָפִים
50	חֲמִשִּׁים	etc.		etc.	
60	שִׁשִּׁים				
70	שִׁבְעִים				
80	שְׁמֹנִים				
90	תִּשְׁעִים			10,000 plural	רְבָבָה רְבָבוֹת,

22.3 Ordinal Numbers from 1 to 10

first	רִאשׁוֹן	sixth	שִׁשִּׁי
second	שֵׁנִי	seventh	שְׁבִיעִי
third	שְׁלִישִׁי	eighth	שְׁמִינִי
fourth	רְבִיעִי	ninth	תְּשִׁיעִי
fifth	חֲמִישִׁי	tenth	עֲשִׂירִי

23 Settled Rules for Nominal Forms

23.1 Characteristics

Sign of the Feminine

The **Taw** (ת) is preserved in the construct state, before suffixes, and before the He locale.

Dual and Plural

A common feature of all suffix forms on dual and plural is a **Jod** (י) immediately before the suffix (→ however §§ 19 and 21).

Segolata

When a form with **doubled final syllable** (e.g. "malk") remains after a dropping of a suffix or He locale, it is a matter of a Segolatum.

23.2 The Vowels of the Lexical Form

Changing Vowels

When in nominal forms the stem vowels in appropriate distance from the primary stress are changed, again **most of the time a** should be used, rarely e. E.g.:

דִּבְרֵיהֶם	(דבר)	from	דָּבָר
זִקְנֵיהֶם	(זקן)	from	זָקֵן
שְׁמָךְ	(שם)	from	שֵׁם

Plurals

In principle, plural forms of the type דְּבָרִים can come from nominals with **changeable** vowels a or e (דָּבָר) or from **Segolata** (דֶּבֶר).

Dagesch Forte

When in forms with an ending the last consonant of the nominal appears **dou-bled** (Dagesch forte → § 20), often a long vowel stands in the uninflected form. At the same time, i becomes long e, a long a, u long o,

e.g.: אִמּוֹתֵינוּ from אֵם: "our mothers"

Monosyllabic nominals with unchangeable long a can be **participles** of 'Ajin-Waw verbs (→ § 41).

e.g.: קָמֵיהֶם (קָם) from קום

24 Verbs: General Comments on Formation

24.1 Terms

A **root** (hebr.: שֹׁרֶשׁ) is the unit of (most of the time) **three consonants**, from which one can reduce all forms of a word of same or similar **meaning**.[1]

A **radical** is an **individual consonant** of a root (lat.: "radix").

A group of verb forms that have the same way of formation is called a **stem**. In a stem, the **fundamental meaning** of a root is modified in particularly regular ways (→ § 29).[2]

"**Conjugation**," "**stem modification**" or "**Binyanim**" (בְּנְיָנִים, singular: בִּנְיָן) are other technical terms for the "stems" of a verb.

The base stem of a verb is the one that carries the **simple**, unmodified, **active** meaning, and is called "Qal" (hebr. קַל = "simple").

24.2 Existence of Forms

Overview

Personal Forms	Perfect Class		Imperfect Class			
	Afformative Conjugation (Perfect)		Preformative Conjugation (Imperfect)		Imperative	
	sing	pl	sing	pl	sing	pl
	3m[3] 3f	3	3m 3f	3m 3f		
	2m 2f	2m 2f	2m 2f	2m 2f	2m 2f	2m 2f
	1	1	1	1		
Nominal Forms	Participles Infinitives					

Personal forms (finite forms) and nominal forms (infinite forms) appear in every stem.

---

1   As all botanical metaphors in linguistics, the term "root" should also not be understand literally: It is not true that all concrete forms are grown out of this root. Rather the root is a theoretically-deduced entity, which does not appear in linguistic reality.

2   Thus, in Hebrew grammar, the term "stem" denotes something different than in German or Latin grammar.

Personal Forms

The personal forms are differentiated according to **person**, number (numerus), and gender (genus):

1st person (speaker(s) and his/their circle):	"I/we"
2nd person (the one(s) addressed):	"you/you"
3rd person (the one the speech is about):	"he/they"[3]

Number (numerus): singular and plural.[4]

Gender (genus): masculine or feminine.[5]

Imperative

Imperative forms appear only in the **2nd person**.

Tenses

There are two systems of conjugation, from which **four tenses** are formed: With suffixes (afformatives) the forms of the **afformative conjugation** (AC) are formed in the two tenses "perfect" and "perfect consecutive" (→ § 27). Mainly with prefixes (preformatives) the forms of the **preformative conjugation** (PC) are formed with the two tenses "imperfect" and "imperfect consecutive"[6] or "Narrativ" (→ § 25).

Nominal Forms

The participles and the infinitives are nominal forms.

Form Classes

Inside of a stem, the perfect form on the one hand and the imperfect form on the other are often formed differently; this affects the vocalization in particular. One

---

3   Forms for the neuter ("es [it]") are not distinguished in Hebrew.
4   No dual appears with the verb. Nominals in the dual are accompanied by verb forms in the plural (→ § 44.6).
5   Masculine and feminine forms were differentiated only in the 2nd and 3rd person.
6   The term "tense" and the names "perfect" and "imperfect" are traditional and do not exactly meet the functions of the verb forms in the text, because the terms "time" (lat.: *tempus*) as well as "complete" (lat.: *perfectum*) and "incomplete" (lat.: *imperfectum*) do not completely describe the use of the verb forms in the text. Nevertheless, they are retained in this grammar, though under the methodological assumption that no fundamentally sufficient explanation for the use of a phenomenon should be gathered from the name for this linguistic phenomenon.
    In the Hebrew grammar of Bauer and Leander the tenses are called "nominal" (perfect) and "aorist" (imperfect). In newer publications on Hebrew grammar, the terms "yiqtol" and "qatal" are read for "imperfect" and "perfect," respectively (these are the same forms of the 3ms → §§ 25.3 and 27.3).

then differentiates forms of the **perfect class** and forms of the **imperfect class**. As a rule, imperatives belong to the imperfect class. Nominal forms belong partly to one class, partly to the other.

24.3 Strong and Weak Verbs

With strong verbs, all **three radicals** are present as consonants in all forms.

With weak verbs, all three radicals are **not preserved in all forms** as consonants (→ §§ 35–40), or the root exists only in **two** radicals (→ §§ 41 and 42).

Different classes of weak verbs are distinguished according to the radical that demonstrates the irregularity.

Classification

The radicals of the verb פָּעַל "do" are used for classification:

פ means that the 1st radical is weak (thus not always present),
ע means that the 2nd radical is weak,
ל means that the 3rd radical is weak.

For example, the name "פ״נ verb" (Pe-Nun) names the verb class whose 1st radical Nun is not preserved as a consonant in all forms.[7]

24.4. Ways of Citing

Root

In the lexicon, every verb is cited as a **root**. As a rule, only the three consonants, **without vowels**, stand next to one another. This is read in such a way that a long a is spoken after the 1st radical, a short a after the 2nd:

כתב : כָּתַב "kâtab"

This is **actually** the form of the 3rd person masculine singular of the perfect in the base stem (Qal): **"He has written."**[8]

However, the German meaning of the root stands in the **lexicon** in the **infinitive**:

כתב "to write."

Also verbs that do not appear at all in the base stem are still cited as a root in this same way.

7　On the name ע״וי and ע״ע → § 41.1 and § 42.1, note.
8　One exception → § 41.1.

25 The Forms of the Preformative Conjugation

25.1 Use

The forms of the preformative conjugation (PC) are the most frequent in the text of the Hebrew Bible (ratio of PC to AC 3:2). The imperfect and the narrative tense imperfect consecutive (Narrativ → § 25.4) are built on the forms of the preformative conjugation. In German, we translate the imperfect most of the time with the present, the imperfect consecutive most of the time with preterit (further → § 48).

25.2 Formation

Overview

The personal forms are differentiated through **prefixes** (preformatives), a few additionally through **suffixes** (afformatives). The afformatives and the consonants of the preformatives are the same in all stems.

Verb forms are cited in the following **order**: 3rd—2nd—1st, because the form of the 3rd person is the simplest.[1]

fem		masc		Singular
	••• ת		••• י	3rd
י ••• ת		••• ת		2nd
		••• א		1st
				Plural
נָה ••• ת		וּ ••• י		3rd
נָה ••• ת		וּ ••• ת		2nd
		••• נ		1st

Preformatives

Preformatives are the consonants:

Jod (י) for the **3rd person**,

Alef (א) and **Nun** (נ) for the **1st person**,

Taw (ת) for all **remaining** forms.

---

1 In this grammar, tables are furthermore oriented from right to left, when the order of the Hebrew linguistic signs plays a role.

Afformatives

Vocal afformatives are **i** (יְ◌) for **2**[nd] **f. s.** and **u** (וּ) for the **masculine** plural forms. נָה is the consonantal afformative for the **feminine** plural forms.[2]

25.3 The Forms in the Base Stem (Qal)[3]

קטֹל	to kill[3]
כבד	to be heavy

Features

Characteristic are the following: only one vowel with the 2nd radical and a closed preformative syllable with short i or (rarely) a.

The vowel with the 2nd radical (imperfect vowel) is long o (lengthened from u) or short a. The imperfect vowel a appears with intransitive verbs and with verbs with gutturals. Imperfect vowel e (lengthened from i) appears only with a few weak verbs (→ §§ 36 and 38).

Most of the time, the vowel in the preformative syllable is i, with gutturals also a or ä.

The Qal Imperfect

Imperfect Vowel a		Imperfect vowel o		
f	m	f	m	
תִּכְבַּד	יִכְבַּד	תִּקְטֹל	יִקְטֹל	3 s
תִּכְבְּדִי	תִּכְבַּד	תִּקְטְלִי	תִּקְטֹל	2 s
	אֶכְבַּד		אֶקְטֹל	1 s
תִּכְבַּדְנָה	יִכְבְּדוּ	תִּקְטֹלְנָה	יִקְטְלוּ	3 pl
תִּכְבַּדְנָה	תִּכְבְּדוּ	תִּקְטֹלְנָה	תִּקְטְלוּ	2 pl
	נִכְבַּד		נִקְטֹל	1 pl

---

2   The origin of the preformatives and afformatives from pronominals is clear (outside of the Jod).
3   קטל is the traditional verb used for examples. We follow this on a practical basis: In contrast to כתב (in earlier editions of this grammar) attention does not have to be given to the BeGaDKe-FaT consonants and to the Dagesches. קטל means "to kill," but appears only four times in the Bible; it is thus nothing more than a symbol for "the verb." When the examples of form however are translated, then כתב "to write" serves as the example verb.

Accent

The **imperfect vowel** u is **lengthened** to o in the tone syllable; a is preserved short. The **consonantal** afformative נָה is added **unaccented**. The imperfect vowel disappears before the accented, added **vocal** afformatives ◌ִי and וּ. The **preformative vowel** in the 1ˢᵗ person singular undergoes ablaut to ä with the guttural א.

25.4 Imperfect Consecutive or Narrativ

Narrativ

In biblical prose, imperfect consecutive is the **narrative tense** ("Narrativ" from lat. narrare: to tell). In German narratives, the preterit corresponds to it most of the time.

In the form of the Hebrew imperfect consecutive, the prefix "wa-" represents the succession of narrative, which can be introduced in German translation with succession particles such as "da [then]," "dann [then]," "und [and]," "dass [that]" (further on the use → § 48).

Forms

The proclitic element ◌ַו (Waw with Patach and following Dagesch forte: "Waw consecutive") goes before imperfect form. This is unique to imperfect forms:

יִכְתֹּב   he writes

וַיִּכְתֹּב   and he wrote

Before the א of the 1ˢᵗ person there is **compensatory lengthening** (→ § 09) of the ־ַו to וָ:

וָאֶכְתֹּב

Loss of the **Dagesch forte** (→ § 05.2) occurs before יְ:

וַיְדַבֵּר

In the uninflected forms of the imperfect consecutive, the **next to last syllable** can be **accented** instead of the last syllable.[4] It is prerequisite that the next to last syllable is open and the last closed.

A long vowel in the last syllable then appears shortened.

e.g.: Impf. יֵלֵךְ Impf cons. וַיֵּלֶךְ

---

4   This "tone reversal" does not appear in the 1ˢᵗ person singular.

26 Further Personal Forms of the Imperfect Class

26.1 Imperative

Imperative forms appear only in the 2ⁿᵈ person and are distinguished according to number (sing/plur) and gender (m/f).

Imperative forms have the **vocalization** and the afformatives of the **imperfect forms**, but not their preformatives.[1]

Forms

The **vowel afformatives** i (ִֹי) and u (וּ) are **accented**, and in front of these the vowel of the stem syllable disappears.

With the 1ˢᵗ radical arises then a closed syllable with **short i** (→ § 10.4).

כְּבַד	קְטֹל	m s
כִּבְדִי	קִטְלִי	f s
כִּבְדוּ	קִטְלוּ	m pl
כְּבַדְנָה	קְטֹלְנָה	f pl

26.2 Modi

In the course of the development of a language, independent modus-forms (for demand, wish, etc.) are to a great extent lost. In Biblical Hebrew other linguistic devices have taken over their functions. Details → on this § 51.

Remnants of such older modi are still preserved, but they have lost their functions in part (→ §§ 32.2, 39.3, 41.3).

Jussive

Hebrew grammars conventionally call forms of the 2ⁿᵈ and 3ʳᵈ person of the imperfect, with which a **demand** is expressed, "**Jussive**" (from lat. iubeo/iussi: "to command"). The term is also used when they are not formally distinguished from "normal" imperfect forms.

In **this grammar** then, the term "Jussive" is only used when it is actually a matter of a **separate form** (→ § 32.2) or when in the syntax the speech-intention of a specific clause was intended as inviting in a specific text (→ § 51.4).

---

1   Rule of thumb: Impv is the same as PC minus P.

He Cohortativum (Cohortative)

Forms of the 1st person imperfect can be expanded through the afformative הָ◌ ("He cohortativum" from lat.: cohortari: "to encourage") and thus expresse a wish, desire, i.e. a self request:

| אֶכְתֹּב | I write | אֶכְתְּבָה | I may/will write |
| נִכְתֹּב | we write | נִכְתְּבָה | we will/want to write/let us write! |

He cohortativum is **accented** and the imperfect vowel disappears. Occasionally, He cohortativum also occurs as a jussive ending of the **3rd person**. In Narrativ forms, a cohortative function is no longer recognizable.

Imperative with He Cohortativum

The uninflected form of the **imperative** can be **strengthened** through He cohortativum.[2] Form: The afformative is accented, the imperfect vowel disappears, and a short vowel appears in the first syllable (→ § 10.4): i or å.

| קְטֹל | > | קָטְלָה |
| כְּבַד | > | כִּבְדָה |

Nun Paragogicum

Remnants of an older modus form are the (always accented) endings ין◌ (2 f s) and ן◌ 3/2 m pl), which are used occasionally instead of the normal vowel afformatives י◌ and ו (Nun paragogicum from Greek paragogé: "ending"). The imperfect vowel is often preserved before such endings: Particular functions, however, are no longer recognized.

| | תִּקְטְלִין | or | יִקְטְלוּן |
| | | also | תִּקְטֹלֶן |

---

2   In this position, the He is also called "He adhortativum."

27 The Forms of the Afformative Conjugation

27.1 Use

*Two tenses are derived from the forms of the afformative conjugation (AC). The **perfect** is a past-time tense in narrative texts and other texts. The **perfect consecutive** is a non past-time tense and appears above all in discourse texts. All German equivalents cannot all in all be cited. They depend on the context (→ § 48).*

27.2 Formation

The personal forms are distinguished through added endings (afformatives). Only the form of the 3rd person, masculine, singular (3ms) appears without an ending. The afformatives are derived in part from personal pronouns,[1] in part from nominal endings.

fem	masc	
ה ◌ָ●●●	●●	3rd sing
ת ◌ָ●●●[2]		
תְּ ●●●	תָּ ●●●	2nd
	תִּי ●●●	1st
	וּ ●●●	3rd pl
תֶּן ●●●	תֶּם ●●●	2nd
	נוּ ●●●	1st

27.3 The Forms in the Basic Stem (Qal)

קָטַל	to kill
יָכֹל	to be able
זָקֵן	to be old

---

1 This is everywhere clearly recognized; with תִּי < אָנֹכִי exists a sound change k > t.
2 תְ before suffixes → § 33.4 and with Lamed-He weak verbs → § 39.2.

Overview

Type Qatel (mediae e)	Type Qatol (mediae o)		Type Qatal (mediae a)		
	f	m	f	m	
זָקֵן	יָכְלָה	יָכֹל	קָטְלָה³	קָטַל	3s
etc.	יָכֹלְתְּ	יָכֹלְתָּ	קָטַלְתְּ	קָטַלְתָּ	2s
as		יָכֹלְתִּי		קָטַלְתִּי	1s
קָטַל		יָכְלוּ		קָטְלוּ⁴	3pl
יְכָלְתֶּן		יְכָלְתֶּם	קְטַלְתֶּן	קְטַלְתֶּם	2pl
		יָכֹלְנוּ		קָטַלְנוּ	1pl

Vowels

Characteristic for the Qal is the **long a** (pre-tone Qámes → § 10.1) **with the 1ˢᵗ radical**, which appears in most of the forms.

With the 2ⁿᵈ radical stands short a (mediae a verbs: קָטַל), long e (mediae e verbs: זָקֵן), or long o (mediae o verbs: יָכֹל).[5]

The following gives detail in how the place of accent influences the vocalization (→ in principle § 10):

Stress

If the consonantal **afformatives** תֶּם and תֶּן are stressed, then the long a disappears in the first syllable. (Examples → table § 27.3). Otherwise it is preserved: The other consonantal afformatives appear unaccented. The **vowel afformatives** הָ and ו are indeed **stressed**, but the **long a** is **preserved** with the 1ˢᵗ radical through a Meteg while the second vowel disappears. In pause forms, the vowel before a vocalic afformative can also be accented and lengthened: e.g. קָטָלָה.

Special feature of **mediae e** verbs: The e appears only in the form of the **3ʳᵈ person masculine** singular and in pause forms, otherwise the forms are the same as those of קָטַל.

Special feature of **mediae o** verbs: Before an accented consonantal afformative (תֶּם and תֶּן), the **o** of the second syllable is shortened **to å**.

---

3   The Qámes here and in the 3ʳᵈ person plural denotes long â (qâteláh—qâtelú).
4   The Qámes here and in the 3ʳᵈ person singular denotes long â (qâteláh—qâtelú).
5   They are the short base vowels (→ § 2.2) a, i (lengthened to ê) and u (lengthened to ô).

27.4 The Perfect Consecutive

כָּתַב	"he has written"
וְכָתַב	"and he writes"
	"then he will/shall write"

Use

Through a small **proclitic pre-syllable**, וְ, on the "perfect" tense, which is mainly a looking-back tense, is given the "Perfectum consecutivum," which is a tense that has a **different aim**, mainly that of looking-ahead. It is also called "consecutive perfect" or "Waw-AC."

Form

In the perfect consecutive, the **afformatives** תִּי and תָּ are often **accented**, but in this case the long vowel in the first syllable is preserved (Meteg):

וְכָתַבְתִּי
וְכָתַבְתָּ

28 Nominal Forms of the Verb

28.1 Infinitives

The Hebrew verb has two infinitive forms in all stems: the infinitivus absolutus (inf a) and the infinitivus constructus (inf c). In order to avoid unwieldy Latin expressions, in this grammar the infinitivus constructus is denoted simply as "infinitive," the infinitivus absolutus as "infinitive absolute."[1]

Infinitive Absolute

The infinitive absolute

1. stands **isolated** in the clause (lat. absolutus = removed),
2. cannot be connected to suffixes and prepositions, and
3. introduces **only the meaning of the verb** into the clause (details on use → §§ 49.2 and 50.4).

In the Qal, the form belongs to the **perfect class** (→ § 24.2). The vowels do not change.

קָטֹל

Infinitive (Infinitivus Constructus)

The infinitive (inf c) is used in a way similar to German and English. For details on this, see § 12 and § 33 (prepositions and suffixes) as well as §§ 49.3 and 50.5 (syntax).

In the Qal, the forms belong to the **imperfect class** (→ § 24.2): Schwa mobile stands in the 1st radical, the imperfect vowel *o* (lengthened < *u*) in the 2nd. This is also true with verbs having the imperfect vowel *a*.[2]

יִקְטֹל	קְטֹל
יִכְבַּד	כְּבֹד

At times infinitive forms are formed with a **feminine ending**.

With some weak verbs an **infinitive ending** ת also appears (→ §§ 36, 38 and 39).

יְרָאָה	ירא (to fear)
אַהֲבָה	אהב (to love)
לֶכֶת	הלך (to go)

---

1   Also abbreviated: "inf c" and "inf a."
2   Occasionally, infinitive forms also appear with a. Thus, many times an infinitive and an imperative are the same (m s).

28.2 Participles

Participles can carry out the function of all nominal component parts of a clause. Frequently they appear as predicates in nominal clauses (details → § 49). In the base stem (Qal), there is an active and a passive participle. Both are related to the perfect class.

Form Overview

mediae e	mediae o	mediae a		
		fem	masc	
זָקֵן	יָכֹל	קֹטְלָה	קֹטֵל	active ptcp
		קֹטֶלֶת		
		קֹטְלוֹת	קֹטְלִים	
			קֹטְלֵי	
–	–	קְטוּלָה	קָטוּל	passive ptcp

The Forms of the Active Participle

With mediae a verbs, the participle has **unchangeable o** in the first syllable and changeable e in the second: קֹטֵל.

With mediae e and o verbs, the form of the participle is the **same** as the Qal perfect **3rd person** masculine singular: The other forms are formed like other nominals with changeable vowels (→ § 17).

Apart from the feminine ending הָ◌/תָ◌ (→ § 16.2), the **feminine ending ת** appears with many participles in the singular, which is added without a vowel. At the same time, **Segolat** forms arise (→ § 18).

The Forms of the Passive Participle

The passive participle has **pre-tone Qámes** in the first syllable, unchangeable **long u** in the second: קָטוּל.

(formation as other nominals → § 17)

29 The Derived Stems of the Verb

29.1 Function

Through regular change of the base stem's form, the meaning of a verb can be modified.[1]

Seven derived stems (stem modifications, **Binyanim**, conjugations) are used most frequently. Stems that only appear occasionally are referred to on a case by case basis (→ e.g. §§ 39.6, 41.8, 42.8).

All seven stems are not supported for every root. As a result, the **lexicon** only gives information for each one that exists. In principle, **all verb forms** can appear in each stem. The **passive** stems Puʿal and Hofʿal have **no imperatives**.

29.2 Overview

	Base Stem	N-Stem	Doubled Stems (Intensive Stems[2])			Causative Stems (H-stems)	
Names	Qal	Nifʿal	Piʿel	Puʿal	Hithpaʿel	Hifʿil	Hofʿal
Forms	קַל	נִפְעַל	פִּעֵל	פֻּעַל	הִתְפַּעֵל	הִפְעִיל	הָפְעַל
	קָטַל	נִקְטַל	קִטֵּל	קֻטַּל	הִתְקַטֵּל	הִקְטִיל	הָקְטַל
	יִקְטֹל[3]	יִקָּטֵל	יְקַטֵּל	יְקֻטַּל	יִתְקַטֵּל	יַקְטִיל	יָקְטַל
Meanings	active	passive, reflexive	factitive, resultative	passive for Piʿel	reflexive for Piʿel	causative	passive for Hifʿil

29.3 The Names of the Stems

The base stem is called Qal (hebr. קַל "simple"). The names of the remaining stems are derived from the verb פעל "to do": The form of פעל in the **3ms AC** of the stem in question serves as its **name**.

Nifʿal—נִפְעַל

The prefix נ (< na) forms a closed syllable with the 1ˢᵗ radical.

נִקְטַל

A common feature of the **doubled stems** is the doubling of the middle radical through a **Dagesch forte**.[4]

---

1 Similar to German: essen/fressen, schneiden/schnitzen, fahren/führen/gefährden.
2 Old meaning, as the "intensive" meaning was believed to be predominate.
3 Imperfect forms here only for the sake of completeness; in detail → §§ 30–32.
4 Occasionally, doubled stems are formed differently, e.g. as "Pilpel" (= repetition of two radicals) of the verb: כִּלְכֵּל.

Pi'el—פִּעֵל[5]

In the Pi'el perfect, **i** stands in the hard syllable. The second vowel e is changeable.

| קִטֵּל |

Pu'al—פֻּעַל

In the hard syllable, Pu'al has the u that is characteristic of passive forms.

| קֻטַּל |

Hithpa'el—הִתְפַּעֵל

The pre-syllable הִת is characteristic.

| הִתְקַטֵּל |

A common feature of the **causative stems** (H-stems) is the **prefix consonant He** (ה).

Hif'il—הִפְעִיל

Preformative vowel in AC is i (< a), **long i** with the 2nd radical, which is not always preserved, however.

| הִקְטִיל |

Hof'al—הָפְעַל

Preformative vowel is **u** or å (**sign of passive**).

| הֻקְטַל or הָקְטַל |

29.4. The Meanings of the Stems

Only rough guidelines can be given. In each **individual case, the lexicon gives** information.

In the base stem **Qal**, the verb has it **simple**, unmodified active meaning.[6]

Nif'al

The **Nif'al** is reflexive or passive of the Qal:

Qal	שׁמר	to keep	Ni	נִשְׁמַר	to keep oneself, to be kept

Pi'el

For the doubled stems, the **Pi'el** has the active meaning. It is disputed today whether the intensive meaning is the predominant one, e.g.:

Qal	קָבַר	to bury	Pi	קִבֵּר	to bury many/much

---

5   With פעל, the doubling is not revealed because of the guttural ע.
6   Remnants of a Qal passive have been preserved with a few verbs (→ § 36.4).

Very frequently it is the **factitive** meaning (lat. facere: to make): to make some-thing/someone something, e.g.:

Qal	גָּדַל	to be great	Pi	גִּדַּל	to make great

In this meaning, the Pi'el touches on the Hif'il (see below). Rule of thumb: With intransitive Qal, **Pi'el is about the same as Hif'il**; with transitive Qal **Pi'el is about the same as Qal**. Otherwise, with the Pi'el, as with Hif'il, it depends less on the action as on the **result** of the action.

Pu'al

The **Pu'al** is passive of the Pi'el:

Pi	גָּנַב	to steal	Pu	גֻּנַּב	to be stolen

Hithpa'el

The **Hithpa'el** is mainly reflexive of the Pi'el:

Pi	הִלֵּל	to praise	Hitp	הִתְהַלֵּל	to praise oneself

Hif'il

For the causative stems, the **Hif'il** presents the **active causative** meaning (does something for an action or state of being) e.g.:

Qal	אָבַד	to perish	Hi	הֶאֱבִיד	to destroy
Qal	לָבֵשׁ	to dress	Hi	הִלְבִּישׁ	to dress with (to cause something to clothe someone)

Hof'al

The **Hof'al** is **passive** of the Hif'il:

Hi	הִשְׁלִיךְ	to throw down	Ho	הָשְׁלַךְ	to be thrown down

30 The Forms of the Nifʻal

30.1 Overview

Nifʻal PC		Nifʻal AC		
f	m	f	m	
תִּקָּטֵל	יִקָּטֵל	נִקְטְלָה	נִקְטַל	3s
תִּקָּטְלִי	תִּקָּטֵל	נִקְטַלְתְּ	נִקְטַלְתָּ	2s
	אֶקָּטֵל		נִקְטַלְתִּי	1s
תִּקָּטַלְנָה	יִקָּטְלוּ		נִקְטְלוּ	3pl
תִּקָּטַלְנָה	תִּקָּטְלוּ	נִקְטַלְתֶּן	נִקְטַלְתֶּם	2pl
	נִקָּטֵל		נִקְטַלְנוּ	1pl
	וַיִּקָּטֵל [וַיִּלָּחֶם]			Narrativ
	וָאֶקָּטֵל			Narr. 1s
הִקָּטְלִי	הִקָּטֵל			impv s
הִקָּטַלְנָה	הִקָּטְלוּ			impv pl
	הִקָּטֵל			inf c
[נִקְטֹל]	הִקָּטֵל			inf a
		נִקְטָלָה	נִקְטָל	participle

30.2 Afformative Conjugation

Prefix "ni"

The feature of the stem, the **prefix נ** (on "na" → § 10.4), forms a closed syllable with the 1ˢᵗ radical. It is unchanged in all perfect forms.

As in the Qal, the a with the 2ⁿᵈ radical is preserved before consonantal afformatives; it disappears before vowel afformatives.

30.3 Preformative Conjugation

In the forms of the imperfect class, the Nun of the prefix **assimilates** to the 1ˢᵗ radical. After the doubling of the 1ˢᵗ radical stands a long â.

Imperfect

In the imperfect forms, the **typical sequence of vowels** is i¹—â—ê. The e before consonantal afformatives undergoes ablaut to a; before vowel afformatives it disappears. With some verbs, in uninflected forms of the Narrativ (impf cons), the next to last syllable can be accented (→ § 25.4).

Imperative

A prefixed הִ stands in the imperative;² vocalization is the same as in the imperfect.

30.4 Nominal Forms

Participle

The Nifʿal participle belongs to the **perfect class**. It is similar to the form of the 3ms perfect, only that the **a** is **long** (pre-tone Qames): נִקְטָל נִקְטָלִים נִקְטְלֵי.

Infinitive

The infinitive (inf c) belongs to the **imperfect class**. It is the same as the imperative (ms): הִקָּטֵל. After prepositions, ה can drop out: לְ + הִקָּטֵל = לְקָּטֵל (as in the Hifʿil → § 32).

Infinitive Absolute

Two forms appear for the infinitive absolute, one formed according to the AC, one according to the PC: נִקְטֹל and הִקָּטֵל. Thirdly, the **infinitive** (construct) is also used **as an infinitive absolute**.

---

1 Also ä after the Alef (א) of the 1st person: אֶקָּטֵל → § 25.3.
2 The Nifʿal prefix may have originally been read הִן. The He (ה), preserved in the initial sound, was then dropped out after preformative consonants (as with the article or in the Hifʿil → § 32.2), while the Nun (נ) always assimilates. The He would also help in a better pronunciation of the lost preformative form.

31　The Forms of the Doubled Stems

31.1　Overview

	Hithpaʻel		Puʻal		Piʻel		
	f	m	f	m	f	m	
Afformative Conjugation	הִתְקַטְּלָה	הִתְקַטֵּל	קֻטְּלָה	קֻטַּל	קִטְּלָה	קִטֵּל	3s AC
	הִתְקַטַּלְתְּ	הִתְקַטַּלְתָּ	קֻטַּלְתְּ	קֻטַּלְתָּ	קִטַּלְתְּ	קִטַּלְתָּ	2s
		הִתְקַטַּלְתִּי		קֻטַּלְתִּי		קִטַּלְתִּי	1s
		הִתְקַטְּלוּ		קֻטְּלוּ		קִטְּלוּ	3pl
	הִתְקַטַּלְתֶּן	הִתְקַטַּלְתֶּם	קֻטַּלְתֶּן	קֻטַּלְתֶּם	קִטַּלְתֶּן	קִטַּלְתֶּם	2pl
		הִתְקַטַּלְנוּ		קֻטַּלְנוּ		קִטַּלְנוּ	1pl
Preformative Conjugation	תִּתְקַטֵּל	יִתְקַטֵּל	תְּקֻטַּל	יְקֻטַּל	תְּקַטֵּל	יְקַטֵּל	3s PC
	תִּתְקַטְּלִי	תִּתְקַטֵּל	תְּקֻטְּלִי	תְּקֻטַּל	תְּקַטְּלִי	תְּקַטֵּל	2s
		אֶתְקַטֵּל		אֲקֻטַּל		אֲקַטֵּל	1s
	תִּתְקַטַּלְנָה	יִתְקַטְּלוּ	תְּקֻטַּלְנָה	יְקֻטְּלוּ	תְּקַטֵּלְנָה	יְקַטְּלוּ	3pl
	תִּתְקַטַּלְנָה	תִּתְקַטְּלוּ	תְּקֻטַּלְנָה	תְּקֻטְּלוּ	תְּקַטֵּלְנָה	תְּקַטְּלוּ	2pl
		נִתְקַטֵּל		נְקֻטַּל		נְקַטֵּל	1pl
		וַיִּתְקַטֵּל		וַיְקֻטַּל		וַיְקַטֵּל	Narrativ
						וָאֲקַטֵּל	1s
Imperative	הִתְקַטְּלִי	הִתְקַטֵּל			קַטְּלִי	קַטֵּל	Impv s
	הִתְקַטֵּלְנָה	הִתְקַטְּלוּ			קַטֵּלְנָה	קַטְּלוּ	Impv pl
Nominal Forms		הִתְקַטֵּל				קַטֵּל	inf c
		הִתְקַטֵּל				קַטֹּל	inf a
	מִתְקַטְּלָה	מִתְקַטֵּל	מְקֻטָּלָה	מְקֻטָּל	מְקַטְּלָה	מְקַטֵּל	participle
					מְקַטֶּלֶת		

31.2　Common Features

Dagesch Forte

In all forms of the doubled stems, the **middle** radical is **doubled** (Dagesch forte). As a characteristic of formation, the vowels in the strong syllable (thus before the doubled consonant) appear unchanged.

The doubling does not occur when the middle radical is a **guttural** or a **Resch** (→ §§ 9 and 34).

The Dagesch forte can **drop out** when the middle radical does not belong to the group of BeGaDKeFaT and has a Schwa with it (→ § 5.2).

The vowel after the 2nd radical is e or a and disappears before vowel afformatives.

31.3 Pi'el

AC

Only the **perfect forms** belong to the perfect class. They are formed according to the pattern קִטֵּל. The second vowel is only an e[1] in the 3rd person masculine singular, otherwise it is a short a. The second vowel disappears before vowel afformatives.

PC

The preformative forms have the vowel series **Schwa—a—e**. The e with the 2nd radical is preserved before consonantal afformatives; it disappears before vowel afformatives. In the preformative of the 1st person singular, a **Schwa compositum** appears (Chatéf-Pátach).[2] The imperative is the same as the **PC without P**: קַטֵּל.

Nominal Forms

The **participles** of the Pi'el, like all doubled stems, belong to the imperfect class and have a Mem (מ) as a preformative.

The **infinitive** (inf c) is identical to the imperative (ms). Occasionally, the form of the infinitive construct is also used as an infinitive absolute (inf a). The form קַטֹּל also appears as an infinitive absolute.

31.4 Pu'al

Perfect and imperfect classes are not differentiated in vocalization. All forms are formed according to the **pattern** קֻטַּל.

The a with the 2nd radical disappears before vowel afformatives. As a passive stem, the Pu'al has **no imperative**. The Pu'al **participle** has a long a with the 2nd radi-

---

1   With three verbs, ä appears in the 3rd m. s.: דִּבֶּר "to say," כִּפֶּר "to atone," and כִּבֶּס "to wash."
2   Narrativ (impf cs) 1st s וָאֶקְטֵל (compensatory lengthening → § 9.2); imperfect with simple (copulative) Waw: וַאֲקַטֵּל (breaking a syllable → § 9.3).

cal, which is treated as a **pre-tone** Qámes when the tone has been moved up: מְקֻטָּל —מְקֻטָּלִים—מְקֻטָּלֵי. Further nominal forms do not appear in the Puʿal.[3]

31.5 Hithpaʿel

Perfect and imperfect classes are not differentiated in vocalization. All forms are formed according to the pattern הִתְקַטֵּל.

Perfect

The prefix הִתְ is in the perfect. The vowel with the 2nd radical is e or a and has disappeared before vowel afformatives.

If the 1st radical is a **dental** (ד, ט, ת), then the ת of the prefix has **assimilated** (Dagesch forte).

דבר	הִדַּבֵּר

When the 1st radical is a **sibilant** (ז, ס, צ, שׁ), then the ת of the prefix steps behind the 1st radical (metathesis or **transposition**—gr/lat. "reordering").[4]

שמר	הִשְׁתַּמֵּר

Imperfect Classes

In the imperfect and the participle, the preformative consonants, together with the ת of the prefix, form the preformatives and the ה falls out, e.g.: מִתְקַטֵּל, יִתְקַטֵּל. The vowel after the 2nd radical, e or a, disappears before vowel afformatives. Imperative (ms) and both infinitives are identical: הִתְקַטֵּל or הִתְקַטַּל.

3　Outside of an infinitive absolute from גנב: גֻּנֹּב.
4　A single time one such reordering appears with צ (Gen 44:16), and at the same time the ת also changes to ט: צדק Hitp: נִצְטַדָּק "we justify ourselves."

32 The Forms of the Causative Stems

32.1 Overview

	Hof'al		Hif'il		
	f	**m**	**f**	**m**	
Afformative Conjugation	הָקְטְלָה	הָקְטַל	הֻקְטִילָה	הִקְטִיל	3 s perfect
		[הָקְטַל]			
	הָקְטַלְתְּ	הָקְטַלְתָּ	הֻקְטַלְתְּ	הִקְטַלְתָּ	2 s
		הָקְטַלְתִּי		הִקְטַלְתִּי	1 s
		הָקְטְלוּ		הִקְטִילוּ	3 pl
	הָקְטַלְתֶּן	הָקְטַלְתֶּם	הֻקְטַלְתֶּן	הִקְטַלְתֶּם	2 pl
		הָקְטַלְנוּ		הִקְטַלְנוּ	1 pl
Preformative Conjugation	תָּקְטַל	יָקְטַל	תֻּקְטִיל	יַקְטִיל	3 s imperfect
	תָּקְטְלִי	תָּקְטַל	תֻּקְטִילִי	תַּקְטִיל	2 s
		אָקְטַל		אַקְטִיל	1 s
	תָּקְטַלְנָה	יָקְטְלוּ	תֻּקְטֵלְנָה	יַקְטִילוּ	3 pl
	תָּקְטַלְנָה	תָּקְטְלוּ	תֻּקְטֵלְנָה	תַּקְטִילוּ	2 pl
		נָקְטַל		נַקְטִיל	1 pl
Short form				יַקְטֵל	3 s short form (jussive)
		וַיָּקְטַל		וַיַּקְטֵל	3 s Narrativ
Imperative		–	הַקְטִילִי	הַקְטֵל	Impv s
			הַקְטֵלְנָה	הַקְטִילוּ	Impv pl

Nominal Forms		–		הַקְטִיל	Infinitive
		הָקְטֵל		הַקְטֵל	inf a
	מָקְטָלָה	מָקְטָל	מַקְטִילָה	מַקְטִיל	participle

Common Features

Most forms are formed with the **prefix ה**. After other preformative consonants (PC and participle) the ה is omitted. **Participles** have the **preformative מ**.

32.2 Hifʻil

In the Hifʻil, **vowel** afformatives are **always** added **unaccented**; for that reason, the characteristic long i in the 2nd radical is preserved in many of the forms.

AC

Only the perfect forms belong to the **perfect class** of the Hifʻil. A short i (<a) stands in the preformative syllable of the AC Hifʻil. **Long î** stands as the second stem vowel; before consonantal afformatives, it shortens to a short a.[1]

PC

Short a stands in the **preformative syllable**[2] of the Hifʻil **PC** and also in the imperative. Long i stands as the second stem vowel; before the consonantal afformative נָה also long e.[3]

Short Forms

So-called **short forms** or **jussive**-forms appear in uninflected imperfect forms of the 2nd and 3rd person.[4] In these, the second stem vowel is **not i, rather e**: יַקְטִיל—יַקְטֵל.

---

1   To the perfect class belong only the personal forms of the perfect, not the participle.
2   Actually one must differentiate between "preformative" (for the feature of subject) and prefix (for the feature of stem). This appears also whether it is always possible without any problems. With the term "preformative syllable" it is practical to do without the distinction.
3   The original short i is regularly lengthened to e. The lengthening to long e that is predominate in the Hifʻil is otherwise not usual.
4   In principle and for all verbs, the following applies: When in the uninflected PC forms i or u stands in the tone syllable, then it can give in addition a short form (or jussive form) with e or o (→ § 41.3).

Also in the corresponding form of the **imperfect consecutive** stands **e**, just as in the **imperative** (m s).

Nominal Forms

The Hif'il participle has the preformative מַ. Infinitives are הַקְטִיל (inf c)[5] and הַקְטֵל (inf a).

32.3 Hof'al

All forms of the Hof'al are formed according to the pattern הָקְטַל (with Qámes chatuf å in the preformative syllable). In the preformative, the short u can be preserved (הֻקְטַל).

In the Hof'al participle as with the participles of the Nif'al and Pu'al, long a stands as a pre-tone Qámes (→ § 10.4).

Of the infinitives, the absolute only appears with a strong verb. The passive stems do not have imperatives.

32.4 Analytical Features of All the Stems
Table

	Qal	Nif'al	Pi'el	Pu'al	Hithpa'el	Hif'il	Hof'al
AC	קָטַל	נִקְטַל	קִטֵּל	קֻטַּל	הִתְקַטֵּל	הִקְטִיל	הָקְטַל
PC	יִקְטֹל	יִקָּטֵל	יְקַטֵּל	יְקֻטַּל	יִתְקַטֵּל	יַקְטִיל	יָקְטַל

Features

The AC forms (other than Qal) are read as the names of the stems.

Qal PC forms are unmistakable, just like all Pu'al, Hithpael, and Hof'al forms.

Only for the preformative conjugation of Hif'il, Nif'al and Pi'el (in this alphabetical order) one must remember:

---

5   He at the beginning can fall out after prepositions: לְ + הַקְטִיל > לְקַטִיל < (similarly as with the article (→ § 12.3) or with the Nif'al inf (→ § 30.4)).

1. Hif'il   1 feature: preformative syllable closed with short a

2. Nif'al   2 features: 1st radical doubled,

                                 then long a

3. Pi'el   3 features: preformative Schwa,

                                 1st radical with short a,

                                 2nd radical doubled.

33 Verb Forms with Suffixes

33.1 Use

Suffixes on finite verb forms represent the (accusative) object. For that reason, they only appear with transitive verbs, thus also only in the transitive stems Qal, Pi'el, and Hif'il.[1]

Suffixes on the verb cannot apply back to the subject of the same clause (reflexive). For that reason, suffixes of the 1st and 2nd person do not appear on verb forms of the 1st or 2nd person. Reflexive relationships are expressed through the reflexive stems Nif'al and Hithpa'el.

33.2 Forms

The forms of the suffixes are basically the **same** on a nominal, particle, and verb (→ § 11).

Overview

	1st	2nd m	2nd f	3rd m[2]	3rd f
Singular	נִי	ךָ	ךְ	הוּ	הָ
				or וֹ	or
				or יוֹ	הָ
Plural	נוּ	כֶם	–	ם	ן

Connecting Vowels

Between a verb form ending with a consonant and a suffix beginning with a consonant, a **connecting vowel** is inserted. Connecting vowels are: **a in the perfect**, e or ä in the forms of the **imperfect class**.

Accent

The **vowel before the suffix** is generally accented. Only כֶם and ךָ and the contracted forms וֹ, יוֹ, and הָ are final accents.

---

1   (Rare) exceptions e.g.: גְּדֵלַנִי "he was raised by me" (Job 31:18), וְהִתְנַחֲלוּם - Hitp "and they will obtain them as an allotted inheritance" (Is 14:2), וַיִּלְחֲמוּנִי - Nif'al "and they attack me" (Ps 109:3).
2   The forms וֹ and יוֹ are contracted from "a-hu" or "i-hu," the form הָ from "a-ha."

Old Forms

The changeable **vowels are changed** in the verb forms through a different accent (→ § 10). The features of the Pi'el and Hif'il stems are always preserved. **Qal forms** can demonstrate greater differences than forms without a suffix. Notable is the suffix form of the Qal imperative (ms): קָטְלֵנִי with å in the first syllable.[3]

In part, **old** forms of **afformatives** are preserved before suffixes:

The afformative of the 3fs is represented through תֹ. This brings about forms with a helping vowel such as קְטָלָתֶךָ, or with assimilation such as קְטָלַתּוּ (from קָטְלַת and וּה). A short a is preserved before נִי. Instead of 2 f s תְּ, תִּי stands before suffixes.[4]

instead of	נִי ֶ	:	נִי ֹ	קָטַל	קְטָלֵנִי
				קָתַלְתָ	קְטָלְתַּנִי
instead of	ֶ ה	:	ת ֹ	קָטְלָה	קְטָלַתְנוּ
instead of	תְּ	:	תִּי	קָטַלְתְּ	קְטַלְתִּינוּ
instead of	תֶּם	:	תוּ	קְטַלְתֶּם	קְטַלְתּוּנוּ
instead of	נָה	:	וּ	תִּקְטֹלְנָה	תִּקְטְלוּנוּ

Nun energicum

Remnants of a modus ending appears in suffix forms to which a **Nun** has **assimilated**. A difference in meaning to other suffix forms is not recognized: Such suffix forms with "Nun energicum" appear only with imperfect forms that have **lost an ending**, there often in **pause**.

Suffixes with Nun energicum:				Example: on יִקְטֹל
Suffix 1 s	נִי	with Nun energicum	נִּי ֶ	יִקְטְלֵנִי
Suffix 2 m s	ךָ	with Nun energicum	ךָ ֶ	יִקְטְלֶךָ
Suffix 3 m s	הוּ	with Nun energicum	נּוּ ֶ	יִקְטְלֶנּוּ
Suffix 3 f s	הָ	with Nun energicum	נָּה ֶ	יִקְטְלֶנָּה

---

3   Also the infinitive has this form before suffixes (→ also imperative with He cohortativum § 26.2).
4   Especially rare: 2 m pl תוּ instead of תֶּם, and 3/2 f pl וּ instead of נָה.

33.3 Suffixes on Nominal Forms

On the Participle

Suffixes on the **participle** denote the **object** of the action.

שֹׁפֵט one who judges

שֹׁפְטוֹ one who judges him/his judge

On the Infinitive

Suffixes on the **infinitive** denote

לִשְׁפֹּט to judge

sometimes the **object** of the action (as with personal forms of the verb),

לְשָׁפְטוֹ to his judge/
in order to judge him

sometimes the **subject** of the action.

בְּשָׁפְטוֹ in his judging/
as he judges/
because he judges

The forms of the suffixes are basically the same on **nominal forms** of the verb as with all **nominals** (→ § 17). Only with the infinitive, the suffix of the 1s appears in **both forms**:

נִי for the object (לְשָׁפְטֵנִי "in order to judge me") and

י for the subject (לְשָׁפְטִי "so that I might judge").

34 Strong Verbs with Gutturals

34.1 General Comments

When the Masoretes have applied particular rules of vocalization with the gutturals (or laryngeals), forms of strong verbs with gutturals sound in part different than the "normal" forms (→ § 9).

Depending on which radical is a guttural, these verbs are classified into "primae gutturalis" (1ˢᵗ radical), "mediae gutturalis" (2ⁿᵈ radical), and "tertiae gutturalis" (3ʳᵈ radical) verbs.

Special Features

The **special features** of verbs with gutturals are (→ § 09):

- preference for the **vowel a** (with Alef also ä),
- **Schwa compositum** (Chatef vowel) instead of Schwa mobile (Schwa simplex),
- **breaking up** of closed syllables,
- **no Dagesch forte**, rather compensatory lengthening or virtual doubling,
- **a preceding** a guttural **at the end of the word.**

34.2 Verbs with a Guttural as the 1st Radical (Verben primae gutturalis)

In the Qal imperfect, in the Nifʻal perfect and in all Hifʻil and Hofʻal, the guttural closes a preformative syllable. Then a **short aꜘ** or, above all with א, a **short ä**, stands instead of a short i. Most of the time, the closed syllable remains broken open.

Further moved tone	1ˢᵗ guttural forced open		strong verb	
יַעַבְדוּ	יַעֲבֹד	יַעֲבֹד	יִקְטֹל	Qal Impf (o)
	אֶעֱבָד	אֶעֱבֹד	אֶקְטֹל	with Alef
יֶאְסְרוּ	יֶאֱסֹר	יֶאֱסֹר		
יֶחְכְּמוּ	יֶחְכַּם	יֶחְכַּם	יִזְקַן	Qal Impf (a)

---

1   Qal forms can therefore always be differentiated still from Hifʻil forms, because in the Hifʻil the second vowel i remains preserved.

When **"the tone moves further,"** thus the second vowel in corresponding range of the primary stress disappears, a short full vowel with following silent Schwa occurs with the guttural again (→ § 09.3).

In the Imperfect class of the Nif'al, instead of the doubling of the 1st radical, the **i lengthens to ê** (→ § 9.2).

				Nif'al
נֶעֶבְדוּ	נֶעֱבַד	נֶעֱבַד	נִקְטַל	Perf
		יֵעָבֵד	יִקְטֵל	Impf
		הֵעָבֵד	הִקָּטֵל	inf c
				Hif'il
הֶעֱבִיד	הֶעֱבִיד	הֶעְבִיד	הִקְטִיל	Perf
יַעֲבִיד	יַעֲבִיד		יַקְטִיל	Impf
				Hof'al
הָעָבְדוּ²	הָעֳבַד	הָעֳבַד	הָקְטַל	Perf
יָעָבְדוּ	יָעֳבַד	יָעֳבַד	יָקְטַל	Impf

34.3 Verbs with a Guttural as the 2nd Radical (Verben mediae gutturalis)

In the doubled stems, virtual doubling (with ה, ח, ע) or compensatory lengthening appears: i > ê, a > â, u > ô (→ table).

II Guttural		strong verb	
Compensatory Lengthening	Virtual Doubling		Pi'el
בֵּרַךְ	נִחַל	קִטֵּל	Perfect
יְבָרֵךְ	יְנַחֵל	יְקַטֵּל	Imper-fect
וַיְבָרֶךְ			Narrativ
בֹּרַךְ	נֻחַל	קֻטַּל	Pu'al

34.4 Verbs with a Guttural as the 3rd Radical (Verben tertiae gutturalis)

For III-guttural verbs, only the verbs with **'Ajin** (ע), **Chet** (ח) and **consonantal He** (ה) are counted. Alef (א) and He (ה) are otherwise silent at the end of a word (weak verbs, → §§ 39 and 40).

---

2   In the Hof'al, in spite of Meteg, Qámes Chatúf (â) is to be read.

Patach Furtivum

An a must precede a guttural at the **end of** the word. **Patach furtivum** follows vowels i, o, and u.

The **vowel e** is **displaced** through a in the finite forms of the verb and in the construct forms of infinitive and participle. It is **preserved** in pause forms and in the absolute forms of the infinitive and participles (Patach furtivum).

3ʳᵈ Guttural	strong verb	
		Qal
שֹׁלֵחַ	קֹטֵל	ptcp st a
שֹׁלֵחַ	קֹטֵל	ptcp st c
שָׁלוּחַ		ptcp passive
		Nifʿal
הִשָּׁלֵחַ	הִקָּטֵל	inf c
הִשָּׁלֵחַ	הִקָּטֵל	inf a
		Piʿel
שִׁלַּח	קִטֵּל	perfect
שִׁלֵּחַ	קִטֵּל	in pause
יְשַׁלַּח	יְקַטֵּל	imperfect
יְשַׁלֵּחַ	יְקַטֵּל	in pause
		Hifʿil
הִשְׁלִיחַ	הִקְטִיל	perfect
יַשְׁלִיחַ	יַקְטִיל	imperfect

Feminine Forms

With feminine AC and participle forms, Segolat forms can appear:

2fs AC Qal שָׁלַחַתְּ : קָטַלְתְּ

Ptcp f s Qal שֹׁלַחַת : קֹטֶלֶת.

Comprehensive Overview of 34.2–4

3ʳᵈ guttural	2ⁿᵈ guttural	1ˢᵗ guttural			strong verb	
		יַעַבְדוּ	יַעֲבֹד	יַעֲבֹד	יִקְטֹל	**Qal** impf (o)
			אֶעֱבֹד	אֶעֱבֹד	אֶקְטֹל	with Alef
		יֶאֶסְרוּ	יֶאֱסֹר	יֶאֱסֹר		
		יֶחְכְמוּ	יֶחֱכַם	יֶחֱכַם	יִזְקַן	a

3rd guttural	2nd guttural	1st guttural				strong verb	
שֹׁלֵחַ						קֹטֵל	ptcp st a
שֹׁלַח						קֹטֵל	ptcp st c
שָׁלוּחַ							
		נֶעֶבְדוּ	נֶעֱבַד	נֶעֱבָד	נֶעְבַּד	נִקְטַל	**Nifal** perf
				יֵעָבֵד		יִקָּטֵל	Impf
הִשָּׁלַח						הִקָּטֵל	inf c
הִשָּׁלֵחַ						הִקָּטֵל	inf a
שִׁלַּח	בֵּרֵךְ	נִחַל				קִטֵּל	**Pi'el** perf
שִׁלֵּחַ							
יְשַׁלַּח	יְבָרֵךְ	יְנַחֵל				יְקַטֵּל	Impf
יְשַׁלֵּחַ	וַיְבָרֶךְ						
	בֹּרַךְ	נֻחַל				קֻטַּל	**Pu'al**
הִשְׁלִיחַ		הֶעֱבִיד	הֶעֱבִיד	הֶעֱבִיד		הִקְטִיל	**Hif'il** perf
יַשְׁלִיחַ		יַעֲבִיד	יַעֲבִיד	יַעֲבִיד		יַקְטִיל	Impf
		הָעָבְדוּ[3]	הָעֳבַד	הָעֳבַד	הָעֳבַד	הָקְטַל	**Hof'al** perf
		יָעָבְדוּ	יָעֳבַד	יָעֳבַד	יָעֳבַד	יָקְטַל	Impf

35 Weak Verbs with Alef as the 1st Radical (פ״א Verbs)

35.1 Existence

Only 8 verbs with Alef (א) as the 1ˢᵗ radical have weak forms: אבד *"to destroy,"* אבה *"to want,"* אכל *"to eat,"* אמר *"to say,"* אפה *"to bake,"* אהב *"to love,"*[1] *אחז "to grasp,"* אסף *"to gather." The last three form strong and weak forms.*

35.2 Forms

פ״א weak forms appear only in the Qal imperfect, also in the infinitive with אמר. The analysis of the weak forms is not difficult: the Alef is almost always written.[2]

Overview of Qal PC

	Plural		Singular		Imperfect
in pause	f	m	f	m	
	תֹּאמַ֫רְנָה	יֹאמְרוּ	תֹּאמַר	יֹאמַר	3
	תֹּאמַ֫רְנָה	תֹּאמְרוּ	תֹּאמְרִי	תֹּאמַר	2
		נֹאמַר		אֹמַר	1
וַיֹּאכֵ֫לוּ					
וַיֹּאמֶר				וַיֹּ֫אמֶר	Narrativ
				אֱמֹר + לְ > לֵאמֹר	Infinitive

Imperfect

The **1st radical א quiesces** (is silent). Long o[3] stands in the preformative syllable that is now open. The imperfect vowel o (< u) is replaced through one of the other imperfect vowels (a or e). In the form of the **1st person singular**, after the preformative consonant א, the א of the root is only written once.

Infinitive

For אמר, the infinitive (inf c) has the form לֵאמֹר only in combination with לְ.

---

1   With אהב, only the 1ˢᵗ person is weak.
2   אסף *"to gather"* has two weak forms without Alef: וַיֹּ֫סֶף 2 Sam 6:1 and תֹּסֵף Ps 104:29.
3   From the original preformative vowel, a lengthens to â and undergoes ablaut to ô.

36 Weak Verbs with Nun as the 1ˢᵗ Radical (פ״נ Verbs)

With weak forms of פ״נ verbs, the 1ˢᵗ radical either assimilates or falls out.

נפל	to fall
נגש	to draw near
נגע	to touch

36.1 Forms with Assimilation

Feature

A נ (Nun) at the end of a syllable has **assimilated** with the following consonant, which therefore appears doubled (Dagesch forte). For that reason, with Pe-Nun, weak forms appear in every place where the **1ˢᵗ radical closes a preformative syllable**. And this is the case in the Qal imperfect, in the Nif'al perfect, and in the entire Hif'il and Hof'al. A **feature** of the weak forms is a **Dagesch forte** in the first visible radical.[1]

Overview of Assimilation with I-נ Verbs

Qal imperfect	*jin-pol >	יִפֹּל
Nif'al perfect	*nin-pal >	נִפַּל[2]
Hif'il perfect	*hin-pil >	הִפִּיל
Hif'il imperfect	*jan-pil >	יַפִּיל
Hof'al perfect	*hun-pal >	הֻפַּל
Hof'al imperfect	*jun-pal >	יֻפַּל

II-guttural verbs keep the Nun, thus forming **no weak forms**. נִחַם (Ni "to regret") with virtual doubling is an exception.

---

1   The Dagesch forte can fall out when it should stand in a consonant that belongs to the BeGaD-KeFaT group and has a Schwa with it (→ § 05.2).
2   **Nif'al** perfect and **Pi'el** perfect agree: in the Nif'al the **prefix נ** stands with following assimilation, in the Pi'el the **1st radical נ** with following Dagesch of the doubled stem.

36.2 Tables of the Qal PC

	נגע		נגשׁ		נפל		
	f	m	f	m	f	m	
Imperfect		יִגַּע	תִּגַּשׁ	יִגַּשׁ	תִּפֹּל	יִפֹּל	3 s
			תִּגְּשִׁי	תִּגַּשׁ	תִּפְּלִי	תִּפֹּל	2
	etc.			אֶגַּשׁ		אֶפֹּל	1
			תִּגַּשְׁנָה	יִגְּשׁוּ	תִּפֹּלְנָה	יִפְּלוּ	3 pl
			תִּגַּשְׁנָה	תִּגְּשׁוּ	תִּפֹּלְנָה	תִּפְּלוּ	2
				נִגַּשׁ		נִפֹּל	1
Imperatives	גְּעִי	גַּע	גְּשִׁי	גַּשׁ	נְפְלִי	נְפֹל	impv s
	גַּעֲנָה	גְּעוּ	גַּשְׁנָה	גְּשָׁה	נְפֹלְנָה	-	He coh.
				גְּשׁוּ		נִפְלוּ	pl
Infinitives		גַּעַת		גֶּשֶׁת		נְפֹל	inf c
		גַּעְתִּי		גִּשְׁתִּי			+ suffix

36.3 Weak Imperatives and Infinitives

Aphaeresis

Verbs with the imperfect vowel a also have weak imperatives and infinitives in the Qal.[3] In these forms, the **Nun** is not assimilated, rather it **drops out** (aphaeresis). The infinitive has added the **ending** ת, without a connecting vowel. **Segolata** occur with it (→ § 18.1).

Infinitive *gaš - t >	גֶּשֶׁת	
Prefixes with **pre-tone Qámes:**	לָגֶשֶׁת	
Suffix forms on the **base form:**		גִּשְׁתּוֹ
Helping vowel a with **guttural:**	גַּעַת	לָגַעַת	גַּעְתּוֹ

---

3   There are also isolated cases of strongly formed imperative and infinitive forms such as נְגֹל.

36.4 The Verbs נתן, לקח and Doubly Weak Verbs

נתן	to give
לקח	to take
נשׂע	to lift up

Tables of the Qal PC

נשׂא		לקח		נתן		
f	m	f	m	f	m	
תִּשָּׂא	יִשָּׂא	תִּקַּח	יִקַּח	תִּתֵּן	יִתֵּן	3 s
תִּשְׂאִי	תִּשָּׂא	תִּקְחִי⁴	תִּקַּח	תִּתְּנִי	תִּתֵּן	2
אֶשָּׂא		אֶקַּח		אֶתֵּן		1
תִּשֶּׂאנָה	יִשְׂאוּ	תִּקַּחְנָה	יִקְחוּ	-	יִתְּנוּ	3 pl
תִּשֶּׂאנָה	תִּשְׂאוּ	תִּקַּחְנָה	תִּקְחוּ	-	תִּתְּנוּ	2
נִשָּׂא		נִקַּח		נִתֵּן		1
Imperatives שְׂאִי	שָׂא	קְחִי	קַח	תְּנִי	תֵּן	impv s
-		קְחָה		תְּנָה		+ He coh
-	שְׂאוּ	קֶחְנָה	קְחוּ	-	תְּנוּ	pl
Infinitives שְׂאֵת		קַחַת		תֵּת		inf c
לָשֵׂאת		לָקַחַת		לָתֵת		+ ל
שְׂאֵתִי		לְקַחְתִּי		לְתִתִּי		+ suff

The Verb נתן

נתן also has Qal **perfect**[5] weak forms:

The 3rd radical is assimilated following ת.

The **imperfect vowel** (i lengthened to) **e** stands in the Qal imperfect.

2ms *natan-ta > נָתַתָּ
2fs *natan-t > נָתַתְּ
(forms → tables § 36.4)

---

4 The doubling does not occur with non-BeGaDKeFaT with Schwa (→ § 05.2).
5 Of the other forms, only the Nif'al perfect is substantiated: נִתַּן. The Hof'al form יֻתַּן has the meaning of a passive for the Qal, but is cited by the lexicons under Hof'al.

The **imperatives** of the Qal are formed without a
1ˢᵗ radical (see table above).

In the Qal **infinitive** (with ending תּ) the 3ʳᵈ radical is
assimilated to ת.

*tint > *titt > תֵּת
+ suffix: לְתִתִּי

The Verb לקח

In contrast to נתן, לקח forms weak forms as if it were a פ״נ verb (details → above
in the table).

Doubly Weak Verbs

Pe-Nun and Lamed-Alef verbs[6]

נשׂא to lift up
נבא (Ni) to be a prophet

There are doubly weak forms with quiescent (silent) Alef and long vowel (יִשָּׂא,
נִבָּא) in the Qal and Nifʿal (→ § 40). For נשׂא the imperative and infinitive forms
in the Qal are particularly to be noted (→ table in 36.4).

---

6   The verbs נכה (Hi: to strike) and נטה (Qal: to extend, Hi: to bend) → § 39, Lamed-He verbs.

37 Weak Verbs with Jod as the 1st Radical (פ״י Verbs)

יָטַב to be good

Weak forms of the few פ״י verbs appear only in the Qal imperfect and in the Hif'il. Forms of the Qal imperative and infinitive as well as Nif'al and Hof'al forms are not substantiated.[1]

37.1 Weak Forms with i in the Preformative (Qal Imperfect)

All I-י verbs have the **imperfect vowel** a. The accompanying **preformative vowel** i is **contracted** with the Jod to long i.	*jijtab > יִיטַב
The open **preformative syllable** remains **preserved** also before an accented ending.	יִיטְבוּ

37.2 Weak Forms with e in the Preformative (Hif'il)

Hif'il

In the imperfect class of the Hif'il[2] the preformative vowel a is contracted with the Jod to **long e:** "ay" > "ai" > "e"	*jajtib > יֵיטִיב
In the imperfect consecutive, the **next-to-last syllable** can be **accented** in forms without an ending.[3]	וַיֵּיטֶב
Also in Hif'il perfect, unchangeable **long e** stands in the preformative syllable.	הֵיטִיב

---

1 Apart from the frequent verb (יטב, (x139 only the quite rare verbs ילל (Hi) "to wail," ימן (Hi), "to turn to the right," ינק "to suck," יקץ "to awake" and ישן "to sleep" belong to this verb class. The verb ישר "to be straight/right" has Hif'il forms like פ״י verbs (→ § 38.3).

2 Only in the Hif'il forms are the Pe-Jod verbs recognized as such.

3 "withdrawing tone" → § 25.4.

38 Weak Verbs with Original Waw as the 1st Radical (פ״ו Verbs)

יֵשֵׁב	to sit
יָבֵשׁ	to be dry
הלך	to go[1]
יָצַת	to kindle, burn

In initial position, Waw has become Jod. As a result, the פ״ו verbs are listed in the lexicon under Jod (י). Waw appears as a consonant only in the imperfect class of the Nif'al and sometimes in the Hithpael.[2]

There are weak forms where the 1ˢᵗ radical closes a preformative syllable (Qal PC, Nif'al AC, in the entire Hif'il and Hof'al → § 36.1) and also with a few verbs appearing very frequently in the Qal imperative and infinitive (→ § 36.3).

38.1 Qal Forms—Overview

	הלך f	הלך m	ישב f	ישב m	יָבֵשׁ f	יָבֵשׁ m	
Imperfect	תֵּלֵךְ	יֵלֵךְ	תֵּשֵׁב	יֵשֵׁב	תִּיבַשׁ	יִיבַשׁ	3 s
	תֵּלְכִי	תֵּלֵךְ	תֵּשְׁבִי	תֵּשֵׁב	תִּיבְשִׁי	תִּיבַשׁ	2
	אֵלֵךְ		אֵשֵׁב		אִיבַשׁ		1
	תֵּלַכְנָה	יֵלְכוּ	תֵּשַׁבְנָה	יֵשְׁבוּ	תִּיבַשְׁנָה	יִיבְשׁוּ	3 pl
	תֵּלַכְנָה	תֵּלְכוּ	תֵּשַׁבְנָה	תֵּשְׁבוּ	תִּיבַשְׁנָה	תִּיבְשׁוּ	2
	נֵלֵךְ		נֵשֵׁב		נִיבַשׁ		1
	וַיֵּלֶךְ		וַיֵּשֶׁב		וַיִּיבַשׁ		Narrativ
Imperative	לְכִי	לֵךְ	שְׁבִי	שֵׁב			Impv s
	לֵכְנָה	לְכוּ	שֵׁבְנָה	שְׁבוּ			pl
Infinitive	לֶכֶת		שֶׁבֶת				inf
	לָלֶכֶת		לָשֶׁבֶת				with ל
	לְלֶכְתּוֹ		לְשִׁבְתּוֹ				with suffix

---

1   הלך "to go" (→ also § 38.3 and 4) is formed like a פ״ו verb.
2   For example, יתר Ni remains: יִוָּתֵר; ידע reveals its identity: הִתְוַדַּע.

38.2 Qal Forms

with i

Verbs with the **imperfect vowel a** form the same forms as the Pe-Jod verbs (→ §
37): **long, unchangeable i** always stands in the open preformative syllable in the
Qal; the second vowel a is changeable.

with e

Verbs with the **imperfect vowel e** (< i) and הלך and ידע (see below)[3] form all
forms of the Qal PC with aphaeresis of the Waw (→ § 36.3); **unchangeable long
e** always stands in the open preformative syllable.[4]

Aphaeresis

Verbs with the **imperfect vowel e** (< i) and הלך, ירש, and ידע (see below) also
form Qal **imperative** and **infinitive** with aphaeresis of the Waw (as נתן and לקח
→ § 36.3).

Infinitive ending ת

In the infinitive (inf c), the two-radical base, e.g. שֵׁב, receives the ending ת without a connecting vowel (*šibt), and it results in a **Segolat form**: שֶׁבֶת (→ §§ 18
and 36.3).

---

3   Seven verbs have *e* in the Qal PC: יצא, ירד, ישב, ידע, ילד, and הלך. To remember in a story:
    "A man went out (וַיֵּצֵא) from his house, went down (וַיֵּרֶד), dwelled there (וַיֵּשֶׁב), knew (וַיֵּדַע) a
    woman, who bore (וַתֵּלֶד) a child, and he left (וַיֵּלֶךְ)."
4   Probably lengthened from *i* in an open syllable and unchangeable in analogy to the other pre-
    formative vowels of this verb class.

38.3 Forms with o or u in the Open Preformative Syllable (Forms of the Nif'al, Hif'il, and Hof'al) and Forms with Sharpened Preformative Syllable

יצת[5]		הלך		ישב		
f	m		m	f	m	
נִצְּתָה	נִצַּת	no Nif'al		נוֹשְׁבָה	נוֹשַׁב	Nif'al AC
				etc.	נוֹשַׁבְתָּ	
					יִוָּשֵׁב	Nif'al PC
	הִצִּית	no feminine forms	הוֹלִיך	הוֹשִׁיבָה	הוֹשִׁיב	Hif'il AC
3pl	הַצַּתִּי		הוֹלַכְתִּי		הוֹשַׁבְתָּ	
הִצִּיתוּ					etc.	
			יוֹלִיך	תּוֹשִׁיב	יוֹשִׁיב	Hif'il PC
			תּוֹלִיך	תּוֹשִׁיבִי	תּוֹשִׁיב	2s
			אוֹלִיך		אֹשִׁיב	1s
			יוֹלִיכוּ	תּוֹשֵׁבְנָה	יוֹשִׁיבוּ	3 pl
			-	תּוֹשֵׁבְנָה	תּוֹשִׁיבוּ	2 pl
			נוֹלִיך		נוֹשִׁיב	1 pl
			יוֹלֵך		יוֹשֵׁב	jussive
וַיִּצֶּת			וַיּוֹלֶך		וַיּוֹשֶׁב	Narrativ
			הוֹלֵך	הוֹשִׁיבִי	הוֹשֵׁב	impv s
			הוֹלִיכוּ	הוֹשֵׁבְנָה	הוֹשִׁיבוּ	pl
			הוֹלִיך		הוֹשִׁיב	Infinitive
			-		הוֹשֵׁב	inf a
מַצִית		מׁולְכוּת f	מׁולִיך		מושׁיב	participle
הֻצַּת			-		הוּשַׁב	Hof'al

Unchangeable long o stands in the **Nif'al** perfect and in the entire **Hif'il**; in the Hof'al, long u stands in the open preformative syllable.

Forms with Dagesch Forte

Pe-Waw verbs with **Sade** (צ) as the 2ⁿᵈ radical[6] (other than יצא) have weak forms with doubling of the 2ⁿᵈ radical, which then looks like **Pe-Nun verbs**.

---

5   On יצת → below.
6   Only five verbs → lexicon.

38.4 Verbs with Special Features

הָלַךְ **"to go"**	Forms in Tables in §38.1 and 3

In the Qal PC and in the Hifʿil, all forms are formed analogous to the Pe-Waw verb (יָשַׁב).

	Imperfect	Impf Consecutive	Imperative	Infinitive
יָדַע **"to know"**				
In the Qal, all forms of the imperfect class are formed with aphaeresis of the Waw.	יֵדַע	וַיֵּדַע	דַּע	דַּעַת
				לָדַעַת
	יֵדְעוּ		דְּעוּ	לְדַעְתּוֹ
יָרַשׁ **"to take possession"**				
Besides regular PC forms with the imperfect vowel a stand weak imperative and infinitive forms with aphaeresis and e.	יִירַשׁ		רֵשׁ	רֶשֶׁת
			רְשׁוּ	לְרִשְׁתּוֹ
יָצָא **"to go out"**				
In the Qal, it has the imperfect vowel i and forms like a Lamed-Alef verb some forms of a particular kind.	יֵצֵא	וַיֵּצֵא	צֵא	צֵאת
	יֵצְאוּ		צְאוּ	לָצֵאת
	תֵּצֶאנָה			לְצֵאתוֹ
יָרֵא **"to fear"**				
has regular forms:	יִירָא	וַיִּירָא	יְרָא	
	יִירְאוּ			
and irregular forms:			יְראוּ	יִרְאָה
יָכֹל **"to be able"**				
has in the Qal the preformative vowel u, with the Waw contracted to long u, seen as Hofʿal. Infinitive *jekol in addition with ending ת (Segolatum).	יוּכַל			
	יוּכְלוּ			
				יְכֹלֶת

39 Weak Verbs with Final Vowel (ל״ה Verbs)

גלה	to uncover
עשה	to do/make

39.1 General Comments

These verbs are originally ל״ו or ל״י verbs, whose forms have to a large extent become like each other. In forms without an ending, He (ה) has entered as a vowel letter for the final vowel in the place of the 3rd radical.

Verbs with original He (ה) as the 3rd radical are strong verbs and take the He as He mappiqatum (ה → § 34.4).

The unique, strongly-formed form of Lamed-He verbs is the Qal **passive participle**: גְּלוּי. According to the view of the Masoretes, the Jod in this verb form is a consonant.

39.2 Weak Forms

Since the weakness of these verbs affects the end of the verb form, the features are fundamentally the same in all stems.[1]

In forms without afformative, ה stands as a vowel letter for a long vowel in final position.

Final Vowels

		Qal[2]	Ni	Pi	Hi
a	in the perfect	גָּלָה	נִגְלָה	גִּלָּה	הִגְלָה
ä	in the imperfect and	יִגְלֶה	יִגָּלֶה	יְגַלֶּה	יַגְלֶה
	participle st. a.	גֹּלֶה	נִגְלֶה	מְגַלֶּה	מַגְלֶה
e	in the participle st. c.	גֹּלֵה			
	and in the imperative[3]	גְּלֵה	הִגָּלֵה	גַּלֵּה	הַגְלֵה

---

1 Appropriately, the features of the stems are preserved at the beginning of the verb forms. Most of the time, the formation of the preformative syllable resembles that of the strong verb.
2 The table only shows examples, which can be augmented slightly for Puʻal, Hitpaʻel, and Hofʻal.
3 In the infinitive absolute e or o, e.g. (גָּלֹה).

Endings

If accented on the 2nd radical, vowel afformatives and the vowel ending of the participle drop off. (He cohortativum does not appear.)

Qal:	גְּלוּ	יִגְלוּ
	גֹּלִים	
Ni:	נִגְלוּ	יִגָּלוּ
Hi:	הִגְלוּ	יַגְלוּ

ת plus הָ forms the feminine form (3s) AC.

          גָּלְתָה

תָ appears also before the suffix.

with suffix: גָּלַתְנוּ

וֹת- is the infinitive ending in all stems:

Qal inf	גְּלוֹת
Ni inf	הִגָּלוֹת
Hi inf	הַגְלוֹת

Jod[4] with homogeneous vowel[5] stands before the consonantal afformatives:

Qal	תִּגְלֶינָה	גָּלִיתָ
Ni	תִּגָּלֶינָה	נִגְלֵיתִי
Hi	תַּגְלֶינָה	הִגְלִיתָ הִגְלֵיתִי

Suffixes

On verb forms without an afformative (ה falls off), suffixes stand immediately after the 2nd radical.	גָּלָה + הוּ > גָּלָהוּ יִגְלֶה + הוּ > יִגְלֶהוּ

39.3 Short Forms

With forms of the imperfect class that **lack an ending**, besides the "normal" forms in ä or e, there are short forms[6] **without** the **final vowel**. These short forms are frequently, but not exclusively, used as **jussive** (→ §§ 26.2 and 51.4) and in the **Narrativ.**

---

4   The original 3rd radical.
5   In the perfect e or i, in the imperfect ä.
6   not in the Qal imperative as well as Puʻal and Hofʻal.

Nifʿal, Piʿel and Qal	Impf Ni	יִגָּלֶה	Short forms:	יִגַּל
	Impv Ni	הִגָּלֵה		הִגָּל
	Impf Pi	יְגַלֶּה		יְגַל
	Impv Pi	גַּלֵּה		גַּל
	Impf Qal	יִגְלֶה	Short form:	יִגֶל
			The i of the tone syllable can be lengthened to e:	יִגֶל
			The doubled final syllable can be cancelled out through the helping vowel ä (Segolatum → § 18):	יִגֶל
			At the same time, i can also be preserved in the tone syllable:	יִגֶל
Hifʿil	Impf Hi	יַגְלֶה	Short form:	יֶגֶל
			with helping vowel (Segolatum):	יֶגֶל
	Impv Hi	הַגְלֵה	Short form:	הַגְל
			or with helping vowel (Segolatum):	הֶגֶל

39.4 Verbs with Gutturals

		Impf. Qal	Short Form
With verbs with gutturals, most of the time the preformative vowel a also stands with the 1st radical in the Qal.		יַעֲשֶׂה	יַעַשׂ
	but:	אֶעֱשֶׂה	וָאַעַשׂ
Since the differentiating feature of Qal and Hifʿil in the second syllable drops out with short forms, Qal forms are the same as Hifʿil forms.		Hi יַעֲשֶׂה	Hi יַעַשׂ
The short forms of חנה "to camp" and of חרה "to break out" are notable.		יַחֲנֶה	וַיִּחַן
		יֶחֱרֶה	וַיִּחַר

39.5 Tabular Overview of 39.2-4

Overview ל″ה

Final Sound	Hif'il	Pi'el	Nif'al	1st Guttural	Qal			
					f	m		
a	הִגְלָה	גִּלָּה	נִגְלָה	עָשָׂה	גָּלְתָה	גָּלָה	Perfect	3 s
					גָּלִית	גָּלִיתָ		2 s
						גָּלִיתִי		1 s
						גָּלוּ		3 pl
					גְּלִיתֶן	גְּלִיתֶם		2 pl
						גָּלִינוּ		1 pl
ä	יַגְלֶה	יְגַלֶּה	יִגָּלֶה	יַעֲשֶׂה	תִּגְלֶה	יִגְלֶה	Imperfect	3 s
					תִּגְלִי	תִּגְלֶה		2 s
						אֶגְלֶה		1 s
					תִּגְלֶינָה	יִגְלוּ		3 pl
					תִּגְלֶינָה	תִּגְלוּ		2 pl
						נִגְלֶה		1 pl
	יַגֵל	יְגַל	יִגָּל	יַעַשׂ		יִגֶל יֵגֶל	Short Forms	
	יֵגֶל					יִגֶל יֵגֶל		
	וַיַּגֵל	וַיְגַל	וַיִּגָּל	וַיַּעַשׂ		וַיִּגֶל	Narrativ	
e	הַגְלֵה	גַּלֵּה	הִגָּלֵה	עֲשֵׂה	גְּלִי	גְּלֵה	Imperative	s
				עֲשׂוּ	גְּלֶינָה	גְּלוּ		pl
	הַגְל	גַּל	הִגָּל	-		-	Imperative	short form
-ot	הַגְלוֹת	גַּלּוֹת	הִגָּלוֹת	עֲשׂוֹת		גְּלוֹת	Infinitive	
ä	מַגְלֶה	מְגַלֶּה		עֹשֶׂה		גֹּלֶה	Participle	active
e	מַגְלֵה	מְגַלֵּה		עֹשֵׂה		גֹּלֵה		construct
ä			נִגְלֶה	עָשׂוּי		גָּלוּי	Participle	passive
e			נִגְלֵה					construct

39.6 Verbs with Special Characteristics

היה "to be" and חיה "to live"

With the 1st radical, the verbs היה and חיה frequently have i or a sounds[7] in spite of the guttural.

וְהָיוּ impf + ו   הֱיִיתֶם 2 pl AC

הֱיֵה impv

The closed preformative syllable in the Qal PC is many times made through a Meteg: In short forms, the helping vowel i appears, with Jod contracted to long i:

יְהְיֶה imperfect

וִיהִי short form + ו   יְהִי short form

וַיְהִי Narrativ

ראה "to see"

For ראה, short forms with e and with a[8] are common in the Qal:

וַתֵּרֶה 3fs   וַיַּרְא 3ms

הִשְׁתַּחֲוָה "to prostrate onself"/"to worship"

A reflexive Hištaf'el from חוה[9] shows in the verb הִשְׁתַּחֲוָה.
In short forms, the helping vowel u appears.

יִשְׁתַּחֲווּ 3 pl impf   יִשְׁתַּחֲוֶה 3 s impf

וַיִּשְׁתַּחוּ singular!

39.7 Doubly Weak Verbs

With doubly weak ל"ה verbs, the **features** of some other weak verb classes (**at the beginning** of the verb form) are each added to the features of the verb class ל"ה.

Examples

For example, נקה Ni "to be innocent," אבה "to want," ידה Hi "to thank," ירה Hi "teach."

פ"נ   **Assimilation**: Dagesch forte in the first visible Ni radical

נְקֵּיתִי

נִקָּה from   נקה

---

7   These verbs still have other "irregular" forms (e.g. 2fs impv Qal הֲיִי), all of which however present no difficulty for analysis and are cited in a lexicon or concordance.

8   Also here is Qal = Hif'il → § 39.4.

9   Not as in older lexicons, שׁחה.

פ״א	o in the **Qal** imperfect	יאׁבֶה	אבה
פ״ו	o in the **Hif'il**	הוֹדוּ from	ידה
		יוֹרֵנִי from	ירה

Lamed-He and Pe-Nun

Particularly noteworthy are short forms of the verbs נטה "to stretch out," Hi "to bend," and נכה Hi "to strike."

Qal	יֵט	to	יִטֶּה				
	וַיֵּט						
Hi	יֵט	to	יַטֶּה	יַ֫ךְ	to	יַכֶּה	
	וַיֵּט			וַיַּ֫ךְ			
Hi impv	הַט	to	הַטֵּה	הַ֫ךְ	to	הַכֵּה	

40 Weak Verbs with Final Vowel (ל״א Verbs)

ל״א verbs are originally strong verbs, which have later developed weak forms when the א *at the end of the word or syllable had lost its consonantal value.*

40.1 Weak Forms

מצא   to find

In the forms without an ending and before consonantal afformatives, א is silent and the syllable is open with a long vowel.

Examples

Qal	Nif'al	Pi'el	Hif'il	Hof'al
מָצָא	נִמְצָא	*מִצָּא	הִמְצָא	*הֻמְצָא[1]
מָצָאתִי	נִמְצֵאתָ			
תִּמְצֶאנָה				

The analysis of the weak forms offer no problems, because the **Alef** in the text has almost **never fallen out**.

Because many forms of ל״ה and ל״א sound the same (e.g. תִּמְצֶאנָה and תִּגְלֶינָה), there is a **mingling of forms** with ל״ה verbs:

קרה "to meet"	with variant	קרא
	infinitive	לִקְרַאת "**towards**"
יָרֵא "to fear"	imperative pl according to	
	the pattern ל״ה : גְּלוּ	
		יְראוּ

40.2 Tables of the ל״א Qal Forms

Overview

f	m	**AC**	f	m	**PC**
תִּמְצָא	יִמְצָא	3 s	מָצְאָה	מָצָא	3 s
תִּמְצְאִי	תִּמְצָא	2 s	מָצָאת	מָצָאתָ	2 s
	אֶמְצָא	1 s		מָצָאתִי	1 s
תִּמְצֶאנָה	יִמְצְאוּ	3 pl		מָצְאוּ	3 pl
תִּמְצֶאנָה	תִּמְצְאוּ	2 pl	מְצָאתֶן	מְצָאתֶם	2 pl
	נִמְצָא	1 pl		מָצָאנוּ	1 pl
			מִצְאִי	מְצָא	impv s
			מְצֶאנָה	מִצְאוּ	pl
	מֹצֵא	ptcp		מְצֹא	inf c
	מָצוּא	ptcp pass		מָצוֹא	inf a

41 Two Radical Verbs with Long Vowel (Hollow Roots or ע״ו׳ Verbs)

קוּם	to rise
בִּין	to understand
בּוֹא	to go in
בּוֹשׁ	to be ashamed
מוּת	to die

41.1 General Comments

These verbs, which were originally two radicals, have a long vowel in the main syllable, which is often written plene with Waw or Jod. Thus, apparently a vowel letter[1] Waw or Jod stands in the place of the middle radical; hence the name "hollow roots."

In the lexicon, the AC Qal forms are not cited, rather (unvocalized) the forms of the **Qal infinitive** with the vowel letter Waw for the imperfect vowels **u** (קוּם) and **o** (בּוֹשׁ) and Jod for the imperfect vowel **i** (בִּין).

Common Features

The **main syllable** has a **long** vowel, but a also appears short.

Vowel afformatives are **unaccented**.

Vowels of separation (infix vowels) can stand before consonantal afformatives.

The long vowels a and e in the **preformative syllables** are **unchangeable** (pretone vowels).

---

1   Strong verbs with consonantal Jod or Waw as the 2nd radical are only much later forms, e.g. וַיִּגְוַע (Num 20:29), אָיַבְתָּ (Ex 23:22), also Pi'el לְקַיֵּם from קוּם (Ruth 4:7).

41.2 Weak Forms Without Preformative (Qal)

Tables

בין		קום		
f	m	f	m	AC
בִּינָה	בָּן/בִּין	קָמָה	קָם	3 s
בִּינוֹת	בִּינוֹתָ	קַמְתְּ	קַמְתָּ	2 s
	בִּינוֹתִי		קַמְתִּי	1 s
	בִּינוּ		קָמוּ	3 pl
בִּינוֹתֶן	בִּינוֹתֶם	קַמְתֶּן	קַמְתֶּם	2 pl
	בִּינוֹנוּ		קַמְנוּ	1 pl
בִּינִי	בִּין	קוּמִי	קוּם	impv s
-	בִּינוּ	קֹמְנָה	קוּמוּ	pl
	לְבִין		לָקוּם	inf c
			קוֹם	inf a
	בָּן	קָמָה	קָם	ptcp
		קָמֵי/קָמִים		
			[מוּל]²	ptcp passive

Vowels

The a in the **main syllable** predominates in the Qal AC. It is also preserved before the unaccented afformatives. With ʿAjin-Jod verbs, e.g. בִּין, whose imperfect vowel i has pierced into the perfect, the **separation vowel** (infix) ו also appears. **Infinitive** and **imperative** belong to the imperfect class with the vowel u or i.

Participle

The Qal active **participle** has the same form as the 3rd person masculine singular: קָם. The nominal endings are accented; the vowel of the main syllable appears but is unchanged.

41.3 Weak Forms with Long a in the Open Preformative Syllable (Qal and Hif'il PC)

Overview

	Impf Qal (*u*)	Impf Qal (*i*)	Impf Hi	Impv Hi	Inf Hi
Pre-Tone Qames	יָקוּם	יָבִין	יָקִים³	הָקֵם	הָקִים
Suffix accented, afformative not					הֲקִימֹו
	יָקוּמוּ	יָבִינוּ	יָקִימוּ		הָקִימוּ
	תָּקוּמְנָה	תָּבֹנָּה	תָּקֵמְנָה		הָקֵמְנָה
Infix vowel, accented	תָּקֻמֶּינָה		תְּקִמֶּינָה		
Jussive	יָקוּם	יָבֵן	יָקֵם		
Narrativ in pause	וַיָּקֹם	וַיָּבֶן	וַיָּקֶם		
Narrativ in context	וַיָּקָם	וַיָּבֶן	וַיָּקֶם		

The **pre-tone Qames**[4] in the open preformative syllable is **changeable**; thus it disappears in appropriate distance from the primary stress.

Imperfect Vowels

In the Qal, the imperfect vowel u (long) or i (long)[5] stands in the main syllable; in the Hif'il i (long). They are **preserved** in many forms, because the accent does not change (outside of the suffix). In some cases, **u** can undergo ablaut **to o, i to e**, e.g. with the particular **jussive** forms (→ § 32.2), which these verbs can acquire, and in Narrativ forms. In the uninflected **Narrativ** forms (in context), the next-to-last syllable can be accented and the imperfect vowel is shortened (o to å, e to ä).[6]

Infix

In the feminine plural forms, the **separation vowel** (infix vowel) ä (◌ֶי) can appear. It is accented, and the a in the preformative syllable disappears.

---

2 There is no passive for קוּם. This form is also extremely rare with other verbs.
3 With verbs with the imperfect vowel i (e.g. בִין) PC Qal and PC Hif'il are the same.
4 Lengthened in open syllables.
5 On the imperfect vowel a → below (בּוֹשׁ).
6 "Turned Back Tone" → § 25.4.

41.4 Weak Forms with Long e in the Open Preformative Syllable (Hif'il AC)

Hif'il AC

In the open preformative syllable stands long e (lengthened to i).	[הַקְטִיל]	הֵקִים
It is preserved with forms with unaccented vowel afformatives.		הֵקִימָה
It disappears with a moved-up tone, when a separation vowel (infix) and/or suffixes appear.[7]		הֲקִימוֹתָ הֲקִמוֹתוֹ

Participle

Here also the Hif'il participle belongs to the perfect class.   מֵקִים

With an accented nominal ending, the e appears to disappear.   מְקִימִים

41.5 Weak Forms with Open Preformative Syllable: Nif'al and Hof'al

Nif'al and Hof'al forms are highly rare for ע״ו verbs and are not even substantiated for קום.

Nif'al AC

Changeable long a appears also in the preformative syllable in the Nif'al perfect; the stem vowel is o.	נָפוֹץ[8]
Also the separation vowel (infix) o appears.[9]	נְסוּגֹתִי[10]

Hof'al

Unchangeable long u stands in the preformative of all Hof'al forms (as with I-נ verbs).	הוּקַם*

---

7 Different with מות Hi: הֵמַתָּה.

8 From פוץ "to scatter."

9 Before the separation vowel o, the stem vowel o has undergone ablaut to u. It can also be preserved, e.g. in נְפֹצוֹתֶם "you have been scattered."

10 From סוג (Ni "to remain behind").

41.6 Weak Forms with Strengthened Preformative Syllable (Nif'al PC and Aramaized Forms)

Nif'al PC

In the Nif'al (preformative conjugation), forms are regular with Dagesch forte in the first radical (→ § 41.5).	(impf)	יִקּוֹם*
	(inf/impv)	הִקּוֹם*

Also in the other stems, forms that look **like** weak forms of **Pe-Nun verbs** appear with some Ajin-Waw verbs: Instead of open, long preformative syllable, a short, closed preformative syllable is formed through a **Dagesch forte** in the 1st radical. One speaks of "aramaized" forms, because they are formed according to the model of Aramaic verbs.

Aramaized Forms

Such Aramaized forms are found above all in the Hif'il. The important example is the Hif'il of נוּחַ "to rest," which has two different meanings:

נוּחַ	Qal "to rest"	compare with Hif'il:	הֵנִיחַ	"to obtain rest"
			יָנִיחַ	
		also Hif'il:	הִנִּיחַ	"to put/leave"
			יַנִּיחַ	

41.7 Doubled Stems

The normal doubled stems with doubling of the middle radical almost never appear,[11] because there is no middle radical. Instead of this, **parallel stems** are formed.

Polel, Polal, Hitpolel

active: Polel	passive: Polal	reflexive: Hitpolel
קוֹמֵם	קוֹמַם	הִתְקוֹמֵם

Incidentally, the forms are formed as with the doubled stems of the strong verb. At the same time, corresponding forms can appear in Polel and Polal (קוֹמַמְתָּ/קוֹמֵם).

---

11 Still → above, § 41.1, note 1.

41.8 Verbs with Special Characteristics

בּוֹא

The verb בּוֹא "to come/go in"

	Perfect	Participle	Imperfect	Narrativ	Inf/Impv
In the Qal AC (perfect and participle) **long a** stands in all forms,	בָּא	בָּא	יָבוֹא	וַיָּבוֹא	בּוֹא
otherwise always **long o** in the stem syllable.	בָּאוּ	בָּאִים	יָבֹאוּ		
Hif'il forms are regular.			תְּבֹאנָה[12]		

בּוֹשׁ

The verb בּוֹשׁ "to be ashamed"

The verb בּוֹשׁ is one of quite a few[13] in which the stem vowel o appears in the Qal AC:	בּוֹשׁ - בּוֹשָׁה - בּוֹשְׁתָּ
The form יֵבוֹשׁ in the Qal PC is explained by the **imperfect vowel a** (ablauted to o) and the preformative vowel i, in the open syllable lengthened to e.	יֵבוֹשׁ
Compared to the regular **Hif'il** הֵבִישׁ, there is a Hif'il that is formed according to the model of the Pe-Waw verbs: הוֹבִישׁ.	הֵבִישׁ / הוֹבִישׁ

מוּת

The verb מוּת "to die"

As a unique ע"ו verb, מוּת has the stem vowel *e* in the Qal AC:	מֵת	3ms
	מֵתָה	3fs
	מַתָּ	2ms

---

12 Three times also: תְּבֹאֶינָה.
13 Besides e.g. אוֹר "to light" and טוֹב "to be good," which appear mainly in the Hif'il.

41.9 Verbs with Gutturals

3rd Guttural

If a guttural stands as the last radical, then the **vowel e** in uninflected forms is **displaced through a** (→ § 9.4), e.g. in the Jussive and in the imperfect consecutive of the Hif'il. Also in the Qal, the o of the Jussive and the imperfect consecutive is displaced through a, so that **matching** Qal/Hif'il forms appear:

For example נוּחַ "to rest":

Impf Hif'il	יָנִיחַ	Jussive	יָנַח	Impf. Cons.	וַיָּנַח
Impf Qal	יָנוּחַ	Jussive	יָנַח	Impf. Cons.	וַיָּנַח

1st Guttural

If a guttural stands as the 1st radical, then the vowel **Patach—instead of Chatef Patach**—can appear in the preformative of the Hif'il in appropriate distance to the primary stress.

עוּד	Hif'il "to warn"		הֵעִיד	2ms:	הַעִידוֹתָ

42 Two Radical Verbs with Short Vowel
(So-Called ע״ע Verbs)

סבב	to go around
קלל	to be poor
רעע	to be bad

42.1 General Comments

These verbs, which were originally two radicals, have a short vowel in the stem syllable with a doubled 2ⁿᵈ radical (*sabb).

In some forms, the 2ⁿᵈ radical is repeated as the 3ʳᵈ radical, thus the three-radical forms appear. Among others, this is the case in the 3ms Qal afformative conjugation. For that reason, one can refer to these verbs as three-radical roots (סבב).[1]

Strong Forms

The following are always formed strongly:

the **participles** of the Qal,	סֹבֵב - סָבוּב
the **infinitive absolutes** of the Qal,	סָבֹב
and the **doubled stems**.	סִבֵּב - סַבַּב - הִסְתַּבֵּב
In respect to weak forms, Qal AC forms are strong in the 3ʳᵈ person:	סָבַב - סָבְבָה - סָבְבוּ
All other forms are formed **weakly**.	

42.2 Features of the Weak Forms

Common Features

In principle, a **short vowel** stands in the stem syllable (i.e., the syllable that begins with the 1ˢᵗ radical). Only u (Qal) and i (Hifʿil) are lengthened in the tone syllable to o or e, respectively.

---

1   The name Ayin-Ayin (ע״ע) does not mean that the 2ⁿᵈ radical is an Ayin (ע), rather that it appears twice.

In forms with an ending, the **Dagesch forte** appears in the 2nd radical.

Vowel afformatives are **unaccented**.

Separation vowels (**infixes**) stand before consonantal afformatives, in particular in the perfect o (וֹ) and in the imperfect-class ä (יֶ֫).

The long vowels a and e are changeable in the open preformative syllables[2] (**pretone vowels** → § 10).

42.3 Weak Forms Without a Preformative (Qal Perfect and Imperative/Infinitive)

Infinitive	Imperative		Perfect		
	f	m	f	m	
סֹב			סַבָּה	סַב	3 s
with suffix:	סֹבִי	סֹב	סַבּוֹת	סַבּוֹתָ	2 s
סֻבֵּנִי				סַבּוֹתִי	1 s
				סַבּוּ	3 pl
	סֹבֶינָה	סֹבּוּ	סַבּוֹתֶן	סַבּוֹתֶם	2 pl
				סַבּוֹנוּ	1 pl

Stem Vowels

The stem vowels are **short a** in the perfect and **long o** in the imperative/infinitive.

Before endings, the stem vowel appears **preserved** (unaccented o shortens to u) and the second radical shows a **Dagesch forte**.

---

2 Because they are formed by lengthening.

42.4 Weak Forms with a in the Open Preformative Syllable (PC Qal and Hif'il, AC Nif'al)

Overview

Nif'al		Hif'il Imperative		Hif'il PC		Qal PC		
f	m	f	m	f	m	f	m	
נָסַׄבָּה	נָסַב			תָּסֵב	יָסֵב	תָּסֹב	יָסֹב	3 s
	נְסַבֹּׄתָ	הָסֵׄבִּי	הָסֵב	תָּסֵׄבִּי	תָּסֵב	תָּסֹׄבִּי	תָּסֹב	2 s
	נְסַבֹּׄתִי				אָסֵב		אָסֹב	1 s
נָסֹׄבּוּ				תְּסִבֶּׄינָה	יָסֵׄבּוּ	תְּסֻבֶּׄינָה	יָסֹׄבּוּ	3 pl
otherwise there are no Nif'al forms substantiated		הָסִבֶּׄינָה	הָסֵׄבּוּ	תְּסִבֶּׄינָה	תָּסֵׄבּוּ	תְּסֻבֶּׄינָה	תָּסֹׄבּוּ	2 pl
					נָסֵב		נָסֹב	1 pl
					וַיָּׄסֵב		וַיָּׄסָב	Narr
Nif'al Participle								
נְסַׄבָּה	נָסָב							

Vowels

The lengthened preformative vowel **a is changeable**, thus it disappears in appropriate distance from the principle stress (in the Hi to Chatef-Patach).

Long vowels (o, e) stand in the accented **stem syllables**; short vowels (å, u, i, ä) in unaccented syllables.

42.5 Weak Forms with e in the Open Preformative Syllable (PC Qal and AC Hif'il)

The preformative vowel i—lengthened to e in the open syllable—appears in the Qal with verbs with imperfect vowel a (e.g. קלל) and in the Hif'il perfect and participle.

	Qal Impf	Hi Perf	Hi Ptcp
	יֵקַל	הֵסֵב	מֵסֵב
	יֵקַׄלּוּ	הֵסֵׄבָּה	מְסִבָּה
	תְּקַלֶּׄינָה	הֲסִבּׄוֹת	

Changeable e

The e is a pre-tone vowel and disappears in appropriate distance from the primary stressed syllable.

42.6 Weak Forms with u in the Open Preformative Syllable (Hofʿal)

As forms analogous to the פ״ו verbs, all Hofʿal forms have **unchangeable** u in the preformative syllables.

42.7 Weak Forms with Strengthened Preformative Syllable (PC Nifʿal and Aramaized Forms)

In the PC of the Nifʿal, sharpened preformative syllables are regular, e.g. יִסַּב.

Looks like Pe-Nun

Also in other stems, PC forms have been formed according to the pattern of **Aramaic**, in which the 1st radical is doubled. The forms look like forms of פ״נ verbs (→ § 41.6).

e.g. compared with Qal Impf	יִסֹּב:	תִּסֹּבְנָה	יִסֹּבוּ	יִסֹּב
	from תמם "to be complete"		וַיִּתְּמוּ	יִתֹּם
		compared to	יִתֹּמוּ	
compared to Hifʿil	יָסֵב:		וַיַּסֵּבוּ	יַסֵּב
compared to Hofʿal	יוּסַב:			יַסֵּב

42.8 Doubled Stems

Poʿel, Poʿal, Hithpoʿel

There are the normal doubled stems. Frequently there are parallel stems, formed in a similar way to the ע״וי verbs (→ § 41.7).

Piʿel:	סִבֵּב	Puʿal:	סֻבַּב	Hithpaʿel:	הִסְתַּבֵּב
Poʿel:	סוֹבֵב	Poʿal:	סוֹבַב	Hithpoʿel:	הִסְתּוֹבֵב

42.9 Verbs with Gutturals

2nd and 3rd Gutturals

An a must go ahead of a guttural as the last radical (→ § 09.4). Most of the time, the e of the Hifʿil is displaced, or a Patach furtivum is found:

E.g. רעע: **Qal**   **Hif'il**

	Perfect	רַע	הֵרַע
	Imperfect	יֵרַע	יָרַע
	Infinitive	רֹעַ	הָרַע

Instead of the doubling of the 2nd radical, compare with
compensatory lengthening almost always
occurs.

compare	סָבָּה	הֲסִבֹּתָ
with	רָעָה	הֲרֵעוֹתָ

Primae Gutturalis

With ח as the 1st radical, Patach can appear instead
of Chatef-Patach.

For example חלל "to start":   הַחִלּוֹתָ

With 1st guttural verbs, the stem vowel u can   compare   יִסְבֵּנִי
ablaut in the Qal PC to â.

For example חנן "to be gracious":   with   יְחָנֵּנִי

43 Features for the Analysis of Weak Verb Forms

The most important feature for the analysis of weak verb forms is the existence and the form of a preformative syllable.

*The preformative syllable can be **closed** (with strong verbs and Lamed-He and Lamed Alef verbs) with the exception of the sharpened syllables (Dagesch forte in the first visible radical); or the preformative syllable can be **open** with long vowel (with weak verbs), with the exception of the upbeat syllable (Schwa mobile).*

Qal/Pi'el AC and Infinitive/Imperative forms do not have a preformative.

43.1 Forms with Strengthened Preformative Syllable

	strong verb	ל״ה	פ״נ	(צ) פ״ו	ע״וי	ע״ע
Qal PC			יִפֹּל	יֵצֵת		יָסֹב
Nif'al AC			נָפַל	נִצַּת		
Nif'al PC	יִקָּטֵל	יִגָּל			יִקּוֹם	יִסַּב
Hif'il			הִפִּיל	הִצִּית	הִנִּיחַ	
			יַפִּיל	יַצִּית	יַנִּיחַ	יָסֵב
Hof'al			הֻפַּל			יֻסַּב

In addition to the Nif'al, a Dagesch forte appears in the first visible radical especially with פ״נ **verbs**.

Forms that otherwise look like weak forms of פ״נ verbs can be **Aramaized** forms of two-radical verbs or can come from verbs with Jod (פ״נ) and **Sadé**.

43.2 Forms with Preformative

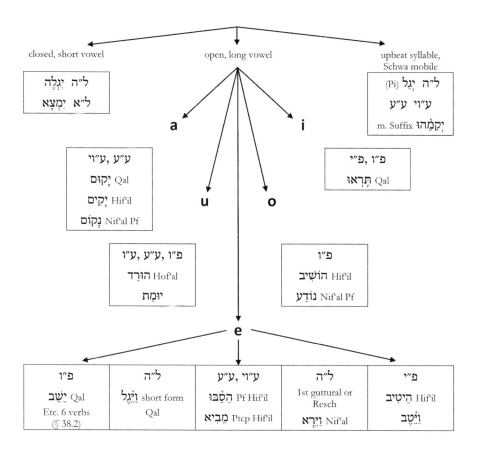

43.3 Forms without Preformative

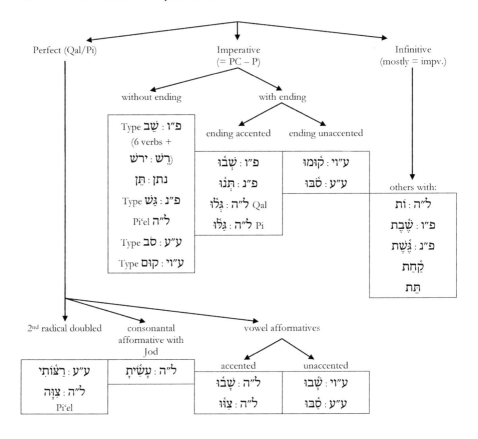

PART III

Texts

Clauses and Parts of Clauses 44–51

Text Syntax 52–54

44 Types of Clauses

44.1 Classification

For grammatical analysis we usually subdivide texts into smaller units, which we call "clauses." In this grammar it has not been attempted to define what a clause is. We know intuitively what a clause is, and this is sufficient to make grammatically practical statements.

Clauses

בְּרֵאשִׁית בָּרָא אֱלֹהִים אֵת הַשָּׁמַיִם וְאֵת הָאָרֶץ:	a	In the beginning God created the heavens and the earth.
וְהָאָרֶץ הָיְתָה תֹהוּ וָבֹהוּ	b	And the earth was formless and void.
וְחֹשֶׁךְ עַל־פְּנֵי תְהוֹם	c	And darkness (was) over the depths.
וְרוּחַ אֱלֹהִים מְרַחֶפֶת עַל־פְּנֵי הַמָּיִם:	d	And the Spirit of God (was) something moving over the the waters.
וַיֹּאמֶר אֱלֹהִים	e	
יְהִי אוֹר	f	
וַיְהִי־אוֹר:	g	And God said:
וַיַּרְא אֱלֹהִים אֶת־הָאוֹר	h	"Let there be light!"
כִּי־טוֹב	i	And there was light.
וַיַּבְדֵּל אֱלֹהִים בֵּין הָאוֹר וּבֵין הַחֹשֶׁךְ:	j	And God saw the light
לָאוֹר יוֹם אֱלֹהִים וַיִּקְרָא	k	Yes, (it was) good.
וְלַחֹשֶׁךְ קָרָא לָיְלָה	l	And God separated between the light and the darkness.
וַיְהִי־עֶרֶב	m	And God called the light day;
וַיְהִי־בֹקֶר	n	but the darkness He called night.
יוֹם אֶחָד:	o	And there was evening.
		And there was morning.
(Genesis 1:1–5)		(It was) one day.

The quoted section of text from Genesis 1 is organized according to the parts of the text that we intuitively take as **clauses**.[1] If for the moment "clauses" i (כִּי־טוֹב) and o (יוֹם אֶחָד) are ignored, then **two types** can clearly be distinguished:

---

1   This differentiation does not correspond to the verse division of the Hebrew Bible.

A does B

Type 1: All words in the vicinity of a finite verb that can be related to this verb belong to a clause. One such clause makes a statement of the type: "A does B." Such a clause can be called a "**verbal clause**." The boundary between two clauses is the boundary between the catchment area of both verbs.

A is B

The other type of clause consists of **two nominals** or groups of nominals, which are applied to one another in such a way that a statement occurs of the type "A is B." At the same time, the place that must be filled in a German clause by a form of the helping verb "sein" is not filled in the Hebrew clause: "A—B." Such a clause can be called a "**nominal clause**." To such a clause belong all words that can be related to one of the two parts of the statement.

Inclusive clauses such as כִּי־טוֹב or יוֹם אֶחָד can be described as incomplete, **elliptical** clauses.

This first formal delimitation of the types of clauses is incomplete under the point of view of text-grammar. How the **first position** of a clause is occupied is important for the weight of the clauses in the text and for the structuring of a text. For this reason, in this grammar it is differentiated between **verbal clauses** (VC), which begin with a finite form of the verb, and **nominal clauses** (NC), which do not begin with a finite verb.[2]

Verbal Clauses

With verbal clauses, the focus lies on the **verb**, which describes an **event**.

Nominal Clauses

With nominal clauses, the focus lies on the **nominal** standing at the front, about which a **statement** is made. For that reason we count as "nominal clauses" not only the clauses without a verb (as example c: וְחֹשֶׁךְ עַל־פְּנֵי תְהוֹם), but also such clauses in which even a finite verb form follows the nominal introducing the clause, as in example b: וְהָאָרֶץ הָיְתָה תֹהוּ וָבֹהוּ. Admittedly, the statement about the nominal consists of an entire clause: "it was formless and void," but it describes not an event, rather the **state** of אֶרֶץ "land."

---

2   On "subordinate clauses," which begin with a conjunction, → § 44.2.

Compound Nominal Clauses

Nominal clauses, whose predicate consists of a whole clause, we call "**compound nominal clauses**" (CNC).[3]

The first clause from Genesis 1—בְּרֵאשִׁית בָּרָא אֱלֹהִים אֵת הַשָּׁמַיִם וְאֵת הָאָרֶץ—is also regarded as a CNC. It occurs under the conditions of a text-beginning, where only particular formulations are possible (→ § 54.2). And it shows that it does not depend only on whether a state is described, but also that a (non-verbal) part of a clause, here an expression of time, receives special **focus**.

44.2 The Function of the Clause Types in the Text

In Narratives

In **narratives**, **verbal clauses** form the **foreground** of the narration with emphasis on the event. They are mainly clauses with an imperfect consecutive form at the beginning that tend to form chains.

Nominal clauses (NC and CNC) contain preconditions, descriptions, situations, or notes about acting persons and so deliver the **background** of the narration.[4] They interrupt the imperfect-consecutive chain and provide for framework and structure.

Likewise, verbal clauses, which have only a **conjunction** (אִם, אֲשֶׁר, כִּי) or לֹא in front of the verb, belong to the background of the narrative. They are "subordinate clauses," and they have in common with nominal clauses that they do not begin with the finite form of the verb. On the tense in such clauses → § 48.

The distribution of VC and NC (or CNC) in the text example from **Genesis 1** is **typical** for a great deal of narrative texts: Nominal clauses pile up at the beginning; the verbal clause predominates from clause (e) on. They control—only occasionally interrupted by NC-insertions—the entire creation narrative, which closes in Gen 2:4a with a nominal clause.

---

3   Other grammars call such clauses "inverted verbal clauses." It is however practical to call clause forms using a common term, if they have in the text fundamentally the same function.

4   "Foreground" and "background" are metaphors from the world of the theater. The picture can be described as follows: What is narrated in verbal clauses takes place at the front of the stage. When nominal clauses "appear" (!), a new scene is played, backdrops are painted and pushed in, persons move, or the curtain is raised or lowered.

In Other Forms of Speech

In forms of speech other than narrative, nominal clauses are more frequent. In principle, it also applies in **discourse** texts that **no event** is described in the **nominal clause**.

וְחָלַפְתָּ מִשָּׁם וָהָלְאָה וּבָאתָ עַד־אֵלוֹן תָּבוֹר	a	And if you go on further from there and come to the oak of Tabor,
וּמְצָאוּךָ שָּׁם שְׁלֹשָׁה אֲנָשִׁים עֹלִים		there three men will meet you,
אֶל־הָאֱלֹהִים בֵּית־אֵל		who are going up to God at Bethel.
אֶחָד נֹשֵׂא שְׁלֹשָׁה גְדָיִים		One is carrying three young goats,
וְאֶחָד נֹשֵׂא שְׁלֹשֶׁת כִּכְּרוֹת לֶחֶם		another is carrying three loaves of bread,
וְאֶחָד נֹשֵׂא נֵבֶל־יָיִן׃		and another is carrying a jug of wine.
וְשָׁאֲלוּ לְךָ לְשָׁלוֹם		And they will greet you ...
(1 Samuel 10:3–4a)		

When **sequences of action** are talked about (a), verbal clauses also stand in the foreground, whereas the nominal clauses (NC and CNC) offer background information and do not contribute to the progress of the action.[5]

However, outside narration, the nominal clause **generally cannot** be allocated to the **background** of the speech. There are genres [*Gattungen*] that are structured differently.

In Dialogue

וַיֹּאמֶר אֲלֵהֶם [יוֹסֵף] מְרַגְּלִים אַתֶּם	b	And he (Joseph) said to them: "You are spies; You are coming to spy out the un-
לִרְאוֹת אֶת־עֶרְוַת הָאָרֶץ בָּאתֶם׃		defended parts of the land."
וַיֹּאמְרוּ אֵלָיו		They said to him:
לֹא אֲדֹנִי וַעֲבָדֶיךָ בָּאוּ לִשְׁבָּר־אֹכֶל׃		"By no means, lord! Your servants have
כֻּלָּנוּ בְּנֵי אִישׁ־אֶחָד נָחְנוּ כֵּנִים אֲנַחְנוּ		come to buy food! All of us—sons of *one* man are we; we are regular people,
לֹא־הָיוּ עֲבָדֶיךָ מְרַגְּלִים׃		by no means are your servants spies!"
וַיֹּאמֶר אֲלֵהֶם		

---

5   On the tense in such verbal clauses → §§ 48 and 51.4.

לֹא כִּי־עֶרְוַת הָאָרֶץ בָּאתֶם לִרְאוֹת׃	He said to them:
וַיֹּאמְרוּ	"No! In fact you are coming to spy out
שְׁנֵים עָשָׂר עֲבָדֶיךָ אַחִים אֲנַחְנוּ בְּנֵי	the undefended parts of the land."
אִישׁ־אֶחָד בְּאֶרֶץ כְּנָעַן וְהִנֵּה הַקָּטֹן	They said:
אֶת־אָבִינוּ הַיּוֹם וְהָאֶחָד אֵינֶנּוּ׃	"Your servants are (originally) twelve;
וַיֹּאמֶר אֲלֵהֶם יוֹסֵף	we are brothers; sons of *one* man in
הוּא אֲשֶׁר דִּבַּרְתִּי אֲלֵכֶם לֵאמֹר מְרַגְּ־	the land of Canaan; to be precise, the
לִים אַתֶּם׃	youngest is with our father today; but
	the twelfth is no more."
	And Joseph said to them,
(Genesis 42:9–14)	"It is as I said to you, namely: You are spies!"

Above all in a dialogue (b), in which **alternating partners** contrast their points of view with each other, the NC controls the speech.

וַיֹּאמֶר אֵלָיו	c	He said to him,
אַתָּה יָדַעְתָּ אֵת אֲשֶׁר עֲבַדְתִּיךָ		"You (yourself) know how I have served
וְאֵת אֲשֶׁר־הָיָה מִקְנְךָ אִתִּי׃		you and how it has gone with your cattle
(Genesis 30:29)		with me."

Strikingly frequently in dialogues, the CNC אַתָּה יָדַעְתָּ "you know" is encountered. A VC may just as well have been possible, but the **orientation** of the speaker in the speech act has priority (c).

Prophetic Speech

שִׁמְעוּ שָׁמַיִם וְהַאֲזִינִי אֶרֶץ כִּי יְהוָה דִּבֵּר	d	Hear, O heavens! Take notice, O
בָּנִים גִּדַּלְתִּי וְרוֹמַמְתִּי וְהֵם פָּשְׁעוּ בִי׃		earth! Yes, (it is) Yhwh (who) speaks,
יָדַע שׁוֹר קֹנֵהוּ וַחֲמוֹר אֵבוּס בְּעָלָיו		"Sons—I have reared and brought them up; But they—they broke away
יִשְׂרָאֵל לֹא יָדַע עַמִּי לֹא הִתְבּוֹנָן׃		from me.
		An ox knows its owner and a donkey its master's manger.
(Isaiah 1:2–3)		Israel—it does not know; My people—they do not understand."
כִּי הִנֵּה הָאָדוֹן יְהוָה צְבָאוֹת	e	See, the Lord Yhwh of hosts (is one who)
מֵסִיר מִירוּשָׁלַםִ וּמִיהוּדָה מַשְׁעֵן וּמַשְׁעֵנָה		removes from Jerusalem and Judah
(Isaiah 3:1a)		supply and support.

The nominal clause is also frequent in **prophetic** speech. Not only with the description of the situation in the so-called **oath** (d) but also in the actual announcement of the disaster, nominal clauses can contain the leading statements to the "**threat**" (e).

Hymns

כִּי אֵל גָּדוֹל יְהוָה	f	Yes, a great God is Yhwh
וּמֶלֶךְ גָּדוֹל עַל־כָּל־אֱלֹהִים:		and a great King above all gods!
אֲשֶׁר בְּיָדוֹ מֶחְקְרֵי־אָרֶץ		In whose hand (are) the depths of the earth,
וְתוֹעֲפוֹת הָרִים לֹו:		the peaks of the mountains (are) His also;
אֲשֶׁר־לֹו הַיָּם וְהוּא עָשָׂהוּ		to whom the sea belongs. He, he has made it,
וְיַבֶּשֶׁת יָדָיו יָצָרוּ:		and the dry land—His hands have formed it.
(Psalm 95:3–5)		

For some **psalms**, above all for the written praise songs (hymns), nominal clauses are typical (f). In particular cases, the relationship of NC and VC must at the same time be clarified and interpreted. Above all in poetry, **rhetorical figures** such as chiasmus (d:יְשְׂרָאֵל לֹא יָדַע—יָדַע שׁוֹר) are to be taken into account.

44.3 Clause Construction in the Nominal Clause (NC)

The categories "subject" and "predicate" are only partly useful. They are used here according to the model of the Arabic grammar: Subject is "the known" (arab. Mubtada'); predicate is "the new" (arab. Chabar).[6]

וְרוּחַ אֱלֹהִים מְרַחֶפֶת עַל־פְּנֵי הַמָּיִם: (Genesis 1:2)	a	And the Spirit of God: (he was) moving over the waters.
כִּי־עָפָר אַתָּה (Genesis 3:19)	b	Yes, dust—you (are that)!
וַיֹּאמַר עֶבֶד אַבְרָהָם אָנֹכִי: (Genesis 24:34)	c	He said, "The servant of Abraham—I (am that)."
יְהוָה הָאֹמֵר אֵלַי שׁוּב לְאַרְצֶךָ (Genesis 32:10)	d	Yhwh (it is) who has said to me, "Return to your country."

---

6   With this is roughly the same as with the names "Thema" (the pre-determined) and "Rhema" (some new information), which are used in linguistics.

Information

The **subject** can stand in front (a): Some new information is given about something known. The **predicate** can stand in front (b): The focus lies on some new information, which then is applied to the known through the naming of the subject. As a rule in both cases, the predicate stands without an article or other **determination.**[7]

Identification

If subject **and** predicate are demonstrated as **known** through an article or other determination (c, d), then the new information of the clause exists in the **identification** of two known elements.

וַיהוָה אֱלֹהִים אֱמֶת הוּא־אֱלֹהִים חַיִּים וּמֶלֶךְ עוֹלָם (Jeremiah 10:10)	e	But YHWH (is) God (in) truth; He (is) living God and (King of Eternity) everlasting King.
אָרוּר מַקְלֶה אָבִיו וְאִמּוֹ (Deuteronomy 27:16)	f	Cursed (is) the one who dishonors his father or mother.

Subject and Predicate

Subject and predicate of nominal clauses can be nominals or groups of nominals **in the widest sense**, thus also "adjectives" (→ § 46.3), pronouns, participles (text example f), infinitives, adverbs, and prepositional phrases.

The predicate of a NC can be **expanded** through any groups of nominals (→ §§ 45–47), through אֲשֶׁר-clauses (→ § 53.4), and also through **circumstantial modifiers** (a, e). Participles (text f) can have **objects** with them as subject as well as predicate (→ § 49.1).

---

7   Here it appears right clearly that the "determination" has to do with "known or new" (→ § 52.5). The expression can be kept when it is not taken from it that it is "identifying" definite nominals. It can be defined purely formally: Definite nominals are such that they can come after the object-partical אֵת (→ § 50.1) or an adjective with an article (→ § 46.3). Then to the class of definite nominals belong: (1) nominals with an article, (2) nominals with a suffix, (3) proper names, and (4) nominals in the construct state with 1 to 3.

44.4 Clause Construction in the Compound Nominal Clause (CNC)

יְהוָה בְּהֵיכַל קָדְשׁוֹ	a	Yahweh (is) in His holy temple.
יְהוָה בַּשָּׁמַיִם כִּסְאוֹ		Yahweh—in heaven (is) His throne.
עֵינָיו יֶחֱזוּ		His eyes—they look.
עַפְעַפָּיו יִבְחֲנוּ בְּנֵי אָדָם:		His eyelids—they test the sons of men.
(Psalm 11:4)		
אָנֹכִי אָנֹכִי הוּא מֹחֶה פְשָׁעֶיךָ	b	I, I (am) the one who wipes out your transgressions (= I myself wipe out ...)
(Isaiah 43:25a)		
וַיֹּאמֶר לוֹ אַמְנוֹן	c	Amnon said to him,
אֶת־תָּמָר אֲחוֹת אַבְשָׁלֹם אָחִי אֲנִי אֹהֵב:		"Tamar, the sister of my brother Absalom—I love her."
(2 Samuel 13:4)		

Predicate: a Clause

The statement about a nominal placed first is made in the CNC through a **whole clause**. The predicate of a CNC is thus a clause: **nominal clause** (a, first half) or **verbal clause** (a, second half).

The **overall subject** standing at the front is frequently **referred back to** through a suffix (a) or an independent pronoun (b) in the predicate clause. One such back reference appears particularly then when the subject of the predicate clause is not identical with the overall subject (a, second clause).

Back reference

When the subject of the CNC directly meets the subject of the predicate clause whose subject is a pronoun that refers back to the same (b), the **subject** in particular is strongly **accented**.

Subject with אֵת

When a nominal is marked through the ("accusative"-)particle אֵת as the **object of the action** (c), we would regard it according to the Latin-western category as the direct object. At the beginning of a Hebrew compound nominal clause, it is regarded as a **subject**.

44.5 Clause Construction in the Verbal Clause (VC)

וַיֹּאכַל	a	He ate,
וַיֵּשְׁתְּ		he drank,
וַיָּקָם		he rose,
וַיֵּלֶךְ		he went on his way,
וַיִּבֶז עֵשָׂו אֶת־הַבְּכֹרָה:		he—namely Esau—despised his birthright.
(Genesis 25:34)		
וַיֹּאמֶר אֵלָיו הָאֱלֹהִים בַּחֲלֹם	b	God said to him in the dream,
גַּם אָנֹכִי יָדַעְתִּי		"Also I, I knew (CNC)
כִּי בְתָם־לְבָבְךָ עָשִׂיתָ זֹּאת		that in the integrity of your heart you have done this.
וָאֶחְשֹׂךְ גַּם־אָנֹכִי אוֹתְךָ מֵחֲטוֹ־לִי		And (VC) I also kept you—I myself—from sinning against Me."
(Genesis 20:6)		
כִּי־יֶלֶד יֻלַּד־לָנוּ	c	Yes a child will be born to us,
בֵּן נִתַּן־לָנוּ		a son will be given to us.
וַתְּהִי הַמִּשְׂרָה עַל־שִׁכְמוֹ		The government will rest on His shoulders,
וַיִּקְרָא שְׁמוֹ פֶּלֶא יוֹעֵץ אֵל גִּבּוֹר		and one will call him [he will be called/he named him] Wonderful-Counselor, Mighty-God, Eternal-Father, Prince of Peace.
אֲבִיעַד שַׂר־שָׁלוֹם:		
(Isaiah 9:5)		
שָׁמָּה קָבְרוּ אֶת־אַבְרָהָם וְאֵת שָׂרָה אִשְׁתּוֹ	d	There one has (they have) buried Abraham and his wife Sarah.
שָׁמָּה קָבְרוּ אֶת־יִצְחָק וְאֵת רִבְקָה אִשְׁתּוֹ		There one has buried Isaac and his wife Rebekah.
וְשָׁמָּה קָבַרְתִּי אֶת־לֵאָה:		And there I have buried Leah.
(Genesis 49:31)		

Subject

A **finite** verb form already contains in its person-morpheme the **subject** of the clause (a: 5 clauses). For that reason no further subject needs to follow the predicate of a verbal clause. But if it is given, it follows the verb as an apposition (a, 5th clause). If a pronoun—which is not required in itself—follows the finite verb form as subject (b), then it serves to **emphasize** where placing something first, and for that reason a CNC, is not possible or not intended.

"one"

The **general** subject "one" can be expressed (except by passive forms) through an active verb form of the **third person** masculine, singular (c) or plural (d). [**Ed. note**: This has to do with the German "man."]

44.6 Congruence

Generally, the principle of congruence also applies in Hebrew: A subject and its predicate, a nominal and its attribute (→ § 46.3), a form of reference and the element that is referred to (→ § 52), agree in person, number, and gender.

Correspondingly, a plural stands with multiple subjects, and plural attributes, pronouns, and verb forms occur with nominals in the dual.

וְיֵדְעוּ כָּל־הַקָּהָל הַזֶּה כִּי־לֹא בְּחֶרֶב וּבַחֲנִית יְהוֹשִׁיעַ יְהוָה (1 Samuel 17:47)	a	That (they know, this entire assembly) all this assembly may know that Yhwh does not deliver by sword or by spear.
וַיִּקַּח אַבְרָם וְנָחוֹר לָהֶם נָשִׁים (Genesis 11:29)	b	Then Abram and Nahor took wives for themselves.
וַיַּרְא מֶלֶךְ מוֹאָב כִּי־חָזַק מִמֶּנּוּ הַמִּ־ לְחָמָה (2 Kings 3:26)	c	Then the king of Moab saw that (the struggle [fem.] was stronger [masc.] than him) he did not withstand the attack.
וּלְאַבְרָם הֵיטִיב בַּעֲבוּרָהּ וַיְהִי־לוֹ צֹאן־וּבָקָר וַחֲמֹרִים וַעֲבָדִים וּשְׁפָחֹת וַאֲתֹנֹת וּגְמַלִּים: (Genesis 12:16)	d	But he treated Abram well for her sake; thus (were given [m.s.] to him) he received sheep and oxen and donkeys and male and female servants and female donkeys and camels were his.
קֶשֶׁת גִּבֹּרִים חַתִּים (1 Samuel 2:4a)	e	The bow of the mighty (is) shattered.

Deviation from the Rule of Congruence

With **collectively** used **singulars**, which indicate a large number of individuals, the verbal predicate can stand in the **plural** (a). Inversely, in general the singular—often also the article—stands with the "plural" אֱלֹהִים when the word denotes the (one) God of Israel.

Several Subjects

A verbal predicate at the **beginning** of a clause can also stand in the singular, when it applies to each individual of several subjects (b).

Often the **simpler** masculine singular form stands without consideration of congruence before feminine nominals (c) or before a row of nominals of **different** genders and different numbers (d).

Construct Connection

Occasionally a predicate coincides with the last word of a **construct connection** (e), although it applies only to the first word.

On the problem of congruence with numerical words → § 47.2.

45 Nominal Groups: Construct Connections

45.1 Function

That two (or more) nominals belong closely together is expressed in Hebrew through a construct connection.[1]

בֵּן	(a) Son
בֶּן דָּוִד	the son <u>of David</u> (<u>David's</u> son)

Accent

Both words form a unit of speech and unit of meaning. The last word, which is in the **status absolutus**, carries the full accent and determines the **meaning** of the whole. The meaning of the opening word, which is in the status constructus, limits it.[2] The following are at one's disposal for the **translation** of construct connections into German: **genitive** attributes, **compound** nominals, and **prepositional** attributes (in detail → § 45.4).

45.2 Definiteness

The connection is so close that the **last word** determines the definiteness of or for those that precede as well.

דְּבַר הַמֶּלֶךְ	a	<u>the</u> word of <u>the</u> king
דְּבַר אֲדֹנִי	b	<u>the</u> word of my lord
דְּבַר דָּוִד	c	<u>the</u> word of David
דְּבַר מֶלֶךְ	d	the word of *a* king (*a* king's word)

Definiteness

If the nominal in the status **absolutus** has an article or is otherwise made definite,[3] namely through a **suffix** (b) or as a **proper name** (c), then with this the nominal in the status constructus is also made definite.

---

1   Hebr.: סְמִיכוּת "dependence"
2   Hebr. and Lat. special terms → § 16.1.
3   On the term "definite" → § 44.4 (note).

Before a non-definite status absolutus stands also a non-definite status constructus (d). Certainly in a connection such as (d), German grammar always demands the definite article in initial position.

Compensation through לְ

Inside a construct connection it is **not made definite twice**. For that reason a nominal in the status constructus can have with it **neither an article nor a suffix**.[4] For the connection of definite and indefinite nominals, the preposition לְ is used (→ § 47.1).

45.3 Extensions

וַיִּוָּתֵר יוֹתָם בֶּן־יְרֻבַּעַל הַקָּטֹן (Judges 9:5)	a	Jotham, the son of Jerubbaal, namely the youngest (= the youngest son of Jerubbaal), was left.
רָאשֵׁי בְנֵי־יִשְׂרָאֵל הֵמָּה: (Numbers 13:3)	b	They were heads of the sons of Israel (= leaders of the Israelites).
מְעַט וְרָעִים הָיוּ יְמֵי שְׁנֵי חַיַּי וְלֹא הִשִּׂיגוּ אֶת־יְמֵי שְׁנֵי חַיֵּי אֲבֹתַי (Genesis 47:9)	c	Few and unpleasant were the days of the years of my life, and they have not attained the days of the years of the life of my fathers.

No Interruptions

A construct connection is so tight that no other word can interrupt it. Further **modifiers** stand **after the status absolutus**, even when they refer to the nominal in the status constructus (a).

Chains

Further nominals in the status constructus can be placed before a nominal in the status constructus (b and c), so that they result in complete chains of nominals dependent on each other (c). The **last** nominal (in the status **absolutus**) determines the **sense** of the entire chain.

---

4   The proportionately few exceptions to this rule (e.g. חֶלְקַת הַשָּׂדֶה "a piece of the field" 2Sa 23:11) must each be interpreted on its place in context.

וְיֶ֜תֶר דִּבְרֵ֤י יָֽרָבְעָם֙ אֲשֶׁ֣ר נִלְחַ֔ם וַאֲשֶׁ֖ר מָלָ֑ךְ הִנָּ֣ם כְּתוּבִ֗ים עַל־סֵ֛פֶר דִּבְרֵ֥י הַיָּמִ֖ים לְמַלְכֵ֥י יִשְׂרָאֵֽל׃ (1 Kings 14:19)	d	The rest of the acts of Jeroboam, how he made war and how he reigned, they are still written in the book (of the affairs of the days =) of the annals of the kings of Israel.
בָּר֤וּךְ אַבְרָם֙ לְאֵ֣ל עֶלְי֔וֹן קֹנֵ֖ה שָׁמַ֥יִם וָאָֽרֶץ׃ (Genesis 14:19)	e	Blessed be Abram by the Most High God, creator of <u>heaven and earth!</u>
שִֽׂים־נָ֥א יָדְךָ֖ תַּ֣חַת יְרֵכִ֑י וְאַשְׁבִּ֣יעֲךָ֔ בַּֽיהוָה֙ אֱלֹהֵ֣י הַשָּׁמַ֔יִם וֵאלֹהֵ֖י הָאָֽרֶץ (Genesis 24:2f.)	f	Put your hand under my thigh that I may make you swear by Yhwh, the God of heaven and (the God) of earth.

Compensation through ל

So that the chains are not all too long, the construct connection can be **replaced** from time to time through a connection with ל (d, → also § 47.1).

Two nominals coordinated through ו (e) rarely come after a status constructus. Instead of this, the **status constructus** is usually **repeated** (f). In German translation the governing nominal in every case only appears once.

45.4 Possibilities of Translation

In most cases, construct connections can be rendered in German with a genitive attribute or with the preposition "von." In this way is given also in German the sphere in which the nominal is valid. Often, however, this is not enough.

No Genitive

וַיֹּ֣אמֶר יְהוָ֔ה זַעֲקַ֛ת סְדֹ֥ם וַעֲמֹרָ֖ה כִּי־רָֽבָּה (Genesis 18:20)	a	YHWH said, "The outcry (of) <u>over</u> Sodom and Gomorrah, indeed, it is great."
רַ֣ק הַבְּהֵמָ֔ה בָּזַ֖זְנוּ לָ֑נוּ וּשְׁלַ֥ל הֶעָרִ֖ים אֲשֶׁ֥ר לָכָֽדְנוּ׃ (Deuteronomy 2:35)	b	Only the cattle have we carried away for us and the spoil from the cities that we have captured.
וַיְדַבֵּ֨ר יְהוָ֤ה אֶל־מֹשֶׁה֙ בְּמִדְבַּ֣ר סִינַ֔י לֵאמֹֽר׃ (Numbers 3:14)	c	YHWH spoke to Moses in the wilderness (of) Sinai.

The construct connection can also describe the **sphere** at which the nominal aims (often called "objective genitive") (a) or from which it **comes** (b). In German, other prepositions such as "von" are used for it.

Names

Also the **name** of a person or thing (c) can be added in German not as a genitive, but stand as an **appositive**.

וַתֵּ֫רֶב חָכְמַת שְׁלֹמֹ֔ה מֵחָכְמַת כָּל־בְּנֵי־קֶ֑דֶם (1 Kings 5:10)	d	Thus the wisdom of Solomon was greater than the wisdom of all (sons = members of the east) easterners.
כִּי אִישׁ דָּמִים אָֽתָּה׃ (2 Samuel 16:8)	e	"Yes a (man of bloodshed =) blood-man/ murderer/blood-stained man are you!
הִנֵּה בַּעַל הַחֲלֹמוֹת הַלָּזֶה בָּֽא׃ (Genesis 37:19)	f	See, the (master of dreams) dreamer there! He is right there!
וְאַבְרָם בֶּן־חָמֵשׁ שָׁנִים וְשִׁבְעִים שָׁנָה בְּצֵאתוֹ מֵחָרָ֑ן׃ (Genesis 12:4)	g	But Abram was (a son of seventy-five years) 75 years old when he went out from Haran.

Belonging to a Group

Belonging to a **group** (d, g) or participation in a **quality** (e, f) can be expressed with the status constructus of אִישׁ, בֶּן or בַּעַל. Above all, **past details** are thus formulated. For German translations, definitions must be refined.

Adjectives

וְדֶ֫רֶךְ חַיִּים תּוֹכְחוֹת מוּסָֽר׃ לִשְׁמָרְךָ מֵאֵשֶׁת רָע מֵחֶלְקַת לָשׁוֹן נָכְרִיָּֽה׃ (Proverbs 6:23b, 24)	h	And a way to life are admonition and discipline, that they keep you from (a woman of evil) an evil woman, from (the smoothness of a strange woman) a smooth, strange woman.
וַתִּתֵּן לָהֶם מִשְׁפָּטִים יְשָׁרִים וְתוֹרוֹת אֱמֶת (Nehemiah 9:13)	i	You gave them just ordinances and (instructions of trustworthiness) true laws.
וּבְלֵב כָּל־חֲכַם־לֵב נָתַ֫תִּי חָכְמָה (Exodus 31:6)	j	And in the heart of all (wise of heart), who have expert senses, I have given expertise.

Nominals, which indicate a **characteristic**, can appear in a construct connection as status absolutus (h, i) and as status constructus (j). For **translation** we can consider it first as a substantive **adjective**, in order to render it then as an adjective or in **descriptions**. On numerals in the status constructus → § 47.2.

45.5 Construct Connections with Prepositions and Clauses

The use of the construct connection is **expanded** in cases where, instead of another nominal, another part of a clause follows a nominal in the status constructus.

Preposition

שָׂמְחוּ לְפָנֶיךָ כְּשִׂמְחַת בַּקָּצִיר (Isaiah 9:2)	a	They will rejoice before you like (rejoicers at the harvest) one rejoices at the harvest.
רֹכְבֵי אֲתֹנוֹת צְחֹרוֹת יֹשְׁבֵי עַל־מִדִּין וְהֹלְכֵי עַל־דֶּרֶךְ שִׂיחוּ׃ (Judges 5:10)	b	Those of you riding on white donkeys, those of you sitting on *rich* carpets, and those of you travelling on the road—sing!

אֲשֶׁר-Clause

כֹּה אָמַר יְהוָה בִּמְקוֹם אֲשֶׁר לָקְקוּ הַכְּלָבִים אֶת־דַּם נָבוֹת יָלֹקּוּ הַכְּלָבִים אֶת־דָּמְךָ גַּם־אָתָּה׃ (1 Kings 21:19)	c	Thus says YHWH, "In the place where the dogs licked up the blood of Naboth the dogs will lick up your blood, even yours."

Verbal Clause

תְּחִלַּת דִּבֶּר־יְהוָה בְּהוֹשֵׁעַ (Hosea 1:2)	d	The beginning (of that) which YHWH spoke through Hosea.

A **prepositional** construction (a, b) or a **whole clause** with אֲשֶׁר (c) or without אֲשֶׁר (d) follows instead of a status absolutus. German translation uses prepositional attributes or **descriptions** through clauses.

46 Nominal Groups—Appositions

46.1 Function

An apposition is the further modifying of one nominal through another, which as a rule follows it and is joined with it neither through a preposition nor by means of a construct connection.

Special Cases

כִּי־אַתֶּם בָּאִים אֶל־הָאָרֶץ כְּנַעַן זֹאת הָאָרֶץ אֲשֶׁר תִּפֹּל לָכֶם בְּנַחֲלָה (Numbers 34:2)	a	When you go into the land [namely to] Canaan—this is the land that will fall to you as an inheritance.
וַיִּקְרָא גַּם־פַּרְעֹה לַחֲכָמִים וְלַמְכַשְּׁפִים וַיַּעֲשׂוּ גַם־הֵם חַרְטֻמֵּי מִצְרַיִם בְּלַהֲטֵיהֶם כֵּן: (Exodus 7:11)	b	Then Pharaoh also called to the wise men and sorcerers, and also they, [namely] the magicians of Egypt, did the same with their secret arts.
... אֶל־הָאָרֶץ אֲשֶׁר אָנֹכִי נֹתֵן לָהֶם לִבְנֵי יִשְׂרָאֵל: (Joshus 1:2)	c	... to the land, which I will give to them, [that is] the Israelites.
וַתֹּסֶף לָלֶדֶת אֶת־אָחִיו אֶת־הָבֶל (Genesis 4:2)	d	Then she bore again his brother, Abel.

Appositions **specify** a nominal term (a). Often they further clarify **pronominals** (b) or suffixes (c). Prepositions (c) or the sign of the accusative אֵת (d) can be **repeated** before the apposition.

46.2 Concerning Translation

וַיִּשְׁמַע דָּוִד וַיִּשְׁלַח אֶת־יוֹאָב וְאֵת כָּל־הַצָּבָא הַגִּבֹּרִים: (2 Samuel 10:7)	a	As David heard it, he sent Joab and all (the troops, namely the warriors) the company of warriors.

וַיֹּאמְרוּ לוֹ עֲבָדָיו יְבַקְשׁוּ לַאדֹנִי הַמֶּלֶךְ נַעֲרָה בְתוּלָה (1 Kings 1:2)	b	Then his servants said to him, "Let them seek such a one for my lord, the king, [a maiden, in particular a young one] a young virgin."

Where an apposition is not possible in German, the appropriate rendering can be found through an individual substantive (a), an adjective (b), or a construction beyond that of the helpful translation "nämlich/und zwar."

46.3 Adjectival Attributes

Nominals, which denote characteristics and can be expressed in German among other things with adjectives (e.g.: טוֹב = "goodness/goods/good"), function in the text as other nominals. Their distinctive feature is that they have masculine and feminine forms next to one another.[1] However, forms of comparison (comparative and superlative) are not given. Biblical Hebrew has only a few such "adjectives." What in analogy to German or Latin grammar is regarded as an "attributive adjective" is a special form of apposition (→ § 46.1).

Position and Congruence

אִישׁ טוֹב	a	a man: in particular a good one = a good man
תּוֹרָה טוֹבָה תּוֹרוֹת תּוֹבֹת	b	a law: in particular a good one = a good law laws: in particular good ones = good laws
אִישׁ אֱלֹהִים קָדוֹשׁ (2 Kings 4:9)	c	a man of God, in particular a holy one = a holy man of God

Also the adjectival **attribute follows the nominal** that it further identifies and agrees with it in gender and number (a–c): it is **congruent** with it.[2] If the related word stands inside a construct connection (c), then the "adjective" stands behind the **last** nominal (in the absolute state).

---

1 They also have substantives such as מֶלֶךְ—מַלְכָּה or סוּס—סוּסָה. No separate type of word "adjective" need be accepted in Hebrew.

2 Exceptions to the congruence rule → § 44.6. Exceptions to the rule about position are rare and are to be explained as cases of special accentuation. The nominal רַבִּים "many" can be dealt with as a numeral.

Article and Demonstrative Pronoun

הוּא הָעִיר הַגְּדֹלָה: (Genesis 10:12)	d	That is (the city, in particular, the large one) the large city.
כִּי עֵינֵיכֶם הָרֹאֹת אֶת־כָּל־מַעֲשֵׂה יְהוָה הַגָּדֹל אֲשֶׁר עָשָׂה: (Deuteronomy 11:7)	e	Yes, your eyes have seen all the (work of YHWH, in particular, the great one) great work of YHWH that he did.
וַיְדַבֵּר אֶת־כָּל־הַדְּבָרִים הָאֵלֶּה בְּאָזְנֵיהֶם (Genesis 20:8)	f	Then he spoke all (the words, in particular the ones here) these words in their hearing.
וַיֹּאמֶר מֹשֶׁה אָסֻרָה־נָּא וְאֶרְאֶה אֶת־הַמַּרְאֶה הַגָּדֹל הַזֶּה (Exodus 3:3)	g	Then Moses said, "I must turn aside now and see (the sight, in particular the great one, in particular the one here) this great sight."

If the related word is made **definite** (through article, suffix, as a proper name, in a definite construct connection), then the adjectival attribute receives the **article** (d, e). Demonstrative pronouns (הֵמָּה—הִיא—הוּא—אֵלֶּה—זֹאת—זֶה) are treated as appositions like the adjective (f). An attributive **pronoun** steps into the last place (g).

וַיְהִי־עֶרֶב וַיְהִי־בֹקֶר יוֹם הַשִּׁשִּׁי: (Genesis 1:31)	h	Then there was evening, then there was morning, a day, in particular, the sixth one.
וַיֹּאמֶר לֵךְ בְּכֹחֲךָ זֶה (Judges 6:14)	i	And (Yhwh) said, "Go in (your strength here) this your strength."

No Congruence?

If as an exception an adjective with an **article** stands near an **indefinite** nominal (h), then this connection can be understood in its respective context as apposition.

Often זֶה, which has itself a reference function even like the article (→ § 52.4), also stands **without an article** after a definite nominal (i).

47 Other Nominal Groups

47.1 Prepositional Attributes

In Hebrew, as in German, nominals can also be expanded through a prepositional construction.

Attributes, Not Adverbs

וַיַּעַשׂ שְׁלֹמֹה הָרַע בְּעֵינֵי יְהוָה	a	And Solomon did the in the eyes of Yhwh evil.
(1 Kings 11:6)		= that, which was evil in Yhwh's eyes
		= what Yhwh saw as evil
מִזְמוֹר לְדָוִד	b	A psalm, by David
(Psalm 3:1, etc.)		= a psalm of David

Attention is drawn to the fact that prepositional attributes are not also applied to the verb in translation (a). The (**wrong**) **translation** "he did evil in the sight of Yhwh" would, as an adverb, answer the question "where?"

The prepositional attribute with לְ (b) stands **instead of** a **construct** connection when it is not possible because the definiteness is different for some reason.

Comparative

וַיַּרְא מִיכָה כִּי־חֲזָקִים הֵמָּה מִמֶּנּוּ	c	Then Micah saw that they were (strong, more than him) stronger than he.
(Judges 18:26)		
וַתֵּרֶב חָכְמַת שְׁלֹמֹה מֵחָכְמַת כָּל־בְּנֵי־קֶדֶם	d	And Solomon's wisdom was (great—more than) = greater than the wisdom of all easterners.
(1 Kings 5:10 [Eng 4:30])		

In **comparison**, an adjective (c), also a state of being verb (d), can be expanded through a prepositional expression with מִן. In such comparisons, the **comparative**[1] stands in German, which Hebrew does not know.

---

1   Examples of German superlative → § 45.3, text example a, and § 52.5, text example g.

47.2 Nominal Groups with Numerals

Numerals are strikingly different.

וַיָּבֹאוּ שְׁנֵי הַמַּלְאָכִים סְדֹמָה בָּעֶרֶב (Genesis 19:1)	a	Then the two messengers came to Sodom in the evening
וַיַּעֲבֵר יִשַׁי שִׁבְעַת בָּנָיו לִפְנֵי שְׁמוּאֵל (1 Samuel 16:10)	b	And Jesse made his seven sons pass before Samuel.
וְהַעֲלֵהוּ שָׁם לְעֹלָה עַל אַחַד הֶהָרִים אֲשֶׁר אֹמַר אֵלֶיךָ: (Genesis 22:2)	c	… and offer him there as a burnt offering upon one of the mountains which I say to you.

Genitive?

The numbers from 1 to 10 can stand in **status constructus** before the nominal being counted. In the translation, **no partitive genitive** should be used (a, b: not "two of the messengers," "seven of their sons"!). Only אֶחָד "one" in a construct connection can be translated thus (c).

Inverse Gender

The numerals from 3 to 10 have **the inverse gender** as the thing being numbered (b).

Numerals as Appositions

וַיּוֹלֶד נֹחַ שְׁלֹשָׁה בָנִים אֶת־שֵׁם אֶת־ חָם וְאֶת־יָפֶת: (Genesis 6:10)	d	Noah had three sons: Shem, Ham, and Japheth.
וַיִּתֵּן הָאֱלֹהִים לְהֵימָן בָּנִים אַרְבָּעָה עָשָׂר וּבָנוֹת שָׁלוֹשׁ: (1 Chronicles 25:5)	e	God gave to Heman fourteen sons and three daughters.
אֵלֶּה עָשָׂה בְּנָיָהוּ בֶּן־יְהוֹיָדָע וְלוֹ־שֵׁם בִּשְׁלֹשָׁה הַגִּבֹּרִים: (2 Samuel 23:22)	f	These things Benaiah the son of Jehoiada did, and he had a name as well as the three mighty men.

As apposition to the nominal being counted, the numerals (3–10) also contain the **opposite gender** (d, e). The **order** is as you like. Also, the **definiteness** (f) may not agree.

Compound Numbers

כָּל־הַפְּקֻדִים לְמַחֲנֵה רְאוּבֵן מְאַת אֶלֶף וְאֶחָד וַחֲמִשִּׁים אֶלֶף וְאַרְבַּע־מֵאוֹת וַחֲמִ־שִּׁים לְצִבְאֹתָם (Numbers 2:16)	g	All the numbered men of the camp of Reuben 151,450 by their armies.
וַיִּהְיוּ חַיֵּי שָׂרָה מֵאָה שָׁנָה וְעֶשְׂרִים שָׁנָה וְשֶׁבַע שָׁנִים (Genesis 23:1)	h	The life of Sarah was one hundred and twenty-seven years.
וַיְהִי מֹשֶׁה בָּהָר אַרְבָּעִים יוֹם וְאַרְבָּעִים לָיְלָה: (Exodus 24:18)	i	And Moses was on the mountain forty days and forty nights.

The **order** of the individual sections in compound numbers is as you like (g). Also the linking with ו is not obligatory.

The numbered nominal can also be repeated. Often nominals that are numbered, such as שָׁנָה, יוֹם, לַיְלָה, אִישׁ, as well as אֶלֶף, frequently stand **in the singular** (h, i). Details → § 45.4.

Distinctive Features

וּלְשָׂרָה אָמַר הִנֵּה נָתַתִּי אֶלֶף כֶּסֶף לְאָחִיךְ (Genesis 20:16)	j	But to Sarah he said, "Here, I have given your brother a thousand (shekels) of silver."
וְעַתָּה קְחוּ לָכֶם שְׁנֵי עָשָׂר אִישׁ מִשִּׁבְטֵי יִשְׂרָאֵל אִישׁ־אֶחָד אִישׁ־אֶחָד לַשָּׁבֶט: (Joshua 3:12)	k	And now take for yourselves twelve men from the tribes of Israel, one man per tribe.
וַיְהִי בִּשְׁנַת אַרְבַּע לְדָרְיָוֶשׁ הַמֶּלֶךְ הָיָה דְבַר־יְהוָה אֶל־זְכַרְיָה בְּאַרְבָּעָה לַחֹדֶשׁ הַתְּשִׁעִי בְּכִסְלֵו: (Zechariah 7:1)	l	In the fourth year of King Darius, the word of Yhwh came to Zechariah on the four(th day) of the ninth month, in Chislev.

Familiar **units of measurement** such as shekel and ephah can be left out (j). Repetition of a number and the thing counted, connected with ל, means **distribution**: "per" (k). There are separate **ordinal numbers** only from 1 to 10 (→ § 22.3). The **cardinal numbers** stand instead of these. The cardinal numbers under 10 are frequent in giving of dates (l).

48 The Verbal Part of the Clause—Tenses

48.1 Existence and Distribution of Tense Forms

Four Tenses

The following are differentiated as the tenses of the Hebrew verb: In the Preformative Conjugation (PC), **imperfect** and **imperfect consecutive** (יִקְטֹל and וַיִּקְטֹל), and in the Afformative Conjugation (AC), the **perfect** and **perfect consecutive** (קָטַל and וְקָטַל).

In Narratives

These four "tenses"[1] are distributed differently in texts of different **genres** [*Gattungen*]. In narratives the **imperfect consecutive** (ic) dominates with ca. 75% of all tense forms.[2] For that reason, the imperfect consecutive is also called "**Narrativ**."[3] To this corresponds a low occurrence of imperfect (i) and perfect consecutive (pc) of ca. 2%.

In Other Gattungen

In texts and parts of texts that **do not narrate** (e.g. laws, sermons, prophetic speeches, psalms, also in the dialogue parts of narrations), the **imperfect** (i) predominates with about 50% of all tense forms. After this comes **perfect-consecutive** forms (pc) with 20%. In contrast to these, the ic-forms have only a share of ca. 5%.

In all genres, the perfect (p) is represented quite **regularly** (narration: 22%, non-narration: 28%).

Narrating or Speaking

Thus the imperfect (i) and imperfect consecutive (ic) can be described as the two **primary-tenses**.[4] They control the process of communication,[5] in that they

---

1   On the term "tense" → § 24.2, note.
2   The dialogue parts in narrations are not considered with this, since they themselves are not narrated.
3   From latin: *narrare*, "tell, narrate."
4   This is first understood only quantitatively: the tenses appearing most frequently.
5   This point of view is interested primarily syntactically, that is, with how the speech gives orientation to the partners in the communication. It questions less semantically, that is, not with

characterize the **discourse mode** [*or* linguistic stance] of a text as narrating (ic) or speaking (i). The other tenses have an effect on this orientation (pc in discourse texts) or are **neutral** (p) with regard to it.

Narrative speech allows freedom of **disassociation** to the listener. Discourse speech **engages** him: Speaker and listener have to act and react.[6]

48.2 The Tenses in Narrative Texts

The primary tense in narrative texts is the imperfect consecutive (narrative tense).

Narrativ

וַיֵּרָא אֵלָיו יְהוָה בְּאֵלֹנֵי מַמְרֵא	a	Then[7] Yhwh appeared to him by the oaks
וְהוּא יֹשֵׁב פֶּתַח־הָאֹהֶל כְּחֹם		of Mamre,
הַיּוֹם:		(&)—he was sitting (ptcp) at the tent door
וַיִּשָּׂא עֵינָיו		in the heat of the day—
וַיַּרְא		and he lifted up his eyes
וְהִנֵּה שְׁלֹשָׁה אֲנָשִׁים נִצָּבִים עָלָיו		and he looked,
וַיַּרְא		(&) see, three men were standing (ptcp)
וַיָּרָץ לִקְרָאתָם מִפֶּתַח הָאֹהֶל		opposite him.
וַיִּשְׁתַּחוּ אָרְצָה:		And he saw,
וַיֹּאמַר		and he ran from the tent door to meet them
(Genesis 18:1ff.)		and he bowed himself to the earth,
		and he said: …

Narrativ Chains

In verbal clauses that form the **foreground** of the narrative (→ § 44.2), the predicates stand in the narrative tense (ic) at the front of each clause. Narrative tenses

---

whether and how actions are described through the tenses (as complete, incomplete, or continuous).

6   The functional purpose of the tenses as "discourse mode [linguistic stance]" falls back on the tense-theory of Harald Weinrich, who in his book "Tempus-Besprochene und erzählte Welt" (4th ed. Stuttgart 1985) analyzed the tenses in European linguistics under this point of view and at the same time has done without the use of the categories "time" and "aspect." This theory is not absolutely true; it can however in my opinion best explain the use of the verb forms in the text.

7   The translations of example texts are not models for translation. They should make discernible the Hebrew tense relationships. That is why most of the time "da" or "und" stand before the narrative tense.

do not stand isolated but form chains. For a narrative, the **narrative sequence** is a constitutive element. It is signaled through the tense-morpheme "wa" (waw with pathach and following Dagesch forte).

For German **translation** the German narrative tense preterite can be used. In German it can also get by without a concluding conjunction ("und," "dann," "da").

Interruption of the Narrativ Chain

As soon as some other linguistic sign comes before the verb, another tense form must replace the imperfect consecutive. This is usually a **perfect** form.

וַיָּקָם יוֹנָה לִבְרֹחַ תַּרְשִׁישָׁה מִלִּפְנֵי יְהוָה וַיֵּרֶד יָפוֹ וַיִּמְצָא אֳנִיָּה בָּאָה תַרְשִׁישׁ וַיִּתֵּן שְׂכָרָהּ וַיֵּרֶד בָּהּ לָבוֹא עִמָּהֶם תַּרְשִׁישָׁה מִלִּפְנֵי יְהוָה:	b₁	And Jonah rose up to flee to Tarshish away from Yhwh. And he went down to Joppa, and he found a ship going to Tarshish, and he paid the fare and he went down into it to go with them to Tarshish away from Yhwh.
וַיהוָה הֵטִיל רוּחַ־גְּדוֹלָה אֶל־הַיָּם וַיְהִי סַעַר־גָּדוֹל בַּיָּם	b₂	But Yhwh hurled a great wind on the sea and there was a great storm on the sea.
וְהָאֳנִיָּה חִשְּׁבָה לְהִשָּׁבֵר: וַיִּירְאוּ הַמַּלָּחִים וַיִּזְעֲקוּ אִישׁ אֶל־אֱלֹהָיו ...	b₃	(&) the ship—it was about to break up—(but as...) then the sailors became afraid and every man cried to his god …
...יָרַד אֶל־יַרְכְּתֵי הַסְּפִינָה וַיִּשְׁכַּב וַיֵּרָדַם: וַיִּקְרַב אֵלָיו רַב הַחֹבֵל וַיֹּאמֶר לוֹ ... (Jonah 1:3ff.)	b₄	… But Jonah had gone below into the hold of the ship, and had lain down and fallen sound asleep. Then the captain came to him and he said to him …
וַיַּחְתְּרוּ הָאֲנָשִׁים לְהָשִׁיב אֶל־הַיַּבָּשָׁה וְלֹא יָכֹלוּ כִּי הַיָּם הוֹלֵךְ וְסֹעֵר עֲלֵיהֶם: וַיִּקְרְאוּ אֶל־יְהוָה ... (Jonah 1:13f.)	c	Then the men rowed to return to land but they could not, for the sea was becoming *even* stormier against them. Then they called to YHWH …

Background

Clauses that interrupt the narrative chain contain background information. In them, the story does not progress.

Simple nominal clauses (often with participles—a, second clause) describe contemporaneous circumstances (→ also § 49.1).

Compound nominal clauses (beginning with וְ → § 53.1) can **structure**[8] the narration as the opening of scenes and entire texts (b_2, b_4) or can stress an object or subject (b_2) or can contain a circumstance for the following narrative-tense (b_3). The perfect appears as a **background tense**.

Perspective

Compound nominal clauses (CNC) can also refer back to the chronological background (b_4), that is, they contain **previous information**: The perfect appears as a **perspectival**, looking-back tense.[9]

Subordinate Clauses

Verbal clauses, in which only a **particle** (כִּי, אֲשֶׁר) stands at the front, also contain background information (→ text examples in §§ 53.3 and 53.4). Also a **negated** clause (c) interrupts the imperfect-consecutive chain. To be precise, it does not necessarily contain some background information, but also no new event, rather more likely some commentary of the narrator. From the perfect tense only the perspective (namely, **looking-back**) is in view.

Verbal clauses with a perfect form at the **front** of the clause do **not** occur in narrative.

48.3 The Tenses in Discourse Texts

For the most part, the imperfect predominates in those texts that do not narrate but rather describe in them the world and the behavior of man.[10]

---

8   On the structuring/organizing function of the CNC → § 54.2.
9   Special verb forms for pre-past tense (pluperfect) are not given in Hebrew.
10   There are also discourse genres in which perfects consecutive predominate → § 44.2.

Imperfect and Perfect

וַיַּעֲנוּ אֶת־יְהוֹשֻׁעַ לֵאמֹר	a	They answered Joshua, saying,
כֹּל אֲשֶׁר־צִוִּיתָנוּ נַעֲשֶׂה		"All that you have commanded us we will do;
וְאֶל־כָּל־אֲשֶׁר תִּשְׁלָחֵנוּ נֵלֵךְ:		and wherever you send us we will go!
כְּכֹל אֲשֶׁר־שָׁמַעְנוּ אֶל־מֹשֶׁה		In everything, as we have obeyed Moses,
כֵּן נִשְׁמַע אֵלֶיךָ		we will obey you.
רַק יִהְיֶה יְהוָה אֱלֹהֶיךָ עִמָּךְ		Only that YHWH your God be with you
כַּאֲשֶׁר הָיָה עִם־מֹשֶׁה:		as He was with Moses.
כָּל־אִישׁ אֲשֶׁר־יַמְרֶה אֶת־פִּיךָ		Anyone who rebels against your command
וְלֹא־יִשְׁמַע אֶת־דְּבָרֶיךָ		and does not obey your words,
לְכֹל אֲשֶׁר־תְּצַוֶּנּוּ יוּמָת		in all that you command him, shall be put to
(Joshua 1:16ff.)		death."

Imperfect

The imperfect functions to characterize the speech as **discourse**, as it applies to the discourse situation immediately affecting the listener. Concerning its perspective, it can only be said that it permits fundamentally **no looking-back perspective**; rather it is usually perspectivally indifferent (as the German present tense). The **forward perspective** translated above (a, clauses 3, 5, 7) arises from the contrast in content between it and the looking-back perspective in the clauses with perfect.

Imperfect forms—in contrast to imperfect consecutive forms—are not limited to the beginning of a clause. Imperfects, which do **not** stand at the **beginning of a clause** (as in CNC or subordinate clauses), are **indicative** (simple affirmative clauses); imperfect forms at the **beginning of a clause** are to be regarded as "**volitional**": The speaker wants something.[11]

Foreground and **background** of the speech are denoted not only through the use of tense, but also through **other signs** such as clause position, particles and reference to the speech situation (→ also § 44.2).

Perfect

The perfect has a (**backward-**)**perspectival** function in discourse texts: The speaker refers back to facts of the past in order to include them in the speech situation.

---

11 In a cited text like Joshua 1, it is concerned not with expressions of the will but with agreements. On mood → § 51.4.

Translation

For translation of the **imperfect**, the **present** tense in German is first at one's disposal as a general German speech tense. Only if **additional** signs in the context indicate a modal or temporal orientation, can German **subjunctive** or **modal verbs**[12] also be used.

For translation of the **perfect**, the perspectival tense **perfect** in German[13] is at one's disposal.

Performative Comments

A special form of discourse speech is the **performative** comment. "Performative" means that an **extra-linguistic act** is carried out at the same time with the **linguistic** comment. Or put another way: "Performative comments are such that they themselves describe the speech act that they represent."[14]

בָּרוּךְ הַבָּא בְּשֵׁם יְהוָה בֵּרַכְנוּכֶם מִבֵּית יְהוָה: (Psalm 118:26)	b	Blessed is the one who comes in the name of Yhwh; <u>We bless you</u> from the house of Yhwh.
וַיֹּאמֶר יְהוָה יְהוּדָה יַעֲלֶה הִנֵּה נָתַתִּי אֶת־הָאָרֶץ בְּיָדוֹ: (Judges 1:2)	c	The Yhwh said, "Judah shall go up. (See!) <u>With this I give</u> the land into his hand."

In performative comments, the perfect is used in Hebrew; in German [& English] the present tense. In the speech situation, it can be indicated through a deictic element (→ § 52.4) such as הִנֵּה, הַיּוֹם or וְעַתָּה. The perfect in these comments has no looking-back perspective and no background meaning.

---

12 "Werden" is also a modal verb, with whose help the absent "future" can be expressed in German.

13 The acceptance of a "prophetic perfect," which on must give an account of with German present tense, is not necessary.

14 According to the English linguistic philosopher John L. Austin: "How to Do Things with Words" (1962), German under the title: "Zur Theorie der Sprechakte," Stuttgard, Reclam, 1972.
Marks of the performative comments are in German:
1. The speaker is subject;
2. the verb stands in the present tense,
3. the 2nd person can occur as indirect object,
4. it can be adapted "with this,"
5. the clause is not negative.
Example: "I hereby open the meeting."

Perfect Consecutive

In discourse texts fairly frequently (20%) and in particular genres, the perfect consecutive—that is, forms of the **Afformative conjugation** with proclitic **waw** (→ § 27.4)—is predominant. The perfect consecutive and the imperfect are together the **primary tenses**[15] of discourse texts. Given this, forms of the perfect consecutive are only possible at the **beginning of the clause**. As soon as other elements are at the beginning of the clause, the imperfect occurs, as a rule.

וְעַתָּה	d	But now:
כְּבֹאִי אֶל־עַבְדְּךָ אָבִי		When I come (inf.) to your servant my father,
וְהַנַּעַר אֵינֶנּוּ אִתָּנוּ		
וְנַפְשׁוֹ קְשׁוּרָה בְנַפְשׁוֹ:		and the lad is not with us (NC),
וְהָיָה כִּרְאוֹתוֹ כִּי־אֵין הַנַּעַר וָמֵת		since[16] his life is bound up (ptcp) in the lad's life, Thus it appears: when he sees (inf.) that the lad is not *with us* (NC),
וְהוֹרִידוּ עֲבָדֶיךָ אֶת־שֵׂיבַת עַבְדְּךָ אָבִינוּ בְּיָגוֹן שְׁאֹלָה:		then he will die. Thus your servants will bring the gray hair of your servant our father down to Sheol in sorrow.
כִּי עַבְדְּךָ עָרַב אֶת־הַנַּעַר מֵעִם אָבִי		Yes, your servant became surety for the lad to my father, saying,
לֵאמֹר		
אִם־לֹא אֲבִיאֶנּוּ אֵלֶיךָ		"If I do not bring him *back* to you,
וְחָטָאתִי לְאָבִי כָּל־הַיָּמִים:		then let me bear the blame before my father forever."
(Genesis 44:30ff.)		
וַיֹּאמֶר שְׁמוּאֵל	e	But Samuel said,
אֵיךְ אֵלֵךְ		"How (can) I then go? When Saul hears (of it), he will kill me."
וְשָׁמַע שָׁאוּל וַהֲרָגָנִי		
(1 Samuel 16:2)		

---

15 It is again concerning this indicating that "primary tense" no longer means "numerically over-whelming." Imperfect and perfect consecutive constitute together ca. 70%.
16 Also the translation of perfect-consecutive forms is established stereotypically in this text-example, in particular to "so" or "dann" plus present or future tense (→ note on narrative tense § 48.2).

"If" Clauses

The use of the perfect consecutive in dialogue[17] shows that its original area of application is the conditional structure[18] ("if ... then"): After an "if" clause, the following clause begins with a concluding waw and a form of the Affirmative conjugation.

Forward Perspective

The discourse character of the text is verified mostly through **additional signs** (→ וְעַתָּה and the signs of the 1st person in text d). The following element "we" in front of the perfect form turns the perspective of the perfect around and sends it **to the front**. If the waw is missing, the perfect keeps its looking-back perspective (d, line 9).

In a dialogue, a conditional structure can also be expressed through two consecutive perfects (e), without an apodosis being developed with אִם or כִּי.

וְהָיָה

Before such conditional structures וְהָיָה "so it occurs" can be used as an indicator of tense and as a signal of structure. (Text examples → d, 2nd verse and → § 53.2.)

Law Texts

וְנֶפֶשׁ	f	But anyone
כִּי־תַקְרִיב קָרְבַּן מִנְחָה לַיהוָה		when he presents a grain offering as an offering to Yhwh—his offering shall be of fine flour—so he shall pour oil[19] on it and he shall put frankincense on it.
סֹלֶת יִהְיֶה קָרְבָּנוֹ		
וְיָצַק עָלֶיהָ שֶׁמֶן		
וְנָתַן עָלֶיהָ לְבֹנָה:		
וֶהֱבִיאָהּ אֶל־בְּנֵי אַהֲרֹן הַכֹּהֲנִים		so he shall bring it to Aaron's sons the priests,
וְקָמַץ מִשָּׁם מְלֹא קֻמְצוֹ מִסָּלְתָּהּ וּמִשַּׁמְנָהּ עַל כָּל־לְבֹנָתָהּ		so he shall take from it his handful, namely of its fine flour and of its oil with all of its frankincense.
וְהִקְטִיר הַכֹּהֵן אֶת־אַזְכָּרָתָהּ הַמִּזְבֵּחָה ...		so he the priest shall offer *it* up in smoke *as* its memorial portion on the altar ...
(Leviticus 2:1f.)		

---

17 In literary texts such as the biblical one, the dialogue of the spoken speeches comes at the end.

18 A discussion about whether it acts for conditional or temporal "if"-clauses is pointless. Whether the condition, which the front clause makes, has a temporal component, depends on the meaning of the individual words.

19 It can of course also be translated in such law and sermon texts with "he should..." or "you should..." (→ § 51.4).

The perfect consecutive has a widened range of application in law texts, above all in the **law of the cult** (f): Clauses with perfect consecutive describe the **conduct**, which arises from one particular case that is offered at the beginning (mostly with imperfect).

Sermon Texts

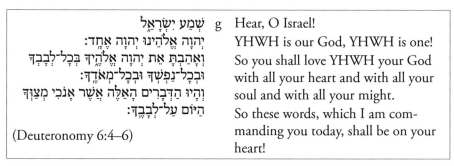

שְׁמַע יִשְׂרָאֵל	g	Hear, O Israel!
יְהוָה אֱלֹהֵינוּ יְהוָה אֶחָד:		YHWH is our God, YHWH is one!
וְאָהַבְתָּ אֵת יְהוָה אֱלֹהֶיךָ בְּכָל־לְבָבְךָ		So you shall love YHWH your God
וּבְכָל־נַפְשְׁךָ וּבְכָל־מְאֹדֶךָ:		with all your heart and with all your
וְהָיוּ הַדְּבָרִים הָאֵלֶּה אֲשֶׁר אָנֹכִי מְצַוְּךָ		soul and with all your might.
הַיּוֹם עַל־לְבָבֶךָ:		So these words, which I am com-
(Deuteronomy 6:4–6)		manding you today, shall be on your heart!

In the **sermonic style** of Deuteronomy and the literature dependent upon it, clauses with perfect consecutive follow frequently after an introductory clause of **fundamental** contents (g). These then contain exhortations and **demands**, which arise from the initial clause.

After Imperative

הַדָּבָר אֲשֶׁר הָיָה אֶל־יִרְמְיָהוּ מֵאֵת	h	The word that came to Jeremiah from
יְהוָה לֵאמֹר:		YHWH, saying,
עֲמֹד בְּשַׁעַר בֵּית יְהוָה		"Stand in the gate of YHWH's house
וְקָרָאתָ שָּׁם אֶת־הַדָּבָר הַזֶּה		and (so you shall proclaim) proclaim there this word
וְאָמַרְתָּ		
שִׁמְעוּ דְבַר־יְהוָה כָּל־יְהוּדָה ...		and (so you shall say) say,
(Jeremiah 7:1f.)		'Hear the word of YHWH, all Judah ....'"

If the **discourse** situation is clear (h, line 1) and the speech begins with an impera-tive (h, line 3), then the **following clauses** can be joined with perfect consecu-tive, which expound and continue the first demand. In German **translation**, the imperative can be followed with "und."

Future Actions

If (future) **actions** are discussed, then clauses with perfect consecutive in a text can **predominate**, while subordinate clauses have imperfects (→ example text a, 1 Sam 10, in § 44.2).

Universal recommendations of translation for the perfect consecutive cannot be given. How it is to be **translated** depends on the clauses coming before and on the **genre** [*Gattung*] of a text. Important is a concluding particle such as "so," "dann," "und."

48.4 Tense Transitions: Narrative to Dialogue

Tense forms cannot change at will. The speech has the tendency to remain in the same tense (ic—ic—ic—ic), at most to transition to a subordinate tense (ic—p—ic—ic), but as far as possible to combine only tenses of the same style of speech (i—pc—impv—pc—pc—i—i). Disruptions of such a tendency deserve higher attention.

Transition: Narrative—Dialogue

A transition between the **primary tense** imperfect consecutive and imperfect inside of one and the same text has particular significance: It signals the change of linguistic stance and at the same time as a rule the transition between the **narrative** of the narrator and the **speech** of the narrative figure.

וַיָּקוּמוּ בַבֹּקֶר	a	And they arose in the morning.
וַיֹּאמֶר		And he said,
שַׁלְּחֻנִי לַאדֹנִי׃		"Send me away to my master."
וַיֹּאמֶר אָחִיהָ וְאִמָּהּ		Then her brother and her mother said,
תֵּשֵׁב הַנַּעֲרָ אִתָּנוּ יָמִים אוֹ עָשׂוֹר		"Let the girl stay[20] with us *a few* days, say ten;
אַחַר תֵּלֵךְ׃		afterward she may go."
וַיֹּאמֶר אֲלֵהֶם		And he said to them,
אַל־תְּאַחֲרוּ אֹתִי		"Do not delay me,
וַיהוָה הִצְלִיחַ דַּרְכִּי		since YHWH has prospered my way.
שַׁלְּחוּנִי		Send me away
וְאֵלְכָה לַאדֹנִי׃		that I may go to my master!"
וַיֹּאמְרוּ		And they said,
נִקְרָא לַנַּעֲרָ		"We will call the girl
וְנִשְׁאֲלָה אֶת־פִּיהָ׃		and consult her wishes."
וַיִּקְרְאוּ לְרִבְקָה וַיֹּאמְרוּ אֵלֶיהָ		And they called Rebekah and asked her,
הֲתֵלְכִי עִם־הָאִישׁ הַזֶּה		"Will you go with this man?"
וַתֹּאמֶר		She said,
אֵלֵךְ׃		"Yes (I will go)!"
וַיְשַׁלְּחוּ אֶת־רִבְקָה אֲחֹתָם		And they sent away their sister Rebekah. ...
(Genesis 24:54ff.)		

---

20 On the volitive clause → § 51.4 (text example c).

Marking

The transition from narrative to dialogue is marked by **tense change**, by **change in person** (1st and 2nd instead of 3rd person), and by a verb for "**to say**" (mostly a form of אמר), which also in a quick change in exchanges is almost never missing and the narrative situation of the narrator also in longer dialogues is kept in mind. In order to indicate the **end** of the literal speech, change in tense or change in person is sufficient.

48.5 Tense Transitions: Foreign Tenses in Narratives

Imperfects and perfects consecutive can appear occasionally in the middle of the narrative context.

A transition of the narrative to **commentary** can be indicated through one such change.

Transition to a Tense Foreign to the Context

וַיֹּאמֶר a	Then he said,	
שִׂימוּ לָחֶם:	"Serve the meal."	
וַיָּשִׂימוּ לוֹ לְבַדּוֹ וְלָהֶם לְבַדָּם	And they served him by himself, and	
וְלַמִּצְרִים הָאֹכְלִים אִתּוֹ לְבַדָּם	them by themselves,	
כִּי לֹא יוּכְלוּן הַמִּצְרִים לֶאֱכֹל אֶת־הָעִ־	and the Egyptians who ate with him by	
בְרִים לֶחֶם	themselves.	
כִּי־תוֹעֵבָה הִוא לְמִצְרָיִם:	Egyptians <u>could</u> not eat bread with the	
(Genesis 43:31f.)	Hebrews,	
	for that is loathsome for Egyptians.	
וַיִּבְחַר מֹשֶׁה אַנְשֵׁי־חַיִל מִכָּל־יִשְׂרָאֵל b	And Moses chose able men out of all Israel	
וַיִּתֵּן אֹתָם רָאשִׁים עַל־הָעָם ...	and made them heads over the people ...	
וְשָׁפְטוּ אֶת־הָעָם בְּכָל־עֵת	So they <u>would judge</u> the people at all times.	
אֶת־הַדָּבָר הַקָּשֶׁה יְבִיאוּן אֶל־מֹשֶׁה	The difficult dispute they <u>would bring</u> to	
וְכָל־הַדָּבָר הַקָּטֹן יִשְׁפּוּטוּ הֵם:	Moses,	
(Exodus 18:25f.)	but every minor dispute they themselves <u>would judge</u>.	

Commentary

A change from the narrative tense to the imperfect or perfect consecutive (a) can show that the author has stepped out of his **speech situation** as narrator and **discussed** something with his hearers/readers, which also should interest them outside of the narrated world.

Notes in the imperfect or perfect consecutive which report **repeated** action are also a kind of **commentary** in the narrative events (b). In German, it is preserved most of the time by the story tense.

Imperfect after Conjunctions

אָז תָּבֹאנָה שְׁתַּיִם נָשִׁים זֹנוֹת אֶל־הַמֶּלֶךְ וַתַּעֲמֹדְנָה לְפָנָיו׃ וַתֹּאמֶר הָאִשָּׁה הָאַחַת ... (1Kg 3:16–17)	c	Then two women who were harlots (once) came to the king and stood before him. Then the one woman said …
וֶאֱלִישָׁע חָלָה אֶת־חָלְיוֹ אֲשֶׁר יָמוּת בּוֹ וַיֵּרֶד אֵלָיו יוֹאָשׁ מֶלֶךְ־יִשְׂרָאֵל (2 Kings 13:14)	d	As Elisha became sick (CNC) with the illness of which he should (later) die, Joash the king of Israel came down to him.
וּשְׁמוּאֵל טֶרֶם יָדַע אֶת־יְהוָה וְטֶרֶם יִגָּלֶה אֵלָיו דְּבַר־יְהוָה׃ (1 Samuel 3:7)	e	But Samuel <u>had</u> not yet known YHWH, nor <u>had</u> the word of YHWH yet been revealed to him.
וַיֵּשֶׁב ... בַּצֵּל עַד אֲשֶׁר יִרְאֶה מַה־יִּהְיֶה בָּעִיר׃ (Jonah 4:5)	f	And he sat … in the shadow until he <u>could see</u> what <u>would happen</u> in the city.

אָז at the Beginning

After the particle אָז "there/then/at that time" the imperfect also occurs frequently in narrative context. At the beginning of the clause, אָז replaces the tense-sign "wa." It is found often before a shorter narrative **note**, when the narrator still wants to insert something on the same theme (e.g. Ex 15:1; Dt 4:41). In two cases, namely 1Kg 3:16 (c) and 1Kg 8:1, really long narratives emerge out of the "insertions."

Relative Future

After some conjunctions the imperfect can appear as a **perspectival** tense. After אֲשֶׁר (d), after עַד אֲשֶׁר "until that" (f), almost always after טֶרֶם "still not" (e), and in subordinate interrogative clauses (f), events that are seen as **future** from the level of the narrative occur in the imperfect.

Perfect with Waw-Copulative

וַיִּקֶן יוֹסֵף אֶת־כָּל־אַדְמַת מִצְרַיִם g לְפַרְעֹה ... וַתְּהִי הָאָרֶץ לְפַרְעֹה: וְאֶת־הָעָם הֶעֱבִיר אֹתוֹ לֶעָרִים ... רַק אַדְמַת הַכֹּהֲנִים לֹא קָנָה כִּי חֹק לַכֹּהֲנִים מֵאֵת פַּרְעֹה וְאָכְלוּ אֶת־חֻקָּם אֲשֶׁר נָתַן לָהֶם פַּרְעֹה עַל־כֵּן לֹא מָכְרוּ אֶת־אַדְמָתָם: (Genesis 47:20–22)	Then Joseph bought all the land of Egypt for Pharaoh ... and the land became Pharaoh's. But the people—he removed them to the cities ... only the land of the priests he did not buy, for the priests had an allotment from Pharaoh, so that they would live off the allotment which Pharaoh gave them. Therefore, they did not sell their land.

Isolated in the narrative context, Afformative conjugation forms can appear with waw, in which there are **no consecutive perfects**. In text example g, line 6, an inversion (CNC) is neither possible nor intended; on the other hand, however, the background character of the clause is retained and a sequence connection is established through the "we" (→ § 53.1).

In later narrative literature (e.g. at the beginning of the book of Job) this use of the perfect with copulative waw gains acceptance in narratives more and more throughout.[21]

48.6 Tense Transitions: Discourse Story Telling

Discourse Narratives

Not all narratives appear distant and in **relaxed** speech style. Even in the Bible the world is discussed many times through story telling, and the situation is interpreted. The narrator can apply his narrative to his **present** with simple syntactical means.

---

21 In medieval Hebrew, the narrative tense is entirely lost and is replaced through the waw-AC.

וַיְהִי	a	(And it came about) after Amaziah came (inf.) from slaughtering the Edomites,
אַחֲרֵי בוֹא אֲמַצְיָהוּ מֵהַכּוֹת אֶת־אֲדוֹמִים		
וַיָּבֵא אֶת־אֱלֹהֵי בְּנֵי שֵׂעִיר		then he brought the gods of the sons of Seir
וַיַּעֲמִידֵם לוֹ לֵאלֹהִים		and set them up as his gods.
וְלִפְנֵיהֶם יִשְׁתַּחֲוֶה		And he would bow down before them
וְלָהֶם יְקַטֵּר:		and burn incense to them.
וַיִּחַר־אַף יְהוָה בַּאֲמַצְיָהוּ ...		Then the anger of YHWH burned against Amaziah ...
(2 Chronicles 25:14f.)		
בִּשְׁנַת־מוֹת הַמֶּלֶךְ עֻזִּיָּהוּ	b	In the year of King Uzziah's death I saw the Lord sitting on a lofty and exalted throne; the train of his robe filling (ptcp) the temple.
וָאֶרְאֶה אֶת־אֲדֹנָי יֹשֵׁב עַל־כִּסֵּא רָם וְנִשָּׂא		
וְשׁוּלָיו מְלֵאִים אֶת־הַהֵיכָל:		
שְׂרָפִים עֹמְדִים מִמַּעַל לוֹ שֵׁשׁ כְּנָפַיִם		Seraphim stood above Him (NC), each having six wings (NC): with two he would cover his face, and with two he would cover his feet, and with two he would fly.
שֵׁשׁ כְּנָפַיִם לְאֶחָד בִּשְׁתַּיִם יְכַסֶּה פָנָיו		
וּבִשְׁתַּיִם יְכַסֶּה רַגְלָיו וּבִשְׁתַּיִם יְעוֹפֵף:		
וְקָרָא זֶה אֶל־זֶה וְאָמַר		So one would call out to another and say,
קָדוֹשׁ קָדוֹשׁ קָדוֹשׁ יְהוָה צְבָאוֹת		"Holy, Holy, Holy, (is) YHWH of hosts!
מְלֹא כָל־הָאָרֶץ כְּבוֹדוֹ:		The whole earth (is) full of His glory."
וַיָּנֻעוּ אַמּוֹת הַסִּפִּים מִקּוֹל הַקּוֹרֵא		Then the foundations of the thresholds trembled at the voice of him who called out, and the temple would fill itself with smoke.
וְהַבַּיִת יִמָּלֵא עָשָׁן:		
וָאֹמַר		Then I said ...
(Isaiah 6:1–4)		

Forcefulness

With engaging story telling, the narrator goes occasionally at **high points** of his narrative to the tenses of discourse speech (a). With it he gives the narration higher **forcefulness.**[22] In example a (lines 5 and 6) a perfect must stand with the same clause position. But as a result, the clauses would move into the background.

---

22 This corresponds to the German and Latin "historical present."

The surprising imperfects emphasize properly the—as unheard of for a king of Israel—activity of Amaziah.

Imagining

Also the calling vision of Isaiah (b) contains such passages: Individual events are not narrated, but a picture is painted and **imagined** in clauses which have the same forceful initial sounds and with the rhyme of the dual-ending "ayim" ("six wings—six wings—with two—with two—with two…"). Also this speech act bears no background clauses.

Individual biblical authors[23] like to use unexpected tense transitions in the introduction or conclusion of a narrative-unit, using them therefore for the **structure** (framework) of a text.

Dreams

וַיַּחֲלֹם יוֹסֵף חֲלוֹם c	Then Joseph had a dream,
וַיַּגֵּד לְאֶחָיו … :	and when he told (it) to his brothers ….
וַיֹּאמֶר אֲלֵיהֶם	
שִׁמְעוּ־נָא הַחֲלוֹם הַזֶּה אֲשֶׁר חָלָמְתִּי:	He said to them,
וְהִנֵּה אֲנַחְנוּ מְאַלְּמִים אֲלֻמִּים בְּתוֹךְ הַשָּׂדֶה	"Please listen to this (important) dream which I have had;
וְהִנֵּה קָמָה אֲלֻמָּתִי וְגַם־נִצָּבָה	
וְהִנֵּה תְסֻבֶּינָה אֲלֻמֹּתֵיכֶם וַתִּשְׁתַּחֲוֶיןָ לַאֲלֻמָּתִי:	Imagine for yourselves: We were binding sheaves in the field. And think only:
(Genesis 37:5ff.)	My sheaf rose up and also stood erect. But think it well: Your sheaves gathered around! Then they bowed down to my sheaf."

How one can speak through "discourse narration" in a threatening situation is shown by the short text excerpt from the Joseph-narrative (c), in which Joseph **apparently tells** his brothers the dream but in reality interprets his position in the circle of the brothers and provokes the brothers. The discourse signals are heaped up to **exaggeration**: A demand to the hearers שִׁמְעוּ־נָא, three times the atten-

---

23 This stylistic device occurs with the Yahwist (e.g. Gen 2) and in the narratives of the throne succession of David (2Sa 9 to 1Kg 2, here above all 2Sa 15).

tion- and significant-indicator[24] וְהִנֵּה, the imperfect תְּסַבֶּינָה as sign for engaged narrative and means of emphasis. Thus the syntax contradicts the semantics ("he narrated").

In other "discourse" narratives, e.g. reduced confessional summaries of the history of Israel as in Deut 26:5–9, the signals relating to the situation are **more sparse** and appear to be missing entirely in the larger narrative works.

Occasionally **semantic** signals appear: theological judgments ("he did what the Lord dislikes") or particular **theological** keywords (as e.g. שׁוּב "turn back/become converted" in the deuteronomistic literature).

48.7 Tense Transitions: Narrative Tense in Speech Context

Also the narrative tense (imperfect consecutive) is not restricted to narrative contexts.

Isolated Narrative Tenses

וַיֹּאמַר	a	Then he [Solomon] said,
יְהוָה אֱלֹהֵי יִשְׂרָאֵל אֵין־כָּמוֹךָ אֱלֹהִים ...		"YHWH, God of Israel, there is no God like You ...
אֲשֶׁר שָׁמַרְתָּ לְעַבְדְּךָ דָוִד אָבִי אֵת		who have kept with Your servant, my
אֲשֶׁר־דִּבַּרְתָּ לּוֹ		father David, that which You have
וַתְּדַבֵּר בְּפִיךָ		promised him; <u>and you spoke</u> with
וּבְיָדְךָ מִלֵּאתָ כַּיּוֹם הַזֶּה:		Your mouth and have fulfilled it with
(1 Kings 8:23–24)		Your hand as (it is) this day."
כִּי־יִשְׁאָלְךָ בִנְךָ מָחָר לֵאמֹר	b	When your son asks you in time to come:
מָה הָעֵדֹת וְהַחֻקִּים וְהַמִּשְׁפָּטִים		"What *do* these testimonies and stat-
אֲשֶׁר צִוָּה יְהוָה אֱלֹהֵינוּ אֶתְכֶם:		utes and judgments which YHWH
וְאָמַרְתָּ לְבִנְךָ		our God commanded you mean?"
עֲבָדִים הָיִינוּ לְפַרְעֹה בְּמִצְרָיִם		then you shall say to your son:
וַיּוֹצִיאֵנוּ יְהוָה מִמִּצְרַיִם בְּיָד חֲזָקָה:		"We were slaves to Pharaoh in Egypt,
וַיִּתֵּן יְהוָה אוֹתֹת וּמֹפְתִים גְּדֹלִים וְרָעִים		and YHWH <u>brought</u> us from Egypt
בְּמִצְרַיִם בְּפַרְעֹה וּבְכָל־בֵּיתוֹ לְעֵינֵינוּ:		with a mighty hand,
וְאוֹתָנוּ הוֹצִיא מִשָּׁם		

---

24 It does not contradict this that וְהִנֵּה is form-typical in dream narratives (→ § 54.3). In antiquity a dream is per se significant. It is the increasing frequency with which Joseph here almost speaks at head and neck.

לְמַעַן הָבִיא אֹתָנוּ לָתֶת לָנוּ אֶת־הָאָרֶץ b	and YHWH <u>did</u> great and distress-
אֲשֶׁר נִשְׁבַּע לַאֲבֹתֵינוּ׃	ing signs and wonders before our
וַיְצַוֵּנוּ יְהוָה	eyes against Egypt, Pharaoh and all
לַעֲשׂוֹת אֶת־כָּל־הַחֻקִּים הָאֵלֶּה	his household.
לְיִרְאָה אֶת־יְהוָה אֱלֹהֵינוּ	But He brought us out from there in
לְטוֹב לָנוּ כָּל־הַיָּמִים לְחַיֹּתֵנוּ כְּהַיּוֹם הַזֶּה׃	order to bring us in, to give us the land
	which He had sworn to our fathers.
(Deuteronomy 6:20–24)	And YHWH <u>commanded</u> us
	to observe all these statutes,
	to fear YHWH our God
	for our good always and for our sur-
	vival, as (it is) today."

Budding Narratives

In a discourse context, additional verbal clauses with narrative tense (as a sequence of events) can follow the perfect (back-perspective). As a result, a narrative appears to develop **secondarily**.

However, the narrative tenses **never** stand **at the beginning** of the speech, and such budding-narratives are mostly very **short** (a). Before a distanced narrative situation can be confirmed, the speech passes again to the perfect or to the discourse tenses. Besides, **deictic** signals (referring to the speech situation)[25] as e.g. the suffix and person morpheme of the 1st and 2nd person or phrases such as הַיּוֹם הַזֶּה occur and characterize the discourse speech.

If in a discourse context a **longer** secondary narrative part appears (b), the references to the situation are particularly numerous and striking.

48.8 The Imperative as Tense

The imperative is indeed not a tense form itself. It is however clearly restricted to discourse contexts, therefore influencing the temporal structure of the texts.

וָאֹמַר הִנְנִי שְׁלָחֵנִי׃ a	Then I said, "Here! I! Send me!"
וַיֹּאמֶר לֵךְ וְאָמַרְתָּ לָעָם הַזֶּה ...	Then He said, "Go! (Thus you will say) and
(Isaiah 6:8f.)	tell this people ...

---

25   On the deixis universal → § 52.4.

כִּי־כֹה אָמַר יְהוָה אַל־תָּבוֹא בֵּית מַרְזֵחַ וְאַל־תֵּלֵךְ לִסְפּוֹד ...	b	Yes, thus says YHWH, "Do not enter a house of mourning, and do not go to the lament ..."
(Jeremiah 16:5)		
וַיְהִי דְבַר־יְהוָה אֵלַי לֵאמֹר: הָלֹךְ וְקָרָאתָ בְאָזְנֵי יְרוּשָׁלַ͏ִם לֵאמֹר	c	Then the word of YHWH came to me, namely: "Go! (thus you shall proclaim) and proclaim in the ears of Jerusalem as follows: ..."
(Jeremiah 2:1f.)		
נַחֲמוּ נַחֲמוּ עַמִּי יֹאמַר אֱלֹהֵיכֶם: דַּבְּרוּ עַל־לֵב יְרוּשָׁלַ͏ִם וְקִרְאוּ אֵלֶיהָ כִּי מָלְאָה צְבָאָהּ כִּי נִרְצָה עֲוֺנָהּ כִּי לָקְחָה מִיַּד יְהוָה כִּפְלַיִם בְּכָל־חַטֹּאתֶיהָ:	d	"Comfort, comfort My people," says your God. "Speak kindly to Jerusalem and call out to her, that her warfare has ended, that her iniquity has been removed; that she has received of YHWH's hand double for all her sins."
(Isaiah 40:1–2)		
וַיְדַבֵּר יְהוָה אֶל־מֹשֶׁה לֶךְ־רֵד כִּי שִׁחֵת עַמְּךָ ...	e	Then YHWH spoke to Moses, "(Go! Go down!) Go down at once; yes, your people have corrupted *themselves* ..."
(Exodus 32:7)		

Not Negated

The imperative stands in a **clear** speech situation, mostly after an אמר-introduction (a), and contains a **direct** demand upon the hearer.[26] The imperative stands only in **affirmative** clauses. In negative clauses (b) אַל must stand with imperfect (→ § 51.4).

In such clear contexts the imperative can also be represented by an infinitive **absolute** (c; → § 49.2).

Tense Signs

Inversely, in a **literary** text, the imperative marks the speech situation, which was predetermined in the spoken language. The beginning of the book of

---

26 On other markers for a demand → § 51.4; on the continuation of the demand through perfect consecutive → § 48.3, text example h.

Deutero-Isaiah (d) is characterized by a chain of imperatives. The clauses following in this context are at the same time clearly related to the discourse speech.

Stereotypically and as a kind of tense-sign—to be precise mood-sign—the imperatives of familiar verbs of movement such as בּוֹא, קוּם, and לֵךְ are used with some other, often unrelated imperative (e) or cohortative. Such dual imperatives serve to **stress** the request and are not understood as two requests.

48.9 Overview

Overview of Tenses

		Context: discourse		Context: narrative
Primary Tense	יִכְתֹּב	he writes **Imperfect**	וַיִּכְתֹּב	he wrote **Narrativ** (imperfect consecutive)
Perspective: Looking back	כָּתַב	he has written **Perfect**	כָּתַב	he wrote, had written **Perfect**
Perspective: Looking forward	וְכָתַב	and he will/then he should write **Perfect Consecutive**	יִכְתֹּב	he would/should write **Imperfect**

49 The Verbal Part of the Clause—Verbal Nominals

*The participle and the infinitive are verbal nominals. They cannot accept the person morphemes of the preformative conjugation or afformative conjugation and are called for that reason "non-finite" forms. They are called verbal-**nominals**, because they can adopt the functions of nominal parts of clauses and can accept the suffixes typical with nominals.*

Verbal nominals occur in texts of all Gattungen *fairly regularly and give no indication of the (narrative or discourse) linguistic stance of the text.*

49.1 Participles

Participles indicate that which the action performs or that which—with passives—is affected by it.

As Parts of Clauses

וְרוּחַ אֱלֹהִים מְרַחֶפֶת עַל־פְּנֵי הַמָּיִם׃ (Genesis 1:2b)	a	… and the Spirit of God (was) <u>something hovering</u> over the waters.
וַיֵּרָא אֵלָיו יְהוָה בְּאֵלֹנֵי מַמְרֵא וְהוּא יֹשֵׁב פֶּתַח־הָאֹהֶל כְּחֹם הַיּוֹם׃ וַיִּשָּׂא עֵינָיו... (Genesis 18:1f.)	b	YHWH appeared to him by the oaks of Mamre, (but he sat) <u>while he was sitting</u> [and he was one sitting] at the tent door in the heat of the day. He lifted up his eyes …
אִם־יְהוָה לֹא־יִשְׁמָר־עִיר שָׁוְא שָׁקַד שׁוֹמֵר׃ (Psalm 127:1b)	c	If YHWH does not guard the city, <u>a watchman</u> keeps awake in vain.

Participles can take on the functions of any nominal part of a clause. Participles appear frequently as **predicates** in a nominal clause (a, b). In narratives, such participial clauses play the role of **adverbial clauses** (b). In nominal clauses, as well as verbal clauses, participles can also appear as **subjects** (c).

Translation

וּמֵת כָּל־בְּכוֹר בְּאֶרֶץ מִצְרַיִם מִבְּכוֹר פַּרְעֹה הַיֹּשֵׁב עַל־כִּסְאוֹ עַד בְּכוֹר הַשִּׁפְחָה אֲשֶׁר אַחַר הָרֵחָיִם (Exodus 11:5a)	d	Then all the firstborn in the land of Egypt shall die, from the firstborn of the Pharaoh (the one sitting) <u>who sits</u> on his throne, even to the firstborn of the slave girl who (sits) behind the millstones.

וַיֵּדַע קַיִן אֶת־אִשְׁתּוֹ	e	Cain had relations with his wife
וַתַּהַר		and she conceived,
וַתֵּלֶד אֶת־חֲנוֹךְ		and gave birth to Enoch;
וַיְהִי בֹּנֶה עִיר		and he was <u>a builder</u> of a city,
וַיִּקְרָא שֵׁם הָעִיר כְּשֵׁם בְּנוֹ חֲנוֹךְ׃		and he called the name of the city Enoch,
(Genesis 4:17)		after the name of his son.

Participles that are used **appositionally** or **attributively** (d) can be rendered in German with relative clauses (**attributive clauses**). Participles in clauses with the verb היה "to be" (e) stand as **predicate nominatives**.

Participles with Objects

דִּבֶּר הָאִישׁ אֲדֹנֵי הָאָרֶץ אִתָּנוּ קָשׁוֹת	f	The man, the lord of the land, spoke
וַיִּתֵּן אֹתָנוּ כִּמְרַגְּלִים אֶת־הָאָרֶץ׃		harshly with us, and took us to be <u>spies</u>
(Genesis 42:30)		<u>of the land</u> [lit. like those who scout the land].
וְתָסֵךְ עָלֵימוֹ וְיַעְלְצוּ בְךָ אֹהֲבֵי שְׁמֶךָ׃	g	And may You shelter them, that they
(Psalm 5:12)		may exult in you, <u>those who love Your name</u> [the lovers of your name].
וַאֲבָרְכָה מְבָרְכֶיךָ וּמְקַלֶּלְךָ אָאֹר	h	And I will bless <u>those who bless you</u>,
(Genesis 12:3)		And <u>the one who curses you</u> I will curse.

As verbal forms, participles can have **objects** (e, f) and **adverbial qualifications** (a, b, d) with them. As nominal forms they can accept a **construct connection** with the object of the action (g) and can accept the pronominal object as a suffix (h).

49.2 Infinitive Absolute

Infinitives indicate the action as such. The infinitive absolute stands isolated in the clause and introduces only the meaning of the verb into the clause.

Replacement for a Finite Form

כֹּה אָמַר יְהוָה	a	Thus YHWH said,
הָלוֹךְ וְקָנִיתָ בַקְבֻּק יוֹצֵר חָרֶשׂ		"[Going…you shall go] <u>Go</u>, and buy a
(Jeremiah 19:1a)		potter's earthenware jar."

כִּי אֵין־אֱמֶת וְאֵין־חֶסֶד	b	There is no faithfulness, no kindness,
וְאֵין־דַּעַת אֱלֹהִים בָּאָרֶץ:		No knowledge of God in the land.
אָלֹה וְכַחֵשׁ וְרָצֹחַ וְגָנֹב וְנָאֹף		*There is* <u>swearing</u>, <u>deception</u>, <u>murder</u>, <u>steal-</u>
פָּרָצוּ וְדָמִים בְּדָמִים נָגָעוּ:		ing and <u>adultery</u>. [or, They swear, deceive,
(Hosea 4:1b–2)		murder, steal, and commit adultery.] They
		employ violence, so that bloodshed follows
		bloodshed.

The infinitive absolute can replace a finite verb form. In a **clear** speech situation the infinitive absolute under the same **context** conditions as the **imperative** stands at the beginning of a clause expressing a wish, desire, or command (a). In **series** (b), infinitives absolute of several verbs gather together and describe a **complex event**. Person and tense arise from the connection of the verbs with the text surrounding them.[1]

49.3 Infinitive (Infinitivus constructus)

The infinitive construct combines with other parts of clauses.

Infinitives after Prepositions

וַיֹּאמְרוּ אִישׁ אֶל־אָחִיו	a	They said to one another:
הִנֵּה שָׂכַר־עָלֵינוּ מֶלֶךְ יִשְׂרָאֵל אֶת־מַלְכֵי		"The king of Israel has hired against
הַחִתִּים וְאֶת־מַלְכֵי מִצְרַיִם לָבוֹא עָלֵינוּ:		us the kings of the Hittites and the
(2 Kings 7:6b)		kings of the Egyptians, <u>to come</u> upon
		us [<u>that</u> they might come against us]."
וַיְהִי כְּבוֹא אַבְרָם מִצְרָיְמָה	b	<u>When Abram came</u> into Egypt,
וַיִּרְאוּ הַמִּצְרִים אֶת־הָאִשָּׁה כִּי־יָפָה הִוא		the Egyptians saw that the woman
מְאֹד:		was very beautiful.
(Genesis 12:14)		

---

1   On the infinitive absolute as a replacement for a finite verbal form → § 50.4.

| אִישׁ מִמֶּנּוּ אֶת־קִבְרוֹ לֹא־יִכְלֶה מִמְּךָ מִקְּבֹר מֵתֶךָ: (Genesis 23:6) | c | None of us will refuse you his grave (from burying) <u>for burying</u> your dead |
| כִּי הִקְשׁוּ אֶת־עָרְפָּם לְבִלְתִּי שְׁמוֹעַ אֶת־דְּבָרָי: (Jeremiah 19:15) | d | Yes they have stiffened their necks (to the not hearing) <u>so as not to heed</u> My words |

The infinitive (infinitive construct) frequently stands after prepositions, for the most part expanding on other parts of a clause. In German, such infinitive constructions correspond most to an adverbial **subordinate clause**.

לְ, כְּ, בְּ

The preposition לְ before the infinitive denotes **goal or purpose** (a); German "dass/damit" or—with same subject—"um zu."

An **expression of time** is expressed with בְּ or כְּ before the infinitive (German **temporal clause**), above all after introductory וַיְהִי or וְהָיָה (b).

מִן and בִּלְתִּי

The preposition מִן before the infinitive is often a **negation** (c). However, the negation בִּלְתִּי also stands with the infinitive; on that occasion, other prepositions can stand ahead of it (d).

Many other prepositions can occur before the infinitive (→ also below text example e). In German the sense-appropriate **conjunction** must be found (e.g. "nachdem" for "nach").

Subject, Object, Suffixes

| וַיְהִי דְבַר־יְהוָה אֶל־יִרְמְיָהוּ אַחֲרֵי שְׂרֹף הַמֶּלֶךְ אֶת־הַמְּגִלָּה (Jeremiah 36:27) | e | The word of YHWH came to Jeremiah (after the king's burning the scroll) <u>after the king had burned</u> the scroll. |
| וַיִּשְׁלַח שָׁאוּל מַלְאָכִים אֶל־בֵּית דָּוִד לְשָׁמְרוֹ וְלַהֲמִיתוֹ בַּבֹּקֶר (1 Samuel 19:11a) | f | Saul sent messengers to David's house (for his watching and for his death) <u>to watch him</u>, in order to put him to death in the morning. |

גֹּאֵל הַדָּם הוּא יָמִית אֶת־הָרֹצֵחַ	g	The blood avenger, he shall put the mur-derer to death!
בְּפִגְעוֹ־בוֹ הוּא יְמִיתֶנּוּ׃		(With his meeting him) he shall put him
(Numbers 35:19)		to death <u>when he meets him.</u>

The subject and object of the action can **follow** the infinitive (e). In principle the same **suffixes** indicate the pronominal object (f) and the pronominal subject (g).[2]

Special Cases

וַיֹּאמֶר יְהוָה אֱלֹהִים	h	Then YHWH God said,
לֹא־טוֹב הֱיוֹת הָאָדָם לְבַדּוֹ		"It is not good for the man <u>to be</u> alone
(Genesis 2:18a)		[the being alone of man]."
יְהִי־אַחֲרִיתוֹ לְהַכְרִית	i	Let his posterity be <u>cut off</u>;
בְּדוֹר אַחֵר יִמַּח שְׁמָם׃		In a following generation let their
(Psalm 109:13)		name be blotted out!
כִּי בְּכָרְתִי אֶת־כְּנַף מְעִילְךָ וְלֹא הֲרַגְתִּיךָ	j	For (through my cutting off) in that I
דַּע וּרְאֵה כִּי אֵין בְּיָדִי רָעָה וָפֶשַׁע		<u>cut off</u> the edge of your robe and did
(1 Samuel 24:12)		not kill you,
		know and perceive that there is no evil
		or rebellion in my hands.

The infinitive can appear as the subject or predicate of a **nominal clause** (h). The infinitive, sometimes with ל, stands as a kind of **predicate nominative** in clauses with the verb היה (i).[3] From time to time an infinitive construction is **continued through finite verb forms** (j).

---

2   Only with suffixes of the 1ˢᵗ person singular is there differentiation between the object-suffix נִי and the subject-suffix יֹ◌ (→ § 33.3).

3   On the infinitive as complement, above all after relative verbs, → § 50.5.

50 Extensions of the Verbal Part of the Clause

50.1 Objects

The verbal part of a clause (finite and nominal forms) can have with it a nominal as direct object ("accusative"), which gives the object of the action.

Marking

בְּרֵאשִׁית בָּרָא אֱלֹהִים אֵת הַשָּׁמַיִם וְאֵת הָאָרֶץ: (Genesis 1:1)	a	In the beginning God created the heavens and the earth.
וַיִּשְׁלַח־שָׁמָּה סוּסִים וְרֶכֶב וְחַיִל כָּבֵד (2 Kings 6:14)	b	And he sent horses and chariots and a great army there.
כִּי־מָלְאָה הָאָרֶץ דֵּעָה אֶת־יְהוָה (Isaiah 11:9)	c	Yes, the land will be full of (knowing YHWH) the knowledge of YHWH.

The particle אֶת/־אֵת (**sign of the accusative** → § 12.4) can make a direct object identifiable, but it only stands before **definite** objects (a) and is rare in poetry. If אֵת is missing, the function of such a nominal as an object must be deduced from the **context**, above all from the meaning of the verb (b).

Like verbal-substantives (→ § 49), substantives that are **derived from verbs** can also have objects with them (c).

Pronominal Objects (Suffixes)

וַיָּמָת שְׁמוּאֵל	d	And Samuel died;
וַיִּקָּבְצוּ כָל־יִשְׂרָאֵל		and all Israel gathered together
וַיִּסְפְּדוּ־לוֹ		and mourned for him,
וַיִּקְבְּרֻהוּ בְּבֵיתוֹ בָּרָמָה		and buried him at his house in Ramah.
(1 Samuel 25:1)		

---

1   Ed. note: The אֹתָם is assumed and has been added; it does not appear in the text.

וַיָּבֹאוּ יָבֵשָׁה	e	And they came to Jabesh
וַיִּשְׂרְפוּ אֹתָם שָׁם:		and burned them there.
וַיִּקְחוּ אֶת־עַצְמֹתֵיהֶם		And they took their bones
וַיִּקְבְּרוּ [אֹתָם]¹ תַּחַת־הָאֶשֶׁל בְּיָבֵשָׁה		and buried (them) under the tamarisk
(1 Samuel 31:12f.)		tree at Jabesh …

Pronominal objects are added as **suffixes** onto the verb form (d) or onto the particle אֵת (e). The object from the **preceding clause** does **not** have to be repeated as a pronoun (e).

Special Cases

וְלֹא־יִקָּרֵא עוֹד אֶת־שִׁמְךָ אַבְרָם	f	(One shall no longer call you) No longer
וְהָיָה שִׁמְךָ אַבְרָהָם		shall your name be called Abram,
(Genesis 17:5)		rather your name shall be Abraham.
וְאָנֹכִי וּבֵיתִי נַעֲבֹד אֶת־יְהוָה:	g	But I and my house, we will serve YHWH.
(Joshua 24:15)		
וַיִּקַּח אֵלִיָּהוּ שְׁתֵּים עֶשְׂרֵה אֲבָנִים …	h	And Elijah took twelve stones …
וַיִּבְנֶה אֶת־הָאֲבָנִים מִזְבֵּחַ בְּשֵׁם יְהוָה		And he built an altar with the stones in the name of YHWH [he built the stones (into) an altar] …
(1 Kings 18:31f.)		

Accusative with the Passive

Also in clauses with a **passive** predicate, the **object** of the action (the subject according to western-latin understanding) can be marked through the "**accusative**"-sign (f). Direct objects also stand with many verbs, whose German parallel does not require the accusative (g [ed. note: the word for "serve" in German takes the dative, not the accusative]).

Double Accusative

With a verb, there can also stand **two objects** ("double accusative") (h). Also here in German translation some other construction must be chosen most of the time. The **lexicon** gives detailed information about the possible constructions of a verb.

50.2 Adverbial Substantives

The verbal part of a clause can have with it a nominal (or preposition), which explains the action as an adverbial qualification.[2]

וַיֵּלֶךְ הָאִישׁ אֶרֶץ הַחִתִּים וַיִּבֶן עִיר (Judges 1:26)	a	And the man went (into) the land of the Hittites and built a city.
וְהַמֶּלֶךְ לָאַט אֶת־פָּנָיו וַיִּזְעַק הַמֶּלֶךְ קוֹל גָּדוֹל (2 Samuel 19:5)	b	But the king covered his face; then the king cried out (with) a loud voice.
וַיִּשְׁלַח יְהוֹשֻׁעַ מַלְאָכִים וַיָּרֻצוּ הָאֹהֱלָה (Joshua 7:22)	c	And Joshua sent messengers, and they ran to the tent.
מַצּוֹת יֵאָכֵל אֵת שִׁבְעַת הַיָּמִים (Exodus 13:7)	d	Unleavened bread shall be eaten (throughout) the seven days.

Context Notice

The adverbial function of such a nominal arises from the **context**, particularly from the relationship of its meaning to the meaning of the preceding **verb**, e.g. "go" and "land," "cry" and "voice" (a, b). With expressions of **place** and **time** the adverbial nominal can be marked through *he locale* (→ § 16.3) (c); and sometimes also the **particle** אֵת stands before an adverbial nominal (d).

On adverbial substantives in the **nominal clause** → § 44.3.

50.3 Prepositional Additions

The verbal part of a clause can also be expanded through substantives with prepositions. The lexicon gives information about the many and diverse meanings of the individual prepositions.[3] *Only the syntactically-conspicuous applications are presented in this chapter.*

---

2   Such an adverbial nominal is also called "accusativus adverbialis."
3   According to Lucien Tesnière (*Structural Syntax*, Stuttgart: Klett, 1980) and Harald Weinrich (*Textgrammatik der deutschen Sprache*, Mannheim; Leipzig; Wien; Zürich: Dudenverlag, 1993), prepositions belong perfectly well in syntax, in particular in the chapter about "Junktionen," because they—like conjunctions, relative pronouns, or construct connections—connect parts of speech with one another in specific ways. For Hebrew grammar, however, it has still not been systematically treated by this chapter.

Preposition ל

The most frequent preposition ל[4] indicates a general and unspecified relationship between events, things, and partners: "**concerning**."

a וַיִּקַּח אַבְרָהָם צֹאן וּבָקָר וַיִּתֵּן לַאֲבִימֶלֶךְ (Genesis 21:27)	Abraham took sheep and oxen and gave (them) to Abimelech.
b וַיְהִי־לִי שׁוֹר וַחֲמוֹר צֹאן וְעֶבֶד וְשִׁפְחָה (Genesis 32:6)	[There is to me] I have oxen and donkeys *and* flocks and male and female servants
c גַּם־לְרֵעֵהוּ יִשָּׂנֵא רָשׁ וְאֹהֲבֵי עָשִׁיר רַבִּים׃ (Proverbs 14:20)	The poor is hated even by his neighbor, But those who love the rich are many.
d וַיֹּאמֶר יְהוָה אֶל־אַבְרָם לֶךְ־לְךָ מֵאַרְצְךָ (Genesis 12:1)	YHWH said to Abram, "Go <u>you</u> (in particular interest of you) from your land..."

Dative

The preposition ל is used after the verb in order to show the indirect object, for which some other languages, including German, have the **dative** at their disposal (→ eng. "he gave it **to** Abimelech").

ל can denote that to which something comes or **belongs**, the **owner** (b).[5] The acting person in the **passive clause** (c) can also be indicated through ל (German "von").

Striking is ל with a suffix of the 2nd person after imperatives (d): This so-called "**dativus ethicus**" indicates a particular inner connection and thus a stress upon the person who is called upon. It is hardly translatable.

On ל as a replacement of a construct connection[6] → §§ 45.2 and 47.1.

---

4   It occurs in the Bible ca. 20,700 times.
5   As Latin or German the "dativus possessoris" is regionally linguistically used: "Das ist mir."
6   Also even a construct-connection expresses a very general and unspecific relationship.

Other Prepositions

וּבְעוֹד שִׁשִּׁים וְחָמֵשׁ שָׁנָה יֵחַת אֶפְרַיִם מֵעָם: (Isaiah 7:8)	e	Now within another 65 years Ephraim will be shattered, (away from the people) *so that it is* no longer a people
וַיַּבְדֵּל אֱלֹהִים בֵּין הָאוֹר וּבֵין הַחֹשֶׁךְ: (Genesis 1:4)	f	And God divided between the light and the darkness.

Preposition מִן

As a preposition of **separation** ("away from"), the preposition מִן can have the value of a **negation** (e).[7]

Preposition בֵּין

The preposition בֵּין "**between**" is usually **repeated** before the second nominal (f). Instead of the second בֵּין can also stand ל or לְבֵין.

On prepositional attributes → § 47.1, on a preposition with an infinitive → § 49.3, on the connection of a preposition and the relative particle אֲשֶׁר → § 53.4.

50.4 Infinitive Absolute (Infinitivus absolutus)

The verbal part of a clause can be expanded through the infinitive absolute of the same verb or of another verb.

לִמְדוּ הֵיטֵב דִּרְשׁוּ מִשְׁפָּט (Isaiah 1:17)	a	Learn (good-doing) <u>to do good</u>! Seek justice!
כֹּה תְבָרֲכוּ אֶת־בְּנֵי יִשְׂרָאֵל אָמוֹר לָהֶם: יְבָרֶכְךָ יְהוָה וְיִשְׁמְרֶךָ: (Numbers 6:23f.)	b	Thus you shall bless the sons of Israel: (<u>saying</u> to them:) in that you say to them: "YHWH bless you and keep you."

---

7   On מִן as a negation with the infinitive → § 49.3. On מִן "more than" in comparisons → § 47.1.

The infinitive absolute can stand as an **object** with a verb (a). Mostly it denotes an **adverbial qualification** (b) and can be expanded again through another nominal part of the clause.

Figura Etymologica

וְעַתָּה הִנֵּה יָדַעְתִּי כִּי מָלֹךְ תִּמְלוֹךְ (1 Samuel 24:21)	c	But now, surely, I know that you will be king.
שִׁמְעוּ שָׁמוֹעַ בְּרֹגֶז קֹלוֹ וְהֶגֶה מִפִּיו יֵצֵא: (Job 37:2)	d	Hear! Hear! the thunder of His voice, and the rumbling that goes out from His mouth.
אֹמְרִים אָמוֹר לִמְנַאֲצַי דִּבֶּר יְהוָה שָׁלוֹם יִהְיֶה לָכֶם (Jeremiah 23:17)	e	They keep saying to those who despise Me, "YHWH has said, 'You will have peace.'"
טָרֹף טֹרַף יוֹסֵף: (Genesis 37:33)	f	Torn (Qal), torn (Pu'al) is Joseph! [or] Joseph has surely been torn to pieces.

Very often the infinitive absolute is used in a "figura etymologica": To a **finite** form of the verb or a participle steps in the infinitive absolute of the **same verb**. As a result the verb in the clause receives particular **focus**.

The infinitive absolute can stand before (c, f) or behind (d, e) the accompanying finite verb or participle (e). The infinitive absolute of the **base stem** [i.e., Qal] can stand with forms of the **derived stems** (f).

Double Expressions

וַיֵּצֵא יָצוֹא וָשׁוֹב עַד־יְבֹשֶׁת הַמַּיִם מֵעַל הָאָרֶץ: (Genesis 8:7)	g	It (the raven) flew (went out—going out and returning) here and there until the water was dried up from the earth.
וַיָּשֻׁבוּ הַמַּיִם מֵעַל הָאָרֶץ הָלוֹךְ וָשׁוֹב (Genesis 8:3)	h	The water returned—going and returning— = the water receded steadily from the earth.

וְהִנֵּה מִשָּׁם אִישׁ יוֹצֵא ... i	Then a man came out from there ...
וּשְׁמוֹ שִׁמְעִי בֶן־גֵּרָא	whose name was Shimei, the son of
יָצָא יָצוֹא וּמְקַלֵּל:	Gera; he came out (coming out and
(2 Samuel 16:5)	cursing) cursing continually as he
	came.

Two Events in One

A *figura etymologica* can be expanded through the infinitive absolute of a **second verb**. In this way, it is expressed that two events are **closely combined** with one another (g–i).

Often in such constructions הלך appears as a **modal verb** and expresses continuation, repetition, or **intensification** (h). The place of one of the two infinitives can also be taken through another form of the verb (i).

On the use of the infinitive absolute as an **independent** part of the clause → § 49.2.

50.5 Infinitive (Construct) and Finite Forms of Relative Verbs

The infinitive (construct) can complete a verbal predicate.

וַתֹּאמֶר שָׂרָה a	Sarah said,
צְחֹק עָשָׂה לִי אֱלֹהִים	"God has made (a) laughter for me."
(Genesis 21:6)	

An infinitive can step in as an **object** without a preposition (a).

Relative Verbs

וַיֹּאמֶר יִצְחָק אֶל־בְּנוֹ b	Isaac said to his son,
מַה־זֶּה מִהַרְתָּ לִמְצֹא בְּנִי	"What is this you have hastened to
(Genesis 27:20)	find, my son?"
הַיּוֹם הַזֶּה אָחֵל תֵּת פַּחְדְּךָ וְיִרְאָתְךָ c	(Today I will begin: putting) This day I
עַל־פְּנֵי הָעַמִּים	will begin to put the dread and fear of
(Deuteronomy 2:25)	you upon the peoples
וַיָּחֶל עוֹד שִׁבְעַת יָמִים אֲחֵרִים d	Then he waited yet another seven days;
וַיֹּסֶף שַׁלַּח אֶת־הַיּוֹנָה מִן־הַתֵּבָה:	then (he did again: sending) again he
(Genesis 8:10)	sent out the dove from the ark.

Relative verbs are such that they describe the **nature** of and **ways** of an event as e.g. (the **lexicons** provide more detail):

חלל	(Hi) "begin,"
חדל	"end,"
יסף	(Hi) "leave/do still more/do still again,"
שוב	"return/do once again,"
שכם	(Hi) "do early/eagerly,"
מהר	(Pi) "do hastily/quickly."

These verbs often have an **infinitive** as object with (b) or without (c, d) ל; sometimes also a finite form of the verb (e).

Translation

The **relative** verb has the **general** meaning, the "subordinate" verb the specific meaning. For that reason in German translation the "subordinating" (of the infinitive) is to the main verb, the **relative** verb to the **adverb** ("still more," "still again," "quickly").

Relative Verbs in a Text[8]

וַיְהִי־הוּא טֶרֶם כִּלָּה לְדַבֵּר e	[15] Then—before he had finished <u>speaking</u>,
וְהִנֵּה רִבְקָה יֹצֵאת ... וְכַדָּהּ עַל־שִׁכְמָהּ:	behold, Rebekah … came out with her[8] jar on her shoulder.
וְהַנַּעֲרָ טֹבַת מַרְאֶה מְאֹד	[16] The girl was very beautiful,
בְּתוּלָה וְאִישׁ לֹא יְדָעָהּ	a virgin, and no man had had relations with her.
וַתֵּרֶד הָעַיְנָה	She went down to the spring,
וַתְּמַלֵּא כַדָּהּ וַתָּעַל:	filled her jar, and came up.
וַיָּרָץ הָעֶבֶד לִקְרָאתָהּ וַיֹּאמֶר	[17] Then the servant quickly ran to meet her, and said,
הַגְמִיאִינִי נָא מְעַט־מַיִם מִכַּדֵּךְ:	"Please let me drink a little water from your jar!"

---

8 In contrast to Hebrew (and English), in German parts of the body and objects carried close to the body are not connected with the possessive pronoun, thus not: "<u>ihren</u> Krug auf <u>ihrer</u> Schulter."

וַתֹּאמֶר שְׁתֵה אֲדֹנִי וַתְּמַהֵר וַתֹּרֶד כַּדָּהּ עַל־יָדָהּ וַתַּשְׁקֵהוּ: וַתְּכַל לְהַשְׁקֹתוֹ וַתֹּאמֶר גַּם לִגְמַלֶּיךָ אֶשְׁאָב עַד אִם־כִּלּוּ לִשְׁתֹּת: וַתְּמַהֵר וַתְּעַר כַּדָּהּ אֶל־הַשֹּׁקֶת וַתָּרָץ עוֹד אֶל־הַבְּאֵר לִשְׁאֹב וַתִּשְׁאַב לְכָל־גְּמַלָּיו: (Genesis 24:15–20)	[18] She said, "Drink, my lord!"; and she <u>quickly lowered</u> her jar to her hand, and gave him a drink. [19] Now <u>when she had finished giving</u> him a drink, she said, "I will draw also for your camels until they have finished drinking." [20] So she <u>quickly emptied</u> her jar into the trough, <u>ran</u> back to the well to draw, and drew for all his camels.

Instead of through an infinitive, relative verbs can also be expanded through a **second** verb in the same **finite form**. The text (e) shows both possibilities next to one another.

Text Meaning

The excerpt of text (from the narrative of the courting of a bride for Isaac) shows as well the **textual** and **stylistic** performance of the grammatical phenomenon "relative verb." The construction "כלה + infinitive" serves to **structure the text** (15 and 19). The construction "מהר + imperfect consecutive" identifies the **narrative speed** with the non-relative verb (רוץ: 2x). The impression of busy bustle with an actual, ordinary, unspeculative activity results through the increasing frequency of the imperfect consecutive forms along with the characteristic "quickly."

On **extended** infinitive constructions, above all on infinitives with **prepositions**, → § 49.3.

51 Description of the Statement of Intent (Mood)

Outside of the imperative (→ § 48.8) and some remaining jussive-forms (→ § 51.4), the Hebrew verbal system has no separate verb form (mood) to mark the statement of intent. If modality is to be expressed through syntactical signs at all, particles are at one's disposal. Sentence position also plays a role.

The attention of the hearer is controlled through indicators, which lie on the **level of meaning** of the text (→ also § 52.2). Verbs with a modal meaning—as for example יכל "can"—also belong here, as well as relative verbs (→ § 50.5).

No Subjunctive

The Hebrew language does not have syntactical markers for the modal categories "**real/unreal/ possible**" (Realis/Irrealis/Potentialis); also there is no "**subjunctive**" as a syntactical marker of internal dependency.

51.1 Strengthening

וַיֹּאמֶר יְהוָה	Then YHWH said,
זַעֲקַת סְדֹם וַעֲמֹרָה כִּי־רָבָּה	"The outcry of Sodom and Gomorrah—indeed—it is great, and their sin—indeed—it is very grave."
וְחַטָּאתָם כִּי כָבְדָה מְאֹד:	
(Genesis 18:20)	

Particles

An important strengthening particle is כִּי "**yes/in truth/so it is**" (→ § 53.3). For further strengthening adverbs and particles such as, for example, אַף "even," הֵן "behold," etc., the **lexicon** is to be consulted.

The connection of a finite verb with an **infinitive absolute** (→ § 50.4) also has a strengthening effect.

On the **rhetorical question** as a statement with a strengthening sense → § 51.3.

51.2 Negation

Verbal Clause

וַיֹּאמֶר אֲבִימֶלֶךְ	a	Abimelech said,
לֹא יָדַעְתִּי מִי עָשָׂה אֶת־הַדָּבָר הַזֶּה		"I do not know who has done this thing;
וְגַם־אַתָּה לֹא־הִגַּדְתָּ לִּי		and also you did not tell me,
וְגַם אָנֹכִי לֹא שָׁמַעְתִּי בִּלְתִּי הַיּוֹם:		and I did not hear of it (except) until today."
(Genesis 21:26)		

וְאַתָּה בֶן־אָדָם אַל־תִּירָא מֵהֶם	b	But you, son of man, do not fear them,
וּמִדִּבְרֵיהֶם אַל־תִּירָא		and also do not fear their words!
(Ezekiel 2:6)		

אַל and לֹא

Verbal predicates are negated in verbal clauses and compound nominal clauses with the particles לֹא and אַל (a, b). At the same time, אַל is restricted to denying clauses (as lat. "ne"). Negative clauses with אַל stand instead of **negative imperatives** (b), which are not possible in Hebrew.

Nominal Clause

וַאֲנַחְנוּ יַחְדָּו אֵין־זָר אִתָּנוּ בַּבַּיִת זוּלָתִי	c	But we were together; no stranger
שְׁתַּיִם־אֲנַחְנוּ בַּבָּיִת׃		(was) with us in the house; only the
(1 Kings 3:18b)		two of us (were) in the house.
וַיֹּאמֶר מֹשֶׁה אֶל־יְהוָה	d	Moses said to YHWH,
בִּי אֲדֹנָי לֹא אִישׁ דְּבָרִים אָנֹכִי		"Please, Lord, I (am a non-word-man)
(Exodus 4:10)		have never been eloquent."[1]
וְזֶה דְּבַר הָרֹצֵחַ אֲשֶׁר־יָנוּס שָׁמָּה וָחָי	e	But this is the case of the manslayer
אֲשֶׁר יַכֶּה אֶת־רֵעֵהוּ בִּבְלִי־דַעַת וְהוּא		who may flee there and live: when he
לֹא־שֹׂנֵא לוֹ מִתְּמֹל שִׁלְשֹׁם׃ ...		kills his friend unintentionally, not
הוּא יָנוּס אֶל־אַחַת הֶעָרִים־הָאֵלֶּה וָחָי׃		hating him previously—
(Deuteronomy 19:4f.)		... he should flee to one of these cities
		and live;

Particle אֵין/אַיִן

Individual **nominals** and nominal clauses are negated with the particle אֵין/אַיִן "nonexistence/there is not" (c).

Infinitive

לֹא can also appear in a **nominal clause**. In that case, it negates not the existence of a thing or person rather its **concept** (d). לֹא can stand before the participle (e: לֹא שֹׂנֵא) but **not** before the **infinitive** (e: בְּלִי דַעַת). Frequently, לְבִלְתִּי is also used as a negator of the infinitive (→ § 49.3).

---

1   Thus the "Einheitsübersetzung," "Gute Nachricht": "Ich habe noch nie gut reden können."

Double Negation

וָאֹמַר	f	I said,
עַד־מָתַי אֲדֹנָי		"Lord, how long?"
וַיֹּאמֶר		He answered,
עַד אֲשֶׁר אִם־שָׁאוּ עָרִים מֵאֵין יוֹשֵׁב		"Until cities are devastated *and* without
וּבָתִּים מֵאֵין אָדָם		inhabitant,
וְהָאֲדָמָה תִּשָּׁאֶה שְׁמָמָה:		and houses are without people,
(Isaiah 6:11)		and the land is utterly desolate."
הַצִּילֵנִי נָא מִיַּד אָחִי מִיַּד עֵשָׂו	g	Deliver me, I pray, from the hand of my
כִּי־יָרֵא אָנֹכִי אֹתוֹ פֶּן־יָבוֹא וְהִכַּנִי אֵם		brother, Esau!
עַל־בָּנִים:		I fear him, that he will come and attack
(Genesis 32:12)		me *and* the mothers with the children.

Several negations (e: מִן and אֵין) are not cancelled out, rather strengthen one another. For that reason, a negation can stand **once again** in the subordinate clause after a **verb**, which already contains a **negative** concept, as for example ירא "fearing" (g: פֶּן).[2]

Further Particles

The **lexicon** gives further information about other, **rarer** particles of negation as e.g. אֶפֶס, בְּלִי, בַּל. On the negative adverb טֶרֶם "**not yet**" → § 48.4; on the negative meaning of מִן → §§ 49.3 and 50.3. On the negative **vow clause** with אִם → § 53.5.

51.3 Questions

וַיֹּאמֶר יְהוָה אֶל־קַיִן	a	YHWH said to Cain,
אֵי הֶבֶל אָחִיךָ		"Where is Abel your brother?"
וַיֹּאמֶר		He said,
לֹא יָדַעְתִּי הֲשֹׁמֵר אָחִי אָנֹכִי:		"I do not know. Am I my brother's keeper?"
(Genesis 4:9)		
וַיִּשְׁלַח מַלְאָכִים וַיֹּאמֶר אֲלֵהֶם	b	Then he sent messengers and said to them,
לְכוּ דִרְשׁוּ בְּבַעַל זְבוּב אֱלֹהֵי עֶקְ־		"Go, inquire of Baal-zebub, the god of
רוֹן אִם־אֶחְיֶה מֵחֳלִי זֶה:		Ekron, whether I will recover from this
(2 Kings 1:2b)		sickness."

---

2 On פֶּן → also below § 51.4.

וַיֹּאמֶר אֲלֵהֶם	c	And he said to them,
עֲלוּ זֶה בַּנֶּגֶב וַעֲלִיתֶם אֶת־הָהָר:		"Go up there into the Negev and then go
וּרְאִיתֶם אֶת־הָאָרֶץ מַה־הִוא		up into the hill country and see what the
וְאֶת־הָעָם הַיֹּשֵׁב עָלֶיהָ הֶחָזָק הוּא		land: how it is and the people who live
הֲרָפֶה הַמְעַט הוּא אִם־רָב:		in it, whether they are strong or weak,
(Numbers 13:17bf.)		whether they are few or many."

וַיֹּאמֶר אָכִישׁ אֶל־עֲבָדָיו	d	Achish said to his servants,
הִנֵּה תִרְאוּ אִישׁ מִשְׁתַּגֵּעַ		"You see yet: A madman!
לָמָּה תָּבִיאוּ אֹתוֹ אֵלָי: חֲסַר		Why do you bring him to me?
מְשֻׁגָּעִים אָנִי		Do I lack madmen, that you have brought
כִּי־הֲבֵאתֶם אֶת־זֶה		this one?"
(1 Samuel 21:15f.)		

Interrogative Words and Interrogative Clauses

An interrogative question[3] can be recognized by the introductory **interrogative word**, such as e.g., אֵי "where" (a), מַה "what/how?" (c), מִי "who," or לָמָּה "why" (d). An interrogative clause can be recognized in general by the introductory הֲ (a), the *he interrogativum* (on the form → § 13.3). In the German interrogative clause, modal verbs (a: "Should I be my brother's keeper?") or subjunctives, which stress the element of uncertainty, frequently appear. These are peculiarities of the German language, which have no parallel in Hebrew.

Indirect Questions, Double Questions

Dependent interrogative clauses (b, c) **do not differ** formally from independent ones. אִם appears frequently (b) as an introduction apart from הֲ (c). Double questions (c) are introduced through הֲ ... הֲ or through הֲ ... אִם (c).[4] The **interrogative** character of a clause can also remain **unmarked** (d), where it arises from the context.

---

3   Interrogative words demand as an answer <u>one</u> word; interrogative clauses, a clause or yes/no.
4   On אִם before simple, direct questions → § 53.5.

Answers

וַיֹּאמֶר לָהֶם	e	He (Jacob) said to them,
הַיְדַעְתֶּם אֶת־לָבָן בֶּן־נָחוֹר		"Do you know Laban the son of Nahor?"
וַיֹּאמְרוּ		They said,
יָדָעְנוּ:		"(We know) Yes."
וַיֹּאמֶר לָהֶם		And he said to them,
הֲשָׁלוֹם לוֹ		"Is it well with him?"
וַיֹּאמְרוּ		They said,
שָׁלוֹם		"(It is well) Yes."
(Genesis 29:5f.)		
וַיֹּאמְרוּ לוֹ אַנְשֵׁי־גִלְעָד	f	Then the men of Gilead said to him,
הַאֶפְרָתִי אַתָּה		"Are you an Ephraimite?"
וַיֹּאמֶר		And he said,
לֹא:		"No."
(Judges 12:5)		
וַיֹּאמֶר דָּוִד אֶל־אַבְנֵר	g	David said to Abner,
הֲלוֹא־אִישׁ אַתָּה		"(Are you not) You are yet a man, and
וּמִי כָמוֹךָ בְּיִשְׂרָאֵל		(who) nobody is like you in Israel!
וְלָמָּה לֹא שָׁמַרְתָּ אֶל־אֲדֹנֶיךָ הַמֶּלֶךְ		Why then have you not guarded your lord
(1 Samuel 26:15)		the king?"
וַיֵּצֵא בַּיּוֹם הַשֵּׁנִי	h	And as he went out the next day,
וְהִנֵּה שְׁנֵי־אֲנָשִׁים עִבְרִים נִצִּים		he came by chance upon two Hebrews
וַיֹּאמֶר לָרָשָׁע		fighting with each other.
לָמָּה תַכֶּה רֵעֶךָ:		He said to the offender,
וַיֹּאמֶר		"Why are you striking your companion?"
מִי שָׂמְךָ לְאִישׁ שַׂר וְשֹׁפֵט עָלֵינוּ		He said,
(Exodus 2:13f.)		"Who made you a prince or a judge
		over us?"

Answer clauses are **elliptical**: As an answer is only repeated the **catchword** of the question and all others are left out (e). With a negative answer the ellipse can go so far (as in German) that only the negative לֹא or אֵין is left (f).

Rhetorical Questions

The **he interrogativum** הֲ combined with the negative לֹא introduces rhetorical questions, which actually present a strengthening **assertion** (g). Rhetorical questions with לָמָּה are usually not questions concerning motive, rather they have the character of an **accusation**. They play a role, e.g. before a **court**, when the prosecutor or judge holds before the **charged** his offense (h).[5]

(On rhetorical questions → also § 52.4, text example d)

51.4 Wish—Intent—Request

Apart from the imperative (→ § 48.8), Hebrew has only a few verb forms remaining that can denote the character of a clause as a wish or a request.[6]

Jussive

וַיֹּאמֶר אֱלֹהִים	a	Then God said,
יְהִי אוֹר		"Let there be light."
וַיְהִי־אוֹר:		And there was light.
(Genesis 1:3)		
תָּשֶׁת־חֹשֶׁךְ וִיהִי לָיְלָה	b	You appoint darkness, thus it is night,
בּוֹ־תִרְמֹשׂ כָּל־חַיְתוֹ־יָעַר:		In it all the beasts of the forest prowl about.
(Psalm 104:20)		

Jussive at the Beginning of a Clause

Jussive-forms stand almost exclusively in request clauses (a). They can also occur in poetry in simple statement clauses, thus having no jussive meaning (b); they also occur perhaps on metrical grounds.

It is important, however, that the jussive-forms always appear at the **beginning of a clause**. This is actually an important sign of the statement of intent of a text.

וַיֹּאמֶר	c	And he said,
שַׁלְּחֻנִי לַאדֹנִי:		"Send me away to my master!"
וַיֹּאמֶר אָחִיהָ וְאִמָּהּ		Her brother and her mother said,
תֵּשֵׁב הַנַּעֲרָ אִתָּנוּ יָמִים אוֹ עָשׂוֹר		"Let the girl stay with us *a few* days, say ten;
אַחַר תֵּלֵךְ:		afterward she may go."
(Genesis 24:54–55)		

---

5   Else one can hardly understand (example h) how the one spoken to reacted harshly to such a "harmless" question.

6   The "jussive"-forms are distinguished from other PC-forms only in the Hifʿil (→ § 32.2), as short forms of the verbs lamed-he (→ § 39.3) and with the hollow roots (→ § 41.3).

When in dialogue the finite **imperfect** form stands at the **start** of the clause (verbal clause), it acts as a volitional clause: The **speaker wants** something.[7]

When the imperfect form does not stand at the beginning of a clause, it acts as a speech act of another kind. The last clause in text (c)—אַחַר תֵּלֵךְ "dann mag sie gehen" (Elberfelder Bibel) or "dann sollst du ziehen" (Luther)—is an example of not just a request, rather a **concession**: "Then they can leave because of us (if then they must)!"

In Poetry

הַלְלוּ יָהּ	d	Praise YHWH!
שִׁירוּ לַיהוָה שִׁיר חָדָשׁ		Sing to YHWH a new song—
תְּהִלָּתוֹ בִּקְהַל חֲסִידִים׃		His praise in the congregation of the godly ones!
יִשְׂמַח יִשְׂרָאֵל בְּעֹשָׂיו		<u>Let</u> Israel <u>be glad</u> in his Maker!
בְּנֵי־צִיּוֹן יָגִילוּ בְמַלְכָּם׃		<u>Let</u> the sons of Zion <u>rejoice</u> in their King!
יְהַלְלוּ שְׁמוֹ בְמָחוֹל		<u>Let</u> them <u>praise</u> His name with dancing!
בְּתֹף וְכִנּוֹר יְזַמְּרוּ־לוֹ׃		<u>Let</u> them <u>sing</u> praises to Him with timbrel and lyre!
(Ps 149:1–3)		

The rule of position for jussive imperfect is valid for **prose** (c); it is valid also to a great extent for **poetic texts** (d). However, there one must also account strongly with rhetorical figures such as chiasmus or parallelism.[8]

Mood in Dialogue

וַיַּרְא וַיָּרָץ לִקְרָאתָם מִפֶּתַח	e	As he saw them, he ran from the tent door to
הָאֹהֶל וַיִּשְׁתַּחוּ אָרְצָה׃		meet them and bowed himself to the earth.
וַיֹּאמַר		Then he said,
אֲדֹנָי אִם־נָא מָצָאתִי חֵן בְּעֵינֶיךָ	1	"My lord! May I now find favor in your eyes!
אַל־נָא תַעֲבֹר מֵעַל עַבְדֶּךָ׃	2	Do not pass your servant by!
יֻקַּח־נָא מְעַט־מַיִם	3	One should bring a little water
וְרַחֲצוּ רַגְלֵיכֶם	4	and wash your feet (impv),

---

7   Alviero Niccacci ("A Neglected Point of Hebrew Syntax: Yiqtol and Position in the Sentence," Liber Annuus XXXVII—1987, Studium Biblicum Franciscanum, Jerusalem, pp. 7–19) has pointed to this meaning of the clause position. I have taken from him the expression "volitional."

8   I cannot accept Niccacci's assumption that the compound nominal clause (X—yiqtol), which follows or precedes the volitional clause, must also generally be understood jussive.

וְהִשָּׁעֲנוּ תַּחַת הָעֵץ:	5	and rest yourselves under the tree (impv).
וְאֶקְחָה פַת־לֶחֶם	6	Then I will bring a piece of bread,
וְסַעֲדוּ לִבְּכֶם	7	then you may refresh yourselves (impv).
אַחַר תַּעֲבֹרוּ	8	Then you may go on (impf),
כִּי־עַל־כֵּן עֲבַרְתֶּם עַל־עַבְדְּכֶם	9	since you have visited your servant."
וַיֹּאמְרוּ	10	Then they said,
כֵּן תַּעֲשֶׂה כַּאֲשֶׁר דִּבַּרְתָּ:		"So you should do (impf), as you have said."

(Genesis 18:2ff.)

Particles

The excerpt of dialogue from the narrative of Genesis 18 (e) shows a great deal of **examples** of how the intention of speech can be expressed through particles:

אִם־נָא

The particle ־נָא marks—together with אִם (1)—a **wish** or—together with the imperfect of a verb—a **request** (2) or **intention** (3).

אַל

The negative אַל (2) would also express a negative demand without ־נָא, which is a request with נָא־.

הָ◌

The *he Cohortative* (הָ◌) on a verb form of the first person (6) expresses a **self-challenge** of the speaker: "I will."

Clause Position

The statement of intent of the unmarked imperfect forms תַּעֲבֹרוּ (8) and תַּעֲשֶׂה (10) is made through **clause position** and context. The verb form does not stand at the beginning of the clause; thus, there exists no expression of will. Rather some **permission** is given or a **possibility** is conceded. Only in German translation[9] do we bring instead an additional characterization through modal expressions ("dürfen/mögen/können").

---

9   German has here in its modal verbs a surplus of means of expression, which may be used oc-casionally in translation. The "imperfect" tense does not here specify the statement of intent.

Imperatives with introductory וְ (4, 5, 7) continue the request clauses (**final clauses** → § 53.1).

Further Particles

וַיֹּאמְרוּ אֲלֵהֶם כָּל־הָעֵדָה לוּ־מַתְנוּ בְּאֶרֶץ מִצְרַיִם אוֹ בַּמִּדְ־ בָּר הַזֶּה לוּ־מָתְנוּ: (Numbers 14:2)	f	And the whole congregation said to them, "<u>Would</u> that we <u>had</u> died in the land of Egypt or in the wilderness! <u>Would</u> that we had died!"
בַּבֹּקֶר תֹּאמַר מִי־יִתֵּן עֶרֶב וּבָעֶרֶב תֹּאמַר מִי־יִתֵּן בֹּקֶר (Deuteronomy 28:67)	g	In the morning you shall say, "<u>Would</u> that it were evening!" And at evening you shall say, "<u>Would</u> that it were morning!"
וְעַתָּה אֱסֹף אֶת־יֶתֶר הָעָם וַחֲנֵה עַל־הָעִיר וְלָכְדָהּ פֶּן־אֶלְכֹּד אֲנִי אֶת־הָעִיר וְנִקְרָא שְׁמִי עָלֶיהָ: (2 Samuel 12:28)	h	And now, gather the rest of the people together and camp against the city and capture it, <u>so that</u> I will not capture the city myself and it will be named after me.

לוּ

Also לוּ "if" introduces a, mostly **unrealizable**, wish clause (f). Only in German (through subjunctive II) is it expressed whether the wish is "real" or "unreal."

מִי יִתֵּן

As a set formula, the interrogative clause מִי יִתֵּן "who will give?" (g) introduces a **wish clause**.

פֶּן

The negative פֶּן "lest" can introduce a **negative intention clause** (h).

Mood in Context

וְאִם רַע בְּעֵינֵיכֶם לַעֲבֹד אֶת־יְהוָה בַּחֲרוּ לָכֶם הַיּוֹם אֶת־מִי תַעֲבֹדוּן אִם אֶת־אֱלֹהִים אֲשֶׁר־עָבְדוּ אֲבוֹתֵיכֶם אֲשֶׁר מֵעֵבֶר הַנָּהָר	i	If it is disagreeable in your sight to serve YHWH, then choose for yourselves today whom you will serve:

וְאִם אֶת־אֱלֹהֵי הָאֱמֹרִי אֲשֶׁר אַתֶּם יֹשְׁבִים בְּאַרְצָם וְאָנֹכִי וּבֵיתִי נַעֲבֹד אֶת־יְהוָה: (Joshua 24:15)		(whether) the gods that your fathers served which (lie) beyond the River, or (whether) the gods of the Amorites in whose land you are living! In any case, I and my house, we will serve YHWH.
וַיְדַבֵּר יְהוָה אֶל־מֹשֶׁה לֵּאמֹר: דַּבֵּר אֶל־כָּל־עֲדַת בְּנֵי־יִשְׂרָאֵל וְאָמַרְתָּ אֲלֵהֶם קְדֹשִׁים תִּהְיוּ כִּי קָדוֹשׁ אֲנִי יְהוָה אֱלֹהֵיכֶם: אִישׁ אִמּוֹ וְאָבִיו תִּירָאוּ וְאֶת־ שַׁבְּתֹתַי תִּשְׁמֹרוּ אֲנִי יְהוָה אֱלֹהֵיכֶם: (Leviticus 19:1ff.)	j	YHWH spoke to Moses, saying: "Speak to all the congregation of the sons of Israel and say to them, 'You shall be holy, for I YHWH your God am holy. Every one of you shall reverence his mother and his father, and you shall keep My Sabbaths! I am YHWH your God.'"
לֹא תִּרְצָח: ס לֹא תִּנְאָף: ס לֹא תִּגְנֹב: ס (Exodus 20:13–15)	k	You shall not murder! You shall not commit adultery! You shall not steal!

Verb Meanings

Often the expression of intention of a text or a clause is clearly adequate in a concrete text through the linguistic or situational **context**. The decision of the hearer about the mood of a verbal predicate can be controlled through the **meaning** of the preceding **verb**: For example the request "decide for yourself!" in Joshua 24 (i) already contains the element of the "wish" for the following question: אֶת־מִי תַעֲבֹדוּן and for the concluding clause: וְאָנֹכִי וּבֵיתִי נַעֲבֹד אֶת־יְהוָה.

Genres [Gattungen]

Particular genres [*Gattungen*], as e.g. the challenges of the apodictic **law** (j), are so joined with a speech situation, that as a result the statement of intent is predetermined. In apodictic law clauses, **bans** can also be introduced for that reason with לֹא instead of with אַל (k).[10]

---

10   One can understand such clauses also as—even apodictically—indicative: "You shall not kill!!" (etc.). That 100 long years ago a leading German school book, the Catachism, would translate it with "Du sollst nicht," Moses could not foresee.

52 Orientation in the Meaning Structure of Texts—References in the Text

Texts are not formed by a simple stringing together of words and clauses. They are structured as a sense-unified whole through an interlacing of many and diverse references in addition to the whole clause.[1] *The hearer (reader) is oriented as a result towards every passage of the continually running text, as it has combined the individual signs and their meanings with one another and with the speech situation.*

In this paragraph are described how references occur in the Hebrew text and what is referenced.

52.1 References

Direction of Reference

Inside the text, reference is made in the following ways:

backward (anaphoric)[2] to things already mentioned and known to the hearer/reader,

forward (kataphoric) to an expected new thing, and

out of the text (deictic) to the communication **situation** itself.

Signs

Signs which have a reference function can be summarized as follows:

word-**meaning** and text-**meaning** combined with one another (→ § 52.2),

pronominals, suffixes, and nominals used as pronominals (→ § 52.3 and 4),

deictic particles and conjugation-morphemes (→ § 52.4),

the **article** and determined nominal groups (→ § 52.5).

---

1   "Text grammar" is the keyword for a grammatical description of language, which goes beyond the whole clause and attempts to grasp how texts are constituted, what holds them together, and how they can be distinguished. E.g., pronominals and other particles can only be described text-linguistically in their function.

2   "anaphoric" from Greek: αναφερειν (*anapherein*) "take up," namely to the side where one read up in an area that has already been read; "kataphoric" from καταφερειν "carry down"; "deictic" from δειχνυμι (*deiknumi*) "show."

52.2 The Levels of Meaning of a Text

Semantic Levels

*The **whole** of verb-meaning and nominal-meaning, which occur in a text, forms its level of meaning (semantic level).*

As a result, the hearer (reader) examines newly appearing words as their meanings (and **some** of their mostly many and diverse **meanings**) are **connected** to the meanings of the other members of the context.

וַיְהִי־אִישׁ מֵהַר־אֶפְרָיִם וּשְׁמוֹ מִיכָיְהוּ׃ a	There was a man of the hill country of
וַיֹּאמֶר לְאִמּוֹ	Ephraim named Micah, who said to
אֶלֶף וּמֵאָה הַכֶּסֶף אֲשֶׁר לֻקַּח־לָךְ וְאַתְּי	his mother: "The eleven hundred *pieces*
אָלִית וְגַם אָמַרְתְּ בְּאָזְנָי	of silver which were taken from you—
הִנֵּה־הַכֶּסֶף אִתִּי אֲנִי לְקַחְתִּיו	You even uttered a curse and also said
וְעַתָּה אֲשִׁיבֶנּוּ לָךְ׃	it in my presence—Here! The silver! I
	have it. I myself have taken it, and now
	I will return it to you."[3]
וַתֹּאמֶר אִמּוֹ בָּרוּךְ בְּנִי לַיהוָה׃	Then his mother said: "Blessed be my
	son by YHWH."
וַיָּשֶׁב אֶת־אֶלֶף־וּמֵאָה הַכֶּסֶף לְאִמּוֹ	And he returned the eleven hundred
וַתֹּאמֶר אִמּוֹ	shekels of silver to his mother, and his
הַקְדֵּשׁ הִקְדַּשְׁתִּי אֶת־הַכֶּסֶף לַיהוָה	mother said:
מִיָּדִי לִבְנִי לַעֲשׂוֹת פֶּסֶל וּמַסֵּכָה	"With this I dedicate the silver (solem-
	ly) to YHWH.—From my hand for
	my son!—With it a graven image and
	a molten image is made."
וַיָּשֶׁב אֶת־הַכֶּסֶף לְאִמּוֹ	So he returned the silver to his mother,
וַתִּקַּח אִמּוֹ מָאתַיִם כֶּסֶף	and his mother took two hundred
וַתִּתְּנֵהוּ לַצּוֹרֵף וַיַּעֲשֵׂהוּ פֶּסֶל וּמַסֵּכָה	shekels of silver and gave them to the
וַיְהִי בְּבֵית מִיכָיְהוּ׃	silversmith. He made out of it a graven
	image and a molten image, and they
	were in the house of Micah.
וְהָאִישׁ מִיכָה לוֹ בֵּית אֱלֹהִים	To the man Micah, to him belonged
וַיַּעַשׂ אֵפוֹד וּתְרָפִים	to be exact a house of God. He made
וַיְמַלֵּא אֶת־יַד אַחַד מִבָּנָיו	an ephod and Teraphim and (filled the
וַיְהִי־לוֹ לְכֹהֵן׃	hand) paid one of his sons a salary, that
(Judges 17:1–5)	he might become to him as a priest.

---

3   Text-critical questions as to why e.g. this clause should thus be moved from the end of verse 3b
     to here, remain undiscussed here.

In the cited text, which is the beginning of a longer narrative, the semantic **level** is **established** at the start (vv. 2, 3) through the verbs לקח "take," אלה "curse,"and ברך "bless," and the nominals אֵם "mother" and בֵּן "son," כֶּסֶף "gold/silver," and the name of God יהוה.

In the clauses that follow, this semantic level is **confirmed** and **expanded** through נתן "give," הִקְדִּישׁ "consecrate," פֶּסֶל "idol," מַסֵּכָה "molten image" and צוֹרֵף "gold-smith."

Word Meanings

To the hearer/reader is now, for example, prevented to misunderstand, for instance, the **new word** שׁוּב (Hi) as "fight/give a reply" or even as a form of ישׁב "sit down," or to allocate, for instance, the meaning "cover" from the new nominal מַסֵּכָה.

Text Meaning

And as far as the meaning of the **whole text** goes: What began as a history of family and history of gold, turns out already here to be a history of religion and history of sacred objects.

Discrepancies

Words, whose meanings are **not** or hardly **appropriate** for the semantic level of a text, have for the hearer/reader a particularly high **attention value**. From such a construction **poems** gain effect:

יְהוָה אֲדֹנֵינוּ מָה־אַדִּיר שִׁמְךָ בְּכָל־הָאָרֶץ אֲשֶׁר תְּנָה הוֹדְךָ עַל־הַשָּׁמָיִם:	b	YHWH, our Lord, how majestic is Your name in all the world! That you have displayed Your splendor above the heavens!
מִפִּי עוֹלְלִים וְיֹנְקִים יִסַּדְתָּ עֹז לְמַעַן צוֹרְרֶיךָ לְהַשְׁבִּית אוֹיֵב וּמִתְנַקֵּם:		From the mouth of infants and nursing babes you have established a bulwark for the sake of your enemies, to make an end to the enemy and the avenger.
כִּי־אֶרְאֶה שָׁמֶיךָ מַעֲשֵׂי אֶצְבְּעֹתֶיךָ יָרֵחַ וְכוֹכָבִים אֲשֶׁר כּוֹנָנְתָּה: (Psalm 8:2–4)		When I consider the heavens, the work of Your fingers, moon and stars, which You have ordained …

Various Levels

In the opening clauses of Psalm 8, the semantic level is characterized **on the one hand** through אָדוֹן "Lord," אַדִּיר "wonderful," כָּל־הָאָרֶץ "all the land," נתן "give," יסד "establish," כון "arrange" (sphere: Creator and **Creation**), **on the other hand** through: עֹז "stronghold," צרר "besiege," אוֹיֵב "enemy" (sphere: **battle**). In between stand **suddenly** the words מִפִּי עוֹלְלִים וְיֹנְקִים "from the mouth of children and infants."

Poetry

The **hearer/reader**, being alerted by the semantic discrepancy, must go and see the point in which the statement about these groups of nominals is connected to the semantic level(s) of the text. The poem allows the hearer sizeable freedom to find or to make up such **starting points**.

52.3 Backward (Anaphoric) Referencing Elements

Pronominals and Suffixes

*Pronominals and suffixes of the **third person** refer backward (anaphoric[4]) in the text to aforementioned persons or things, with which a pronoun agrees (is **congruent** to) at the time in **gender** and **number**.*

וַיְהִי־אִישׁ מֵהַר־אֶפְרָיִם וּשְׁמוֹ מִיכָיְהוּ׃ → —— וַיֹּאמֶר לְאִמּוֹ → אֶלֶף וּמֵאָה הַכֶּסֶף אֲשֶׁר לֻקַּח־לָךְ וְאַתְּ אָלִית וְגַם אָמַרְתְּ בְּאָזְנַי הִנֵּה־הַכֶּסֶף אִתִּי אֲנִי לְקַחְתִּיו → —— וְעַתָּה אֲשִׁיבֶנּוּ לָךְ׃ →	There was <u>a man</u> of the hill country of Ephraim, <u>his</u> name: Micah, who said to <u>his</u> mother: "The eleven hundred *pieces* of silver which were taken from you—You even uttered a curse and also said it in my presence—Here! The silver! I have it. I myself have taken <u>it</u>, and now I will return <u>it</u> to you." Then <u>his</u> mother said: "Blessed be my son by YHWH!"

---

4   From Greek: αναφερειν (*anapherein*) "take up," namely on the side, where one reads.

וַתֹּאמֶר אִמּוֹ בָּרוּךְ בְּנִי לַיהוָה:	And he returned the eleven hundred shekels of silver to <u>his</u> mother, and <u>his</u> mother said:
→	
וַיָּשֶׁב אֶת־אֶלֶף־וּמֵאָה הַכֶּסֶף לְאִמּוֹ	"With this I dedicate the silver (solemnly) to YHWH. —From my hand for my son!—With it a graven image and a molten image is made."
→	
וַתֹּאמֶר אִמּוֹ	
→	
הַקְדֵּשׁ הִקְדַּשְׁתִּי אֶת־הַכֶּסֶף לַיהוָה	So he returned the silver to <u>his</u> mother, and <u>his</u> mother took two hundred shekels of silver
מִיָּדִי לִבְנִי לַעֲשׂוֹת פֶּסֶל וּמַסֵּכָה	
וַיָּשֶׁב אֶת־הַכֶּסֶף לְאִמּוֹ	
→	
וַתִּקַּח אִמּוֹ מָאתַיִם כֶּסֶף	and gave <u>them</u> to the silversmith. He made <u>out of it</u> a graven image and a molten image,
וַתִּתְּנֵהוּ לַצּוֹרֵף וַיַּעֲשֵׂהוּ פֶּסֶל וּמַסֵּכָה	and they were in the house of <u>Micah</u>.
→ →	
וַיְהִי בְּבֵית מִיכָיְהוּ:	<u>To the man</u> <u>Micah</u>, <u>to him</u> belonged to be exact a house of God. He made an ephod and Teraphim
→	
וְהָאִישׁ מִיכָה לוֹ בֵּית אֱלֹהִים	
→ → →	
וַיַּעַשׂ אֵפוֹד וּתְרָפִים	and (filled the hand) paid one of <u>his</u> sons a salary,
וַיְמַלֵּא אֶת־יַד אַחַד מִבָּנָיו	
→	
וַיְהִי־לוֹ לְכֹהֵן:	that he might become to <u>him</u> as a priest.
→	

(Judges 17:1–5)

The narrative beginning cited again here shows in an exemplary way what an important contribution pronominal elements make to a text: Of 82 words 23, thus almost **30%**, are **pronominals**, i.e., words with a pronominal suffix. Of these in turn 14, thus more than half, are suffixes of the third person.

Pronominalization

In our example all suffixes of the **third person**, masculine, as far as they are added to nominals, refer to אִישׁ "**a man**" (1st line). All suffixes of the third person, masculine, added to verb forms, refer back to the noun הַכֶּסֶף "**the silver**" (5th or 3rd line). This distribution is given through the meaning of the verbs: לקח "take" and שׁוב (Hi) "give back" are mainly connected to nominals with the characteristic significance of "not human." (→ § 52.2).

All elements, which again establish the noun אִישׁ (line 1), form the **series** (as an exception to read from left to right): אִמּוֹ → אִמּוֹ → אִמּוֹ → אִמּוֹ → שְׁמוֹ → אִישׁ → אִמּוֹ → אִמּוֹ → מִיכָיְהוּ הָאִישׁ מִיכָה → לוֹ → בָּנָיו → לוֹ.

Antecedent

The significance of **congruence** is not enough to settle the antecedent upon which a pronominal refers back. For the last לוֹ of this series, for example, it would be correct both for מִבָּנָיו אֶחָד "one of his sons" and for אֱלֹהִים בֵּית "house of God." The antecedent אִישׁ has **gathered** however in the course of the text further **meaning**, and is referred to throughout. So לוֹ in the last line of our text example means "him" in the sense of: "And the man Micah had a shrine, and he made an ephod and household idols, and consecrated one of his sons that he might become his priest."

First, if the **side effect** is **examined** with the entire, up-to-now growing significance, the referencing pronominal is allocated to the proper antecedent. As a rule, the memory of the hearer/reader accomplishes this **automatically**.

Renominalization

For that reason, however, the **gaps** between the antecedent and the anaphoric pronoun should not be too great. The antecedent can appear several times again in the text (here e.g. הָאִישׁ with article, → § 52.5). Such a **renominalization** is important for the **structuring** of a text; e.g. it marks in Judg 17:5 the end of the introductory part of the text. For that reason, **translations** should handle it carefully and not intervene in the reference-structure of a text without pressing cause.

Further Anaphora

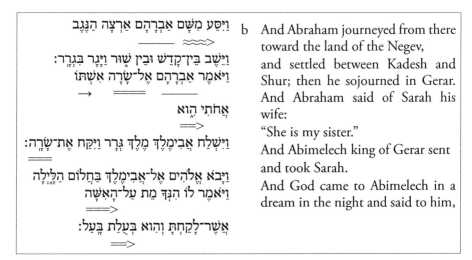

וַיִּסַּע מִשָּׁם אַבְרָהָם אַרְצָה הַנֶּגֶב	b	And Abraham journeyed from there toward the land of the Negev,
וַיֵּשֶׁב בֵּין־קָדֵשׁ וּבֵין שׁוּר וַיָּגָר בִּגְרָר:		and settled between Kadesh and Shur; then he sojourned in Gerar.
וַיֹּאמֶר אַבְרָהָם אֶל־שָׂרָה אִשְׁתּוֹ		And Abraham said of Sarah his wife:
אֲחֹתִי הִוא		"She is my sister."
וַיִּשְׁלַח אֲבִימֶלֶךְ מֶלֶךְ גְּרָר וַיִּקַּח אֶת־שָׂרָה:		And Abimelech king of Gerar sent and took Sarah.
וַיָּבֹא אֱלֹהִים אֶל־אֲבִימֶלֶךְ בַּחֲלוֹם הַלָּיְלָה וַיֹּאמֶר לוֹ הִנְּךָ מֵת עַל־הָאִשָּׁה		And God came to Abimelech in a dream in the night and said to him,
אֲשֶׁר־לָקַחְתָּ וְהִוא בְּעֻלַת בָּעַל:		

וַאֲבִימֶלֶךְ לֹא קָרַב אֵלֶיהָ וַיֹּאמַר
=>

אֲדֹנָי הֲגוֹי גַּם־צַדִּיק תַּהֲרֹג:
הֲלֹא הוּא אָמַר־לִי אֲחֹתִי הִוא
==> →

וְהִיא־גַם־הִוא אָמְרָה אָחִי הוּא
→ =========>

בְּתָם־לְבָבִי וּבְנִקְיֹן כַּפַּי עָשִׂיתִי זֹאת:
≈≈>

וַיֹּאמֶר אֵלָיו הָאֱלֹהִים בַּחֲלֹם
גַּם אָנֹכִי יָדַעְתִּי כִּי בְתָם־לְבָבְךָ עָשִׂיתָ זֹּאת
≈≈>

וָאֶחְשֹׂךְ גַּם־אָנֹכִי אוֹתְךָ מֵחֲטוֹ־לִי
עַל־כֵּן לֹא־נְתַתִּיךָ לִנְגֹּעַ אֵלֶיהָ:
=> ≈≈>

וְעַתָּה הָשֵׁב אֵשֶׁת־הָאִישׁ כִּי־נָבִיא הוּא
→ → ===>

וְיִתְפַּלֵּל בַּעַדְךָ וֶחְיֵה וְאִם־אֵינְךָ מֵשִׁיב דַּע
כִּי־מוֹת תָּמוּת אַתָּה וְכָל־אֲשֶׁר־לָךְ:
וַיַּשְׁכֵּם אֲבִימֶלֶךְ בַּבֹּקֶר וַיִּקְרָא לְכָל־עֲבָדָיו
וַיְדַבֵּר אֶת־כָּל־הַדְּבָרִים הָאֵלֶּה
≈≈≈≈≈≈≈≈>

בְּאָזְנֵיהֶם וַיִּירְאוּ הָאֲנָשִׁים מְאֹד:
(Genesis 20:1–8)

"Now you are a dead man because of the woman whom you have taken; for she is actually married." But Abimelech had not come near her. He said: "Will You also kill an innocent people? Did he not himself say to me: 'She is my sister'? And she—she also said: 'He is my brother.' In the integrity of my heart and with clean hands I have done this." Then God said to him in the dream: "I also know that in the integrity of your heart you have done this; and I also kept you from sinning against Me. For that reason I did not let you touch her. And now: Return the man's wife, for he is a prophet, that he might pray for you so that you might live. But if you do not restore *her*, thus know: You will die, you and all that is yours." And Abimelech arose early in the morning, called all his servants, and told all these things in their hearing. And the men were very frightened.

Series

In the part from Genesis 20 cited here, the anaphoric form of reference forms **two series**: To אַבְרָהָם refers the simple → emphasized elements (3ms), to שָׂרָה the double ==> emphasized elements (3fs). Also here the words of reference again appear in the form of a definite general noun (הָאִשׁ—הָאִשָּׁה) after more pronominals.

Apart from the form of reference for "Abraham," "Sarah," "Abimelech," and "his slaves" arise in the above cited text further anaphoric referencing elements (≈≈>), for which **no single word** in the text is agreed upon as a word of reference:

Adverbs

מִשָּׁם "from **there**" refers back to 18:33: שָׁם וְאַבְרָהָם לִמְקֹמוֹ "However Abraham returned <u>to his place</u>" and this further to 18:1: בְּאֵלֹנֵי מַמְרֵא "in the grove of Mamre."

עַל־כֵּן "**for that reason**" refers to the entire last clause of גַּם אָנֹכִי יָדַעְתִּי up to לִי.

דָּבָר, זֹאת et al.

זֹאת "**this**" and כָּל־הַדְּבָרִים הָאֵלֶּה "**all these things**" refer to the contents of extensive pieces of text that can hardly be differentiated exactly.

The feminine pronoun זֹאת, in the independent form, as well as a feminine suffix הָ־, can refer back to entire clauses and **pieces of text** (→ also § 52.6, text example f). Frequently הַדָּבָר הַזֶּה "it," הַדָּבָר "this" or also the plural כָּל־הַדְּבָרִים הָאֵלֶּה "all these things" are used in this function. Also adverbs such as שָׁם "there," אָז "then," בַּיָּמִים הָהֵם "to the time," and כֵּן "so" occur in an anaphoric function.

52.4 Elements Referenced (Deictically) on the Speech Situation

For the orientation of the speech situation helps above all the person-morphemes and the tense-morphemes of the verbs. As a result, the pronouns and suffixes of the first and second person are initially at one's disposal in order to point[5] to the person involved in the communication and thus to apply the statements to the situation of the communication.

1st and 2nd Person

The person morpheme of the **first person** applies the verb to the **speaker(s)**, the person morpheme of the **second person** to the **one(s) spoken to**.

Tense morphemes instruct the reader to react appropriately to the discourse speech (engaging) or to the narrative speech (distancing) (→ § 48).

The pronouns and suffixes of the first and second person stand mainly in **discourse** texts (dialogue, pronouncement, sermon, law, prayer, etc.). In **narratives** they are an indication that the narrative of the narrator goes over to the speech of the narrated person. (→ §§ 48.3 and 48.4, → as a text example also § 52.7)

---

5   Greek: δειχνυμι (*deiknymi*) "point."

Other Deictic Particles

... וַיַּשְׁכִּימוּ בַבֹּקֶר וַיִּשָּׁבְעוּ אִישׁ לְאָחִיו וַיְהִי בַּיּוֹם הַהוּא וַיָּבֹאוּ עַבְדֵי יִצְחָק ——————→ ... וַיַּגִּדוּ לוֹ עַל־אֹדוֹת הַבְּאֵר אֲשֶׁר חָפָרוּ וַיִּקְרָא אֹתָהּ שִׁבְעָה עַל־כֵּן שֵׁם־הָעִיר בְּאֵר שֶׁבַע עַד הַיּוֹם הַזֶּה: ——————— (Genesis 26:31–33)	a	In the morning they arose early and exchanged oaths … And it came about on <u>the same</u> day, that Isaac's servants came in and told him about the well which they had dug … and he called it[6] Shibah (oath). Therefore the city is named "Beersheba" to <u>this</u> (today) day.
הוֹרֵד אוֹתָם אֶל־הַמַּיִם וְאֶצְרְפֶנּוּ לְךָ שָׁם וְהָיָה אֲשֶׁר אֹמַר אֵלֶיךָ זֶה יֵלֵךְ אִתָּךְ הוּא יֵלֵךְ אִתָּךְ → —— וְכֹל אֲשֶׁר־אֹמַר אֵלֶיךָ זֶה לֹא־יֵלֵךְ עִמָּךְ הוּא לֹא יֵלֵךְ: → —— (Judges 7:4)	b	Bring them down to the water, so that I may test them for you there! Therefore it shall be that he of whom I say to you, "<u>This one</u> shall go with you," <u>he</u> shall go with you; but everyone of whom I say to you, "<u>This one</u> shall not go with you," <u>he</u> shall not go.
הַגִּידָה־נָּא לִי אֵיפֹה הֵם רֹעִים: וַיֹּאמֶר הָאִישׁ נָסְעוּ מִזֶּה —— כִּי שָׁמַעְתִּי אֹמְרִים נֵלְכָה דֹּתָיְנָה (Genesis 37:16–17)	c	"Tell me, please, where they are grazing." And the man said: "They have moved from <u>here</u>. I actually heard them saying: 'Let us go to Dothan.'"
וַיָּבֹא יוֹאָב אֶל־הַמֶּלֶךְ וַיֹּאמֶר מֶה עָשִׂיתָה הִנֵּה־בָא אַבְנֵר אֵלֶיךָ לָמָּה־זֶּה שִׁלַּחְתּוֹ וַיֵּלֶךְ הָלוֹךְ: (2 Samuel 3:24)	d	Joab came to the king and said: ("What have you done? See, Abner came to you; why then have you sent him away and he is gone—already thus!") "<u>How can it be!</u> There is nothing to trust! Then Abner comes to you, and you a fool can run him, and he goes simply thus away!"

---

6 בְּאֵר is feminine.

כֹּה אָמַר יְהוָה	e	Thus says YHWH:
הַשָּׁמַיִם כִּסְאִי וְהָאָרֶץ הֲדֹם רַגְלָי		"Heaven is My throne and the earth My footstool.
אֵי־זֶה בַיִת אֲשֶׁר תִּבְנוּ־לִי		Where <u>then</u> is a house you could
אֵי־זֶה מָקוֹם מְנוּחָתִי:		build for Me, and where <u>then</u> is a place that I may rest?
וְאֶת־כָּל־אֵלֶּה יָדִי עָשָׂתָה		But all this here: My hand has made it and
וַיִּהְיוּ כָל־אֵלֶּה נְאֻם־יְהוָה		by me <u>all this here</u> came into being," declares YHWH.
וְאֶל־זֶה אַבִּיט אֶל־עָנִי וּנְכֵה־רוּחַ		"But to <u>this one</u> I will look: to the wretched, the beaten in spirit,
וְחָרֵד עַל־דְּבָרִי:		who trembles at My word."

(Isaiah 66:1–2)

זֶה and הוּא

The most important deictic pronoun is זֶה. Whereas הוּא refers **anaphorically** (a: הַיּוֹם הַהוּא "the day on which was the speech"), זֶה points to the **speech situation** itself (a: הַיּוֹם הַזֶּה "this day here and now, today") or to the one **immediately** present (b: "the one here").

Interrogative Clauses

זֶה can also denote the communication situation itself and its place: "now, here" (c). It has this function in common with adverbs such as עַתָּה "now,"[7] הִנֵּה "behold!", פֹּה, הֵנָּה "here." As a deictic particle, זֶה also appears **after interrogative words** (d, e). It applies the question directly to the speech situation and demands an urgent answer (German: "Wo denn?", "was denn bloß?"). Most of the time, rhetorical questions with זֶה (d) contain a **severe reproach**.

Anaphoric זֶה?

In Is 66:1 (e) כָּל־אֵלֶּה appears to refer **back** (anaphorically), namely to הַשָּׁמַיִם and הָאָרֶץ at the beginning of a text. However, it lies precisely to see also here a gesture of pointing (**Deixis**): "here are those which a speaker or hearer has simultaneously in view." In the same way one can understand אֶל־זֶה (e, next to last line) **not only**

---

7   On וְעַתָּה and וְהִנֵּה as macrosyntactical signs → § 54.

referring **ahead** (kataphoric[8] → § 52.6): "to which, by which it is valid, that it is respectfully." Also here the deictic understanding is **not excluded**: "to that which is here under my listener and…."

In particular cases with זֶה (זֹאת, אֵלֶּה), the possibility of *Deixis* is **first** considered. Certainly at the same time is to consider that—above all in **later** texts—a difference between זֶה and other pronouns would not be felt greatly and זֶה also is used in an anaphoric or kataphoric function.

52.5 The Article as a Referencing Sign

The article before a noun directs the hearer/reader to apply the meaning of the noun to its previous information.

Previous Information

Previous information can be given through the linguistic context, through speech situation (the situated context), and through general knowledge of things and knowledge of language of the hearer/reader.

וַיֵּשְׁבוּ אֵלָיו וְהוּא יֹשֵׁב בִּירִיחֹו ...	a	They returned to him while he was staying at Jericho …
וַיֹּאמְרוּ אַנְשֵׁי הָעִיר אֶל־אֱלִישָׁע	2	And the men of the city said to Elisha:
הִנֵּה־נָא מֹושַׁב הָעִיר טֹוב כַּאֲשֶׁר אֲדֹנִי רֹאֶה	3	"But of course, the situation of this city is pleasant, as you, lord, see.
וְהַמַּיִם רָעִים וְהָאָרֶץ מְשַׁכָּלֶת:	4	But the water is bad, and the land is unfruitful."
וַיֹּאמֶר קְחוּ־לִי צְלֹחִית חֲדָשָׁה וְשִׂימוּ שָׁם מֶלַח	5	He said, "Bring me a new jar and put salt in it!"
וַיִּקְחוּ אֵלָיו:	6	And they brought (it) to him.
וַיֵּצֵא אֶל־מֹוצָא הַמַּיִם וַיַּשְׁלֶךְ־שָׁם מֶלַח	7	Then he went out to the spring of water, threw salt in it

---

8 From Greek: kataferein (*katapherein*) "take down."

וַיֹּאמֶר כֹּה־אָמַר יְהוָה רִפִּאתִי לַמַּיִם הָאֵלֶּה	8	and said, "Thus says YHWH, 'With this I purify these waters.
לֹא־יִהְיֶה מִשָּׁם עוֹד מָוֶת	9	There shall come from it any longer no death
וּמְשַׁכָּלֶת:	10	and no unfruitfulness.'"
וַיֵּרָפוּ הַמַּיִם עַד הַיּוֹם הַזֶּה	11	And the waters have been purified to this day,
כִּדְבַר אֱלִישָׁע אֲשֶׁר דִּבֵּר:	12	according to the word of Elisha which he spoke.

(2 Kings 2:18–22)

Linguistic Context

The linguistic context provides the previous information in the case of הָעִיר (a, 2 and 3): With "city" is intended the city named in the context of the preceding narrative, "Jericho" (line 1). In the following text (b, lines 5 and 7), the article refers with and "the first time" to the previous chapter (Gen 12), in which it is told about the first building of an altar. The hearer/reader finds the advance information for הַמַּיִם "the water" (a, lines 7, 8 and 10) in the context of the same narrative (line 4).

Situation

In dialogue (a, lines 3–4, 8–10), the **speech situation** itself presents the previous information. הָעִיר, הַמַּיִם, and הָאָרֶץ are things that are **immediately present** to the speech partners, i.e. the city, in which they find themselves, the waters, which they must drink, and the earth, on which they stand. They can point to all of these with their finger.

הַיּוֹם הַזֶּה (a, 11) refers to the day on which the history is told or again told, to the communication situation of the **narrator**.

וַיַּעַל אַבְרָם מִמִּצְרַיִם הוּא וְאִשְׁתּוֹ וְכָל־	b	Then Abram went up from Egypt—he and his wife
אֲשֶׁר־לוֹ וְלוֹט עִמּוֹ הַנֶּגְבָּה:	2	and Lot with him—in the Negev.

וְאַבְרָם כָּבֵד מְאֹד בַּמִּקְנֶה בַּכֶּסֶף	3	But Abram was very rich in livestock, in silver
וּבַזָּהָב: וַיֵּלֶךְ לְמַסָּעָיו מִנֶּגֶב וְעַד־בֵּית־	4	and in gold. He went on his journeys from the Negev as far as Bethel,
אֶל עַד־הַמָּקוֹם אֲשֶׁר־הָיָה שָׁם אָהֳלֹה	5	to the place where his tent had been
בַּתְּחִלָּה בֵּין בֵּית־אֵל וּבֵין הָעָי: אֶל־	6	at the beginning, between Bethel and Ai, to
מְקוֹם הַמִּזְבֵּחַ אֲשֶׁר־עָשָׂה שָׁם בָּרִאשֹׁנֶה	7	the place of the altar which he had made there formerly.

(Genesis 13:1–4)

Knowledge of the Subject and Knowledge of Language

The hearer/reader is referred to his **general knowledge** of things and **languages** when some concrete advance information is determined neither in the linguistic context nor in the speech situation.

הַנֶּגֶב "the southland" (b, line 2) is the land in the south of Palestine well-known to all hearers. With הַמִּקְנֶה "the cattle," הַכֶּסֶף "the silver," הַזָּהָב "the gold" (b, line 3) the hearer, who has **not** been given **special** previous information in a text and situation, is directed to activate all *the* advance knowledge, which provides him the knowledge of his language, in which the words mean the *Gattungen* "cattle/silver/gold."[9]

Article before אֲשֶׁר

In the combination, Article + Noun + אֲשֶׁר-clause (b, line 5), the article functions not back-referencing, rather **forward-referencing** (kataphoric). At the same time,

---

9   With such indications of *Gattung* the German language has the possibility both to set the anaphoric ("determined") article ("das Vieh" etc.) as well as the zero-article ("Vieh/Silber/Gold"). In such cases in German the kataphoric ("undetermined") article is always excluded. (On the syntax of the article in the German language → Harald Weinrich, *Textgrammatik der deutschen Sprache*, Mannheim; Lepizig; Wien; Zürich: Dudenverlag, 1993).

as in German, English and other languages, the **combination** with the **relative clause** first puts *the* information that the hearer needs in order to understand correctly the meaning of the noun in question.[10]

The case is the same as apposition in the combination, Article + Noun + **Participle** (→ below, text f: כֵּלָיו נֹשֵׂא הַנַּעַר "the boy, his weapon holder" = "*the* boy, who holds his weapon").

Additional Elements

When the Hebrew article itself is not shown, whether it is referred to from context, situation, or language, **additional back referencing** (e.g. הַיּוֹם הַהוּא) or **deictic** elements (e.g. a, lines 8–10: לַמַּיִם הָאֵלֶּה or הַיּוֹם הַזֶּה) can join a noun with an article.

Suffix Forms

However, **no article** stands before nominals with suffixes. The anaphoric referencing pronominal suffix adopts the function of the article (→ b, line 1: אִשְׁתּוֹ "his wife").

Proper Nouns

Proper nouns, which are only used when the bearer of the **name** is **well-known** to the hearer, always assume previous information. For that reason they still do not need additionally an article.[11]

Construct-Chains

Because of the **close connection** of nominals which stand in a construct-connection, the article before the last noun does the back-referencing for the preceding nominals.

---

10 Of such a one, we are in the habit in German to stress an article related to a relative clause. For that reason "*die*" would be emphasized through italic type. → also in the text of the last paragraph: "*die* Vorkenntnisse, die…".

11 The use of the article in the case of proper names is however not uniform. On the one hand, names of things and creatures, which it only gives once, without an article are treated as proper names (יָרֵחַ "the moon," שֶׁמֶשׁ "the sun"); on the other hand, above all geographic names are revealed through the article as "the well-known place" (e.g. נֶגֶב "south" compared to הַנֶּגֶב "the—well-known—Southland"). Some names, such as הַיַּרְדֵּן or הָעַי (Gen 13:3) always stand with an article.

For that reason, nominals in the construct state before proper names and before suffix-forms also take **no article**; however, its German equivalent does (→ above a, last line: כִּדְבַר אֱלִישָׁע "according to the word of Elisha").

Indeterminate Nominals

Nominals, with which a **reference** to previous information **is lacking**, signal to the hearer/reader some **new information** that is important for the progress of the communication act. In German, the kataphoric, so-called "**indefinite**" article stands for it (→ § 52.6).

In the narrative from 2Kg 2:19–22 (→ above text a), the nominals without an article are **keywords**, which are **important** for the narrative. From these one can reconstruct the history again: טוֹב "good"—רֹאֶה "one, who sees," רָעִים "unhealthy," מָוֶת וּמְשַׁכָּלֶת "causing a miscarriage," צְלֹחִית חֲדָשָׁה "a new cup," מֶלַח "salt," מָוֶת וּמְשַׁכָּלֶת "death and miscarriage."

Such "indeterminate"[12] nominals appear above all as predicates in nominal clauses, where they impart some new information at the time (→ § 44.3).

In **poetry**, which has an even more relaxed semantic and syntactical structure, the article is used a great deal more **sparingly** than in prose, in part probably also on metrical grounds.

Special Features

הָלוֹךְ הָלְכוּ הָעֵצִים לִמְשֹׁחַ עֲלֵיהֶם מֶלֶךְ	c	Once the trees went forth to anoint a king over them. And
וַיֹּאמְרוּ לַזַּיִת מָלְכָה עָלֵינוּ:		they said to the olive tree, "Reign over us!"
(Judges 9:8)		
וַיְדַבֵּר שְׁמוּאֵל אֶל־הָעָם אֵת מִשְׁפַּט הַמְּלֻ־	d	So Samuel told the people the ordinances of the kingdom; then
כָה וַיִּכְתֹּב בַּסֵּפֶר וַיַּנַּח לִפְנֵי יְהוָה		he wrote it in a book and placed it before YHWH.
(1 Samuel 10:25)		

---

12 On the problem of the term "determination" → § 44.3, note.

וַתִּקַּח יָעֵל אֵשֶׁת־חֶבֶר אֶת־יְתַד הָאֹהֶל _____ וַתָּשֶׂם אֶת־הַמַּקֶּבֶת בְּיָדָהּ וַתָּבוֹא אֵלָיו _____ בַּלָּאט וַתִּתְקַע אֶת־הַיָּתֵד בְּרַקָּתוֹ וַתִּצְנַח ___ ___ בָּאָרֶץ (Judges 4:21)	e	Then Jael, Heber's wife, took a tent peg, then seized a hammer in her hand, and went secretly to him (in the secret) and drove the peg into his temple, that it went through into the ground.
וַיְהִי הַיּוֹם וַיֹּאמֶר יוֹנָתָן בֶּן־שָׁאוּל אֶל־ הַנַּעַר נֹשֵׂא כֵלָיו לְכָה וְנַעְבְּרָה אֶל־ מַצַּב פְּלִשְׁתִּים אֲשֶׁר מֵעֵבֶר הַלָּז (1 Samuel 14:1)	f	(And it came about on the day) One day Jonathan, the son of Saul, said to the young man who was carrying his armor, "Up! Let us cross over to the Philistines' garrison that is on the other side!"
וְדָוִד הוּא הַקָּטָן וּשְׁלֹשָׁה הַגְּדֹלִים הָלְכוּ אַחֲרֵי שָׁאוּל: (1 Samuel 17:14)	g	But David was the youngest, while the three oldest followed Saul (into the war).

Knowledge of the Subject and Knowledge of Language

The article refers in Hebrew very frequently to general knowledge of things and language as in German.

As in German the article is used in particular literary genres [*Gattungen*], e.g. the **fable** (c), where the **actors** ("the trees," "the olive-tree") appear as **types**.

Frequently, as in German where one sits also "**on the table**" or rides "**with the car**," one finds in Hebrew expressions such as (d): כָּתַב בַּסֵּפֶר "writing in a book": back-reference to general knowledge of language plus sheer reference to the verb "write."

Conspicuous is the use of the article in text example e: The article in בָּאָרֶץ "in **the** land" and in בַּלָּט "in **the** secret" is also according to a German linguistic mind a reference to **general** previous knowledge. It is different with the first occurrence of הַיָּתֵד "the stake" and with הַמַּקֶּבֶת "the hammer." We judge in German the view of the—important for the complete information—up-to-now unmentioned concrete **individual thing** and set for that reason no anaphoric, rather the kataphoric "indefinite" article.

Peculiar is the use of the article in the expression: וַיְהִי הַיּוֹם "**one** day" (f). Obviously here the article is used kataphorically (in a similar way to אֲשֶׁר): "the day, on which I was telling in the following" (on introductions to narratives → § 54).

An individual can be set apart out of a group through an **adjective** with an article. For it we can use in German translation the **superlative** (g).

52.6 Forward (Kataphoric) Referencing Elements

What Gives the New?

Less frequent than the elements referring backward (anaphoric) or pointing to the situation (deictic) are such words that refer forward (kataphoric) to **consequences** in the text and thus align the **attention** of the hearer with the new.[13]

וְכִי־יִשְׁאָלְךָ הָעָם הַזֶּה אוֹ־הַנָּבִיא אוֹ־כֹהֵן a לֵאמֹר מַה־מַשָּׂא יְהוָה ← ← וְאָמַרְתָּ אֲלֵיהֶם אֶת־מַה־מַשָּׂא [13] וְנָטַשְׁתִּי אֶתְכֶם נְאֻם־יְהוָה: וְהַנָּבִיא וְהַכֹּהֵן וְהָעָם אֲשֶׁר יֹאמַר מַשָּׂא יְהוָה וּפָקַדְתִּי עַל־הָאִישׁ הַהוּא וְעַל־בֵּיתוֹ: כֹּה תֹאמְרוּ אִישׁ עַל־רֵעֵהוּ וְאִישׁ ← אֶל־אָחִיו מֶה־עָנָה יְהוָה ← וּמַה־דִּבֶּר יְהוָה: ← (Jer 23:33–35)	"But when they ask you—this people of the prophet or priest—as follows, '<u>What</u> is the oracle of YHWH?' then you shall say to them, 'You are the oracle.' YHWH declares, 'Thus I will abandon you.' "But the prophet and the priest and the people—who say, 'The oracle of YHWH,' who I will strike—this man and his house. <u>Thus</u> you shall say (each to his friend and each to his brother) to one another, '<u>What</u> has Yhwh answered?' and, '<u>What</u> has Yhwh spoken?'"

Adverbs

Adverbs such as כֹּה "**thus**" and the adverbially used infinitive of אמר with ל, לֵאמֹר "**as follows:/ namely:**" refer kataphorically.

---

13 Ed. note: Schneider is reading here the alternate reading witnessed to by the LXX and Vulgate.

Questions

Interrogative words (מַה "what?" מִי "who?" אֵי "where?" etc.) also refer to consequences. They declare particular **previous information insufficient** and demand, as an answer, a narrative.

"Indefinite" Pronominals

וְשַׂמְתִּי אֶת־זַרְעֲךָ כַּעֲפַר הָאָרֶץ אֲשֶׁר אִם־ יוּכַל אִישׁ לִמְנוֹת אֶת־עֲפַר הָאָרֶץ ‎——‎ גַּם־זַרְעֲךָ יִמָּנֶה: (Genesis 13:16)	b	Then I will make your descendants as the dust of the earth, so that if anyone can number the dust of the earth, then your descendants can also be numbered.
אִישׁ אִמּוֹ וְאָבִיו תִּירָאוּ וְאֶת־שַׁבְּתֹתַי תִּשְׁמֹרוּ ‎——‎ אֲנִי יְהוָה אֱלֹהֵיכֶם: (Leviticus 19:3)	c	Every one of you shall reverence his mother and his father, and you shall keep My Sabbaths.
הִנֵּה לֹא־יַעֲשֶׂה אָבִי דָּבָר גָּדוֹל אוֹ דָבָר ‎——‎ ‎——‎ קָטֹן וְלֹא יִגְלֶה אֶת־אָזְנִי (1 Samuel 20:2)	d	Know! My father does nothing either great or small without disclosing it to me.
כִּי־יִתֵּן אִישׁ אֶל־רֵעֵהוּ כֶּסֶף אוֹ־כֵלִים ‎——‎ לִשְׁמֹר וְגֻנַּב מִבֵּית הָאִישׁ אִם־יִמָּצֵא הַגַּנָּב יְשַׁלֵּם שְׁנָיִם: (Exodus 22:6)	e	If a man gives his neighbor money or goods to keep *for him* and it is stolen from the man's house—if the thief is caught, he shall pay double.
וַיַּעַל נָחָשׁ הָעַמּוֹנִי וַיִּחַן עַל־יָבֵשׁ גִּלְעָד וַיֹּאמְרוּ כָּל־אַנְשֵׁי יָבֵישׁ אֶל־נָחָשׁ כְּרָת־לָנוּ בְרִית וְנַעַבְדֶךָ: וַיֹּאמֶר אֲלֵיהֶם נָחָשׁ הָעַמּוֹנִי בְּזֹאת ← אֶכְרֹת לָכֶם בִּנְקוֹר לָכֶם כָּל־עֵין יָמִין וְשַׂמְתִּיהָ חֶרְפָּה עַל־כָּל־יִשְׂרָאֵל: → (1 Samuel 11:1–2)	f	Nahash the Ammonite came up and besieged Jabesh in Gilead. And all the men of Jabesh said to Nahash: "Make a covenant with us, then we will serve you." But Nahash the Ammonite said to them: "I will make it with you on this condition, that I will gouge out the right eye of every one of you and bring this as a reproach on Israel."

אִישׁ, דָּבָר etc.

Hebrew does not have "**indefinite**" articles (such as "a/an") and "indefinite" pronouns (such as "something/someone"). Instead words with a very **wide range of meaning** such as דָּבָר "thing," אֶחָד "one," נֶפֶשׁ "living thing," אִישׁ "man," et al., are used

With an article these words would again receive a special noun (anaphoric). **Without an article** they give—basic to their generality—no new, important information, rather open a **framework of information** that is filled in the progress of the text with new, concrete information. For German **translation** the kataphoric pronoun is at one's disposal. Thus, אִישׁ can be expressed with "someone" (b) or "each" (c), דָּבָר with "something" (d), in negative clauses appropriately with "nothing" or "not."

The combination אִישׁ ... רֵעֵהוּ or אִישׁ ... אָחִיו "one … another" is used forward referencing (e); in connection to the plural of a verb however also back referencing (→ above, text example a: "**each other**").

זֶה

Also זֶה (זֹאת, אֵלֶּה) can appear as a **forward** (kataphoric) referencing element (f). A condition for the right view of the direction of reference is on the one hand the fault of concrete elements of relation in the back **context** or in the **speech situation**, on the other hand accent of clause and **use of voice**, which the text cannot portray.

52.7 Analysis of a Text

Signs that show the referencing elements and their direction of reference are here added to the text of Judges 17:1–5 (→ above on § 52.3). It denotes: → anaphoric, ↓ deictic, ← kataphoric elements, === indeterminate nominals.

וַיְהִי־אִישׁ מֵהַר־אֶפְרָיִם וּשְׁמוֹ מִיכָיְהוּ׃
        →   ←

וַיֹּאמֶר לְאִמּוֹ אֶלֶף וּמֵאָה הַכֶּסֶף אֲשֶׁר לֻקַּח־לָךְ↓ וְאַתְּ↓ אָלִית↓ וְגַם אָמַרְתְּ↓ בְּאָזְנַי↓
        —————— → ← ======= →
הִנֵּה↓־הַכֶּסֶף אִתִּי↓ אֲנִי↓ לְקַחְתִּיו↓ וְעַתָּה↓ וַאֲשִׁיבֶנּוּ↓ לָךְ↓׃
      →   →   →

וַתֹּאמֶר אִמּוֹ בָּרוּךְ בְּנִי↓ לַיהוָה׃
     === →

וַיָּשֶׁב אֶת־אֶלֶף־וּמֵאָה הַכֶּסֶף לְאִמּוֹ וַתֹּאמֶר אִמּוֹ הַקְדֵּשׁ הִקְדַּשְׁתִּי↓ אֶת־הַכֶּסֶף
   →   →   → ————— →
לַיהוָה מִיָּדִי↓ לִבְנִי↓ לַעֲשׂוֹת פֶּסֶל וּמַסֵּכָה׃
      =========

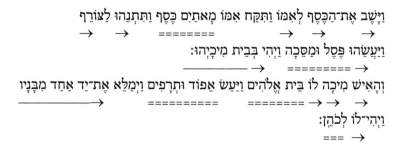

53 Orientation in the Meaning Structure of Texts—Organizing Particles

53.1 The Conjunction וְ (Waw copulativum)

The conjunction וְ is specified the least in its meaning. It has a great deal more range of meaning than German "und" [or the English "and"].

וַיִּקַּח אַבְרָם וְנָחוֹר לָהֶם נָשִׁים שֵׁם אֵשֶׁת־אַבְרָם שָׂרָי וְשֵׁם אֵשֶׁת־נָחוֹר מִלְכָּה (Genesis 11:29)	a	And Abram and Nahor took wives for themselves: Abram's wife was named Sarai; <u>and</u> Nahor's wife was named Milcah.
וְדָוִד הוּא הַקָּטָן וּשְׁלֹשָׁה הַגְּדֹלִים הָלְכוּ אַחֲרֵי שָׁאוּל׃ (1 Samuel 17:14)	b	(&) David—he was the youngest (&) the three oldest—they followed Saul. <u>But</u> David was the youngest, <u>while</u> the three oldest followed Saul.

Just like the German "und," וְ can also connect parts of a text (words, groups of words, clauses) **in the same way** of simply **stringing** together.

However, most of the time, the further range of meaning of וְ is considered, above all when the statements connected through וְ are **not of the same kind** (b) or stand entirely in **contrast** to one another. Particularly between clauses, the meaning of וְ must be determined from the **content** of the clauses.

Rule of Thumb

As a rule of thumb, the following is valid: וְ **binds before a verb**; וְ **separates before a non-verb**.

Waw before Nominal Clauses

The unspecified combination through וְ is common above all then when **nominal clauses** are embedded in a structure of **verbal clauses**.

וַיִּבְרַח אֲדַד הוּא וַאֲנָשִׁים אֲדֹמִיִּים מֵעַבְדֵי אָבִיו וַהֲדַד נַעַר קָטָן ... ׃	c	Then Hadad fled to Egypt (VC), he and certain Edomites of his father's servants ... (&) Hadad was a young boy (NC) ... when Hadad was still a young boy.
(1 Kings 11:17)		

וַיָּבֹאוּ בֵית־אִשָּׁה זוֹנָה וּשְׁמָהּ רָחָב וַיִּשְׁכְּבוּ־שָׁמָּה: (Joshua 2:1)	d	And they … came into the house of a harlot (VC), (&) her name was Rahab (NC) [named Rahab], and lodged there.
הָבָה־לָּנוּ עֶזְרָת מִצָּר וְשָׁוְא תְּשׁוּעַת אָדָם: (Psalm 60:13)	e	Give us help against the adversary! (&) For deliverance by man is in vain.
כֵּן דְּעֶה חָכְמָה לְנַפְשֶׁךָ אִם־מָצָאתָ וְיֵשׁ אַחֲרִית וְתִקְוָתְךָ לֹא תִכָּרֵת: (Proverbs 24:14)	f	Thus is knowledge, it is wisdom for your soul; If you find it (VC), [& then] there will be a future, and your hope will not be cut off.

Temporal Background

Please note again the syntactical function (→ § 44) and the **content** relationship of the verbal clauses and nominal clauses to one another: The nominal clause, as a background clause, can describe a state of being, which existed **before** or **during** the action (c). It is translated in German with "während/als/nachdem."

Description

The nominal clause can make some clarifying statement about **persons** or **things** of the leading clause (d). It is translated in German with "wie/als" or as a relative clause.

Commentary

The nominal clause can contain a **reason** (e) or also (rarely) contain a **result**, above all to a preceding "if"-clause (f). In German, the former is translated with "denn/weil" and the latter with "so/dann/dass."

Waw before Verbal Clauses

לֶךְ־לְךָ מֵאַרְצְךָ …	g	Go, you, from your land …
וְאֶעֶשְׂךָ לְגוֹי גָּדוֹל		thus (<u>then</u>/that) I will make you a great nation,
וַאֲבָרֶכְךָ וַאֲגַדְּלָה שְׁמֶךָ		and I will bless you, and make your name great;
וֶהְיֵה בְּרָכָה: (Genesis 12:1–2)		<u>so that</u> you shall be a blessing;

לֹא אִישׁ אֵל וִיכַזֵּב	h God is not a man, <u>that</u> He should lie,
וּבֶן־אָדָם וְיִתְנֶחָם	nor a son of man, <u>that</u> He should repent (of some-
הַהוּא אָמַר וְלֹא יַעֲשֶׂה	thing);
וְדִבֶּר וְלֹא יְקִימֶנָּה:	has He spoken, without <u>which</u> He acts, or has He
(Numbers 23:19)	spoken, without <u>which</u> He will not make it good?

Final or Consecutive

The concluding function of the element waw as a tense sign (in perfect consecutive and imperfect consecutive) has been discussed in § 48. The **concluding** function of the element waw appears also before verbal clauses with **imperfect** or **imperative**, above all after subjectively particular front clauses with a **demand** (g), **question**, or **negation** (h). In these cases the final remark connected with waw has a consecutive or final sense (German: "dass/so dass/damit").

53.2 The Introductory Formulas וַיְהִי and וְהָיָה

These verb forms stand as introductory formulas when a (mostly temporal) adverbial qualification or an adverbial clause begins with a "main clause." Most of the time, the "main clause" begins with the same tense (imperfect consecutive or perfect consecutive) or with a waw copulative.

וַיְהִי כַּאֲשֶׁר הִקְרִיב לָבוֹא מִצְרָיְמָה	a (And it came about) When he came
וַיֹּאמֶר אֶל־שָׂרַי אִשְׁתּוֹ הִנֵּה־נָא יָדַעְתִּי	near to Egypt, he said to Sarai his
כִּי אִשָּׁה יְפַת־מַרְאֶה אָתְּ:	wife, "See now, I know that you are
וְהָיָה כִּי־יִרְאוּ אֹתָךְ הַמִּצְרִים וְאָמְרוּ	a beautiful woman; (Thus it will be
אִשְׁתּוֹ זֹאת וְהָרְגוּ אֹתִי וְאֹתָךְ יְחַיּוּ:	that) When the Egyptians see you,
אִמְרִי־נָא אֲחֹתִי אָתְּ ...	they will say, 'This is his wife'; and
וַיְהִי כְּבוֹא אַבְרָם מִצְרָיְמָה	they will kill me, but they will let
וַיִּרְאוּ הַמִּצְרִים אֶת־הָאִשָּׁה כִּי־יָפָה	you live. Please say that you are my
הִיא מְאֹד:	sister …."
	(And it came about in their coming)
(Genesis 12:11–14)	When Abram came into Egypt, the
	Egyptians saw that the woman was
	very beautiful.

וַיְהִי אַחַר הַדְּבָרִים הָאֵלֶּה	b (And it came about) After these
וְהָאֱלֹהִים נִסָּה אֶת־אַבְרָהָם	things—(&) God tested Abraham—
וַיֹּאמֶר ...	then he said: …
(Genesis 22:1)	

וַיְהִי הֵם יֹשְׁבִים אֶל־הַשֻּׁלְחָן	c	(And it came about: They were sitting
וַיְהִי דְּבַר־יְהוָה אֶל־הַנָּבִיא		at the table) When they were sitting at
(1 Kings 13:20)		the table, the word of YHWH came to
		the prophet

Expression of Time

In narration context, an expression of time very often stands after an introductory וַיְהִי. Some such expressions of time that are put forward can be formulated as follows:

as a subordinate clause (a, first line),
as an infinitive with a preposition (a, antepenultimate line)—mostly with בְּ or כְּ,
as groups of nominals with a preposition (b), or
as a nominal clause (c).

If after the וַיְהִי the narration does not continue with an imperfect consecutive but rather e.g. (as in text b) with a nominal clause, the actual narrative level is still not reached. These must begin with an imperfect consecutive (→ § 54.2).

וְהָיָה

וְהָיָה כִּי־תָבוֹא אֶל־הָאָרֶץ אֲשֶׁר יְהוָה	d	(Thus it will be) when you enter
אֱלֹהֶיךָ נֹתֵן לְךָ נַחֲלָה		the land which Yahweh your God
וִירִשְׁתָּהּ וְיָשַׁבְתָּ בָּהּ:		gives you as an inheritance, <u>and</u> you
וְלָקַחְתָּ מֵרֵאשִׁית כָּל־פְּרִי הָאֲדָמָה ...		possess it <u>and</u> live in it, <u>then</u> you
(Deuteronomy 26:1–2)		shall take some of the first of all the
		produce of the ground …
וְהָיָה בַּיּוֹם הַהוּא	e	(Thus it will be) in that day—the
שֹׁרֶשׁ יִשַׁי אֲשֶׁר עֹמֵד לְנֵס עַמִּים		root of Jesse, who stands as a signal
אֵלָיו גּוֹיִם יִדְרֹשׁוּ		for the peoples, to him the nations
וְהָיְתָה מְנֻחָתוֹ כָּבוֹד:		will resort—then His resting place
(Isaiah 11:10)		will be glorious.

Before "if"-Clauses

In dialogue parts of narrative and in other discourse texts the וְהָיָה-introduction occurs. It can stand before a **conditional clause** with אִם or כִּי that is placed first or before a **temporal** "if"-clause (a, line 4 and d).

Where Does the "Main Clause" Begin?

As a rule, after an initial clause with וְהָיָה, the **final remark** begins with a **perfect consecutive** (a). This is not always the first perfect consecutive that appears (d). Where the final remark begins must emerge from the content of the clauses. There can also appear verbal clauses with imperfect or imperative as "main clauses." A **nominal clause**—with or without waw—belongs as a rule still to the **front** and not to the "main clause" (e).

In prophetic texts, particularly in Isaiah 1–39, along with Jeremiah and Zechariah, one often finds the introductory formula וְהָיָה בַּיּוֹם הַהוּא "Thus it will come about in that day" (e).

On the text-organizing function of this formula as a macrosyntactical sign → § 54.

53.3 The Particle כִּי

*כִּי draws attention **strongly** to a fact; this is the basic function.*

Fundamental Meaning: "Yes/In Truth"

וַיִּקְרָא אֲבִימֶלֶךְ לְיִצְחָק וַיֹּאמֶר אַךְ הִנֵּה אִשְׁתְּךָ הִוא וְאֵיךְ אָמַרְתָּ אֲחֹתִי הִוא וַיֹּאמֶר אֵלָיו יִצְחָק כִּי אָמַרְתִּי פֶּן־אָמוּת עָלֶיהָ׃ (Genesis 26:9)	a	Then Abimelech called Isaac and said, "Behold, certainly she is your wife! How then did you say, 'She is my sister'?" And Isaac said to him, "<u>Yes</u> I said, 'I might die on account of her.'"
וַתְּכַחֵשׁ שָׂרָה לֵאמֹר לֹא צָחַקְתִּי כִּי יָרֵאָה וַיֹּאמֶר לֹא כִּי צָחָקְתְּ׃ (Genesis 18:15)	b	Sarah denied *it* however, saying, "I did not laugh"; <u>for</u> she was afraid. And He said, "No, <u>but</u> you did laugh."
וַיֹּאמֶר הִנֶּה נָּא־אֲדֹנַי סוּרוּ נָא אֶל־בֵּית עַבְדְּכֶם ... וַיֹּאמְרוּ לֹּא כִּי בָרְחוֹב נָלִין׃ (Genesis 19:2)	c	And he said, "Now behold, my lords, please turn aside into your servant's house, and spend the night ...." They said, "No, <u>rather</u> we shall spend the night in the square."
וַתֹּאמַרְנָה־לָהּ כִּי־אִתָּךְ נָשׁוּב לְעַמֵּךְ׃ (Ruth 1:10)	d	And they said to her, "<u>In truth</u>! We will return with you to your people."

וַיֹּאמֶר [דָּוִד] אֶל־נָתָן חַי־יְהוָה	e	And he said to Nathan, "As Yahweh
כִּי בֶן־מָוֶת הָאִישׁ הָעֹשֶׂה זֹאת:		lives—In truth! The man who has
(2 Samuel 12:5)		done this deserves to die."

When כִּי stands after a **negative** clause (b, c), one uses in German translation an adversative particle "doch/sondern." On the first כִּי in text example b → below on h.

As a strengthening particle, כִּי can introduce a word-for-word speech (d).

Oath Clause

Also in the **oath clause** (e), כִּי serves to strengthen. (For the oath clause with אִם → § 53.5.)

Subject Clauses and Object Clauses

וַיֹּאמֶר יְהוּדָה אֶל־אֶחָיו מַה־בֶּצַע כִּי	f	Judah said to his brothers, "What profit is
נַהֲרֹג אֶת־אָחִינוּ		it that we kill our brother?"
(Genesis 37:26)		
וַיַּרְא אֱלֹהִים כִּי־טוֹב:	g	And God saw: Yes, it was good [= that it
(Genesis 1:10)		was good].

When the final remark begun with כִּי is understood as subject (f) or object (g) for the initial clause, כִּי can be regarded as a **conjunction** and be represented in German with a dependent "**Dass**"-clause.

Adverbial Clauses

וַיֹּאמֶר יְהוָֹה אֱלֹהִים אֶל־הַנָּחָשׁ	h	YHWH God said to the serpent, "(Yes,
כִּי עָשִׂיתָ זֹּאת אָרוּר אַתָּה		you have done this) Because you have done
(Genesis 3:14)		this, you are cursed."
חָנֵּנִי יְהוָה כִּי אֻמְלַל אָנִי	i	Be gracious to me, YHWH (yes, I am sad-
(Psalm 6:3)		dened) for I am saddened.
כִּי נַעַר יִשְׂרָאֵל וָאֹהֲבֵהוּ	j	(Yes, Israel was a youth) When Israel was a
(Hosea 11:1)		youth I loved him.
כִּי תִקְנֶה עֶבֶד עִבְרִי שֵׁשׁ שָׁנִים	k	If you buy a Hebrew slave, he shall serve
יַעֲבֹד		for six years.
(Exodus 21:2)		

The fact to which the כִּי points can serve as an **adverbial** explanation, and as a result the **content** of the כִּי-clause should be examined as to whether it (1) gives a reason, (2) makes an expression of time, or (3) introduces a condition.

Reason

The כִּי-clause can contain a reason (b, h, i) (German: **causal clause** with "da/weil" or clause with "denn")—such a כִּי-clause can also stand in front (h).

Expression of Time
Condition

The כִּי-clause can also make an expression of time (j) or introduce a condition (k). In German, the former is translated with a **temporal clause** with "wenn/als/nachdem"; the latter with a **conditional clause** with "falls/wenn."

As an initial understanding of the context, the fundamental meaning is always applicable: reinforcement ("ja/fürwahr/so ist's").

53.4 *The Particle* אֲשֶׁר

אֲשֶׁר *draws attention to a **fact** which stands in very **close connection** with the preceding (German: "nämlich, dass/die Tatsache, dass/wie").*

Fundamental Function: "The Fact That"

וְדִבַּרְתִּי מִשְׁפָּטַי אוֹתָם עַל כָּל־רָעָתָם	a	And I will pronounce My judgments on them concerning all their wickedness, <u>namely, that</u> they have forsaken Me and have offered sacrifices to other gods,
אֲשֶׁר עֲזָבוּנִי וַיְקַטְּרוּ לֵאלֹהִים אֲחֵרִים		
(Jereremiah 1:16)		

For that reason אֲשֶׁר stands almost exclusively **in sentence final position (*Nachsatz*)**. When the אֲשֶׁר-clause precedes the "main clause" (→ below text example k), then this is probably an **expansion** of the use in cases in which otherwise it was performed by another conjunction (כִּי or אִם).

Relative Clause

זֹאת הָרָעָה | אֲשֶׁר | עָשָׂה הֲדָד	b	This is the evil / אֲשֶׁר / Hadad has done it.
(1 Kings 11:25)		= This is the evil <u>that</u> Hadad did.
וַיֵּלֶךְ...	c	And he went ...
עַד־הַמָּקוֹם | אֲשֶׁר־ | הָיָה שָׁם אָהֳלֹה		to the place / אֲשֶׁר / his tent was there.
→ ←		= He went to the place <u>where</u> his tent was.
(Genesis 13:3)		

The most frequent use of אֲשֶׁר is for **relative clauses**. At the same time, אֲשֶׁר is not a relative pronoun. It shows the connection of two clauses, but does not describe it; it **does not** directly **refer back** to a noun as in German. The clause following after אֲשֶׁר is fundamentally regarded as an **independent** clause. An אֲשֶׁר-clause as an explanation (attribute) to a noun of the clause coming before is expressed through a German relative clause. In the **normal case** the German relative pronoun takes the place of the אֲשֶׁר (b).

In the attributive clause, the antecedent can be **referred back to** through an adverb, a **pronoun**, or a **suffix** (c: שָׁם referring back to הַמָּקוֹם). Then the back-reference must be started in German translation with the relative and should **not** appear **twice**.

The relative שֶׁ (→ § 13.2) can also be used in the same way as אֲשֶׁר.

אֲשֶׁר with Prepositions

אֵינֶנּוּ גָדוֹל בַּבַּיִת הַזֶּה מִמֶּנִּי וְלֹא־חָשַׂךְ מִמֶּנִּי מְאוּמָה כִּי אִם־אוֹתָךְ בַּאֲשֶׁר אַתְּ־אִשְׁתּוֹ (Genesis 39:9)	d	There is no one greater in this house than I, and he has withheld nothing from me except you, [due to the fact that] <u>because</u> you are his wife.
וַיְהִי כַּאֲשֶׁר הִקְרִיב לָבוֹא מִצְרָיְמָה וַיֹּאמֶר אֶל־שָׂרַי אִשְׁתּוֹ (Genesis 12:11)	e	[And it came about the fact that] <u>when</u> he came near to Egypt, he said to Sarai his wife,
וַיֹּאמְרוּ כֵּן תַּעֲשֶׂה כַּאֲשֶׁר דִּבַּרְתָּ׃ (Genesis 18:5)	f	They said, "So do, [as the fact that] <u>as</u> you have said."
מֵאֲשֶׁר יָקַרְתָּ בְעֵינַי נִכְבַּדְתָּ וַאֲנִי אֲהַבְתִּיךָ וְאֶתֵּן אָדָם תַּחְתֶּיךָ וּלְאֻמִּים תַּחַת נַפְשֶׁךָ׃ (Isaiah 43:4)	g	[From the fact that] <u>Since</u> you are precious in My sight, since you are honored and I love you, I will give other men in your place.

אֲשֶׁר is used as a conjunction through its connection with a preposition. The **meaning** of the conjunction arises from the meaning of the **preposition** (d–g).

אֲשֶׁר as a Conjunction

וַיָּמָת בֶּן־הָאִשָּׁה הַזֹּאת לָיְלָה אֲשֶׁר שָׁכְבָה עָלָיו׃ (1 Kings 3:19)	h	This woman's son died in the night, <u>because</u> she lay on him.

הִנֵּה עָשִׂיתִי כִּדְבָרֶיךָ הִנֵּה נָתַתִּי לְךָ לֵב חָכָם וְנָבוֹן אֲשֶׁר כָּמוֹךָ לֹא־הָיָה לְפָנֶיךָ וְאַחֲרֶיךָ לֹא־יָקוּם כָּמוֹךָ: (1 Kings 3:12)	i	See, I have given you a wise and discerning heart, <u>that</u> there has been no one like you before you, nor shall one like you arise after you.
וְשָׁמַרְתָּ אֶת־חֻקָּיו ... אֲשֶׁר יִיטַב לְךָ וּלְבָנֶיךָ אַחֲרֶיךָ (Deuteronomy 4:40)	j	... and you shall keep His statutes ... <u>so that</u> it may go well with you and with your children after you.

אֲשֶׁר can also be used without prepositions

as a conjunction, in particular giving reasons for (h),

as a consecutive clause (i), or

as a purpose clause (j).

וַיֹּאמֶר אֶל־בְּנֵי יִשְׂרָאֵל לֵאמֹר אֲשֶׁר יִשְׁאָלוּן בְּנֵיכֶם מָחָר אֶת־אֲבוֹתָם לֵאמֹר מָה הָאֲבָנִים הָאֵלֶּה: וְהוֹדַעְתֶּם אֶת־בְּנֵיכֶם לֵאמֹר ... (Joshua 4:21f.)	k	He said to the sons of Israel, "<u>When/If</u> your children ask their fathers in time to come, saying, 'What are these stones?' then you shall inform your children, saying ..."
וַיַּרְא שָׁאוּל אֲשֶׁר־הוּא מַשְׂכִּיל מְאֹד (1 Samuel 18:15)	l	Then Saul saw <u>that</u> he was prospering greatly.
וַיֹּאמֶר שָׁאוּל אֶל־שְׁמוּאֵל אֲשֶׁר שָׁמַעְתִּי בְּקוֹל יְהוָה וָאֵלֵךְ בַּדֶּרֶךְ אֲשֶׁר־שְׁלָחַנִי יְהוָה (1 Samuel 15:20)	m	Saul said to Samuel, "( ) I did obey the voice of YHWH, and went on the mission on which YHWH sent me ..."

Rarely—compared to כִּי—אֲשֶׁר can be used conditionally (k) (German: "wenn"), for an object clause (l) (German: "dass"), and for direct speech (m).

Rules of Thumb

Relative Clause: A helpful translation is "...**from which is valid** that."

Conjunction Clause: A helpful translation is "...whereby arises the **fact** that." From the content connection of the clause is given which German conjunction is chosen.

53.5 The Particle אִם

A prerequisite is pointed to with אִם.

Fundamental Meaning: Prerequisite

אִם־חָכַמְתָּ חָכַמְתָּ לָּךְ וְלַצְתָּ לְבַדְּךָ תִשָּׂא: (Proverbs 9:12)	a	<u>If</u> you are wise, you are wise for yourself, And if you scoff, you alone will bear it.
אִם־יוּכַל אִישׁ לִמְנוֹת אֶת־עֲפַר הָאָרֶץ גַּם־זַרְעֲךָ יִמָּנֶה: (Genesis 13:16)	b	(Assuming, someone can count the dust of the earth—also your descendants will be counted.) <u>If</u> anyone can number the dust of the earth, then your descendants can also be numbered.
אֲשֶׁר אִם־צָדַקְתִּי לֹא אֶעֱנֶה לִמְשֹׁפְטִי אֶתְחַנָּן: (Job 9:15)	c	<u>If</u> I (also) were right, I could not answer; I would have to implore the mercy of my judge.
יִשְׂרָאֵל אִם־תִּשְׁמַע־לִי: (Psalm 81:9)	d	Israel! <u>If</u> you would (only) listen to Me!

Condition

The prerequisite can be regarded as a condition (a, b) (German: "wenn"). Whether the condition is intended as **real** (a) or **unreal** (b) can only be deduced from the **context** (→ § 51).

Contrast

The prerequisite can stand in contrast (c) to the content of the following clause (**concessive**) (German "obwohl/wenn auch").

Wish Clauses and Interrogative Clauses

Finally, the prerequisite can also stand alone and be regarded as a wish (d) (German: "wenn doch/wenn nur").

A **hypothetical** prerequisite can also be considered as a **question** (e–g).

וַיִּשְׁלַח מַלְאָכִים וַיֹּאמֶר אֲלֵהֶם לְכוּ דִרְשׁוּ בְּבַעַל זְבוּב אֱלֹהֵי עֶקְרוֹן אִם־אֶחְיֶה מֵחֳלִי זֶה: (2 Kings 1:2)	e	He sent messengers and said to them, "Go, inquire of Baal-zebub, the god of Ekron, (assuming, I will...) <u>whether</u> I will recover from this sickness."

| וַיֵּלֶךְ יְהוֹשֻׁעַ אֵלָיו וַיֹּאמֶר לוֹ
הֲלָנוּ אַתָּה אִם־לְצָרֵינוּ׃
(Joshua 5:13) | f | Joshua went to him and asked him, "Are you for us? <u>or</u> for our adversaries?" |
| וַיֹּאמֶר אָנֹכִי אֲשַׁלַּח גְּדִי־עִזִּים מִן־הַצֹּאן
וַתֹּאמֶר אִם־תִּתֵּן עֵרָבוֹן עַד שָׁלְחֶךָ׃
(Genesis 38:17) | g | He said, therefore, "I will send you a young goat from the flock." She said, moreover, "Will <u>you give</u> to me a pledge until you send it?" |

It follows:

- **Indirect** interrogative clauses (e) (German: "ob"),
- אִם for the second part of a **double question** (f) (German: "oder"), and elliptical clauses, with which the first part of a double question is not articulated (g),
- אִם for a simple **direct** interrogative clause. (On the interrogative clause → also § 51.3).

Oath Clauses

| כֹּה יַעֲשֶׂה־לְּךָ אֱלֹהִים וְכֹה יוֹסִיף אִם־תְּכַחֵד
מִמֶּנִּי דָּבָר מִכָּל־הַדָּבָר אֲשֶׁר־דִּבֶּר אֵלֶיךָ׃
(1 Samuel 3:17) | h | May God do so to you, and more also, <u>if</u> you hide anything from me of all the words that He spoke to you. |

Negatively with אִם

| חֵי פַרְעֹה אִם־תֵּצְאוּ מִזֶּה
(Genesis 42:15) | i | By the life of Pharaoh, (I will be cursed if…) you shall <u>not</u> go from this place! |

A **hypothetical** prerequisite is also made in the **oath** (h). When a self-curse is **concealed** because it is regarded by itself on the speech form of the oath (i), this **elliptical** oath-clause with אִם must be regarded as a **negative** clause. A positive oath clause is introduced appropriately with אִם לֹא.

Rule of Thumb

For translation: In most cases by far, the use of אִם corresponds to German "wenn." In the cases of interrogative clauses and oath clauses, whether they are questions or oaths can be recognized at the time by other signs in the linguistic context.

54 Orientation in the Meaning Structure of Texts—Macrosyntactical Signals

Macrosyntactical signals are words and expressions with which the large structure of texts is marked.[1] *Speakers use such signals in order to make the hearer attentive to the beginning, transitions, high points, and end of the speech.*

If the spoken language (colloquial language) is actually the sphere of such a macrosyntactical sign as well, its action can still be observed also in the literarily-shaped linguistic form of the Hebrew Bible, above all in discourse contexts.

54.1 *Opening Signals and Transition Signals in Dialogue*

וְעַתָּה, וְהִנֵּה, הִנֵּה, הֵן

וַיֹּאמֶר אַבְרָם הֵן לִי לֹא נָתַתָּה זָרַע וְהִנֵּה בֶן־בֵּיתִי יוֹרֵשׁ אֹתִי: (Genesis 15:3)	a Abram said, "See, to me you have given no offspring. [And see] Thus one born in my house is now my heir."
וַיֹּאמֶר יְהוָה אֱלֹהִים הֵן הָאָדָם הָיָה כְּאַחַד מִמֶּנּוּ לָדַעַת טוֹב וָרָע וְעַתָּה פֶּן־יִשְׁלַח יָדוֹ וְלָקַח גַּם מֵעֵץ הַחַיִּים וְאָכַל וָחַי לְעֹלָם: (Genesis 3:22)	b Then YHWH God said, "(See) Now the man has even become like one of Us, so that he knows what is good and evil. (And now) But should he not also still stretch out his hand and take from the tree of life, and eat, and live forever!"
וַיֹּאמֶר [יִצְחָק] הִנֵּה־נָא זָקַנְתִּי לֹא יָדַעְתִּי יוֹם מוֹתִי: וְעַתָּה שָׂא־נָא כֵלֶיךָ תֶּלְיְךָ וְקַשְׁתֶּךָ וְצֵא הַשָּׂדֶה וְצוּדָה לִּי צָיִדה: (Genesis 27:2–3)	c He [Isaac] said, "(Yes see) Thus I know, I am old; I do not know when I must die. (And now) Now take heed! Take your gear, your quiver and your bow, go out to the field and hunt game for me!"

---

1   Such expressions in colloquial German are e.g.: "also," "so!", "also, wie gesagt," "also wissen Sie!", "nicht wahr?", "nein, wirklich!", "pass auf!"; in addition are pauses, clause accents, and use of voice.

Opening

As an opening signal, הֵן or הִנֵּה marks the **start** of the speech;[2] then וְהִנֵּה (a) or וְעַתָּה (b, c) soon leads to the **main point** of the speech. In these cases, the semantic character of a "time-adverb" is hardly still clear with עַתָּה.

וַיִּשְׁלַח מֹשֶׁה מַלְאָכִים מִקָּדֵשׁ אֶל־מֶלֶךְ אֱדוֹם כֹּה אָמַר אָחִיךָ יִשְׂרָאֵל אַתָּה יָדַעְתָּ אֵת כָּל־הַתְּלָאָה אֲשֶׁר מְצָאַ־ תְנוּ: וַיֵּרְדוּ אֲבֹתֵינוּ מִצְרַיְמָה וַנֵּשֶׁב בְּמִצְרַיִם ...וַיֹּצִאֵנוּ [יי] מִמִּצְרַיִם ... וְהִנֵּה אֲנַחְנוּ בְקָדֵשׁ עִיר קְצֵה גְבוּלֶךָ: נַעְבְּרָה־נָּא בְאַרְצֶךָ (Numbers 20:14ff.)	d	Moses sent messengers from Kadesh to the king of Edom: "Thus your brother Israel has said, 'You yourself know all the hardship that has befallen us; that our fathers went down to Egypt, and we stayed in Egypt … and [YHWH] brought us out from Egypt. … (And see) Thus: We are at Kadesh, a town on the edge of your territory. Now let us pass through your land.'"
וַיֵּצֵא הָרוּחַ וַיַּעֲמֹד לִפְנֵי יְהוָה וַיֹּאמֶר אֲנִי אֲפַתֶּנּוּ וַיֹּאמֶר יְהוָה אֵלָיו בַּמָּה: וַיֹּאמֶר אֵצֵא וְהָיִיתִי רוּחַ שֶׁקֶר בְּפִי כָּל־נְבִיאָיו וַיֹּאמֶר תְּפַתֶּה וְגַם־תּוּכָל צֵא וַעֲשֵׂה־כֵן: וְעַתָּה הִנֵּה נָתַן יְהוָה רוּחַ שֶׁקֶר בְּפִי כָּל־נְבִיאֶיךָ אֵלֶּה וַיהוָה דִּבֶּר עָלֶיךָ רָעָה: (1 Kings 22:21–23)	e	Then a spirit came forward, stood before YHWH and said, "I will entice him." YHWH said to him, "How?" He said, "I will go out and be a deceiv- ing spirit in the mouth of all his proph- ets." And He said, "You are to entice him and also prevail. Go and do so!" (And now, see) Thus, therefore, you know it: YHWH has put a deceiving spirit in the mouth of all these your prophets. And YHWH has pro- claimed disaster against you.
וַיֹּאמֶר אֲלֵהֶם יוֹסֵף אַל־תִּירָאוּ כִּי הֲתַחַת אֱלֹהִים אָנִי: וְאַתֶּם חֲשַׁבְתֶּם עָלַי רָעָה אֱלֹהִים חֲשָׁבָהּ לְטֹבָה לְמַעַן עֲשֹׂה כַּיּוֹם הַזֶּה לְהַחֲיֹת עַם־רָב: וְעַתָּה אַל־תִּירָאוּ אָנֹכִי אֲכַלְכֵּל אֶתְכֶם וְאֶת־טַפְּכֶם וַיְנַחֵם אוֹתָם וַיְדַבֵּר עַל־לִבָּם: (Genesis 50:19–21)	f	Joseph said to them: "Do not be afraid! No! Am I in God's place? Particularly: You meant evil against me; God meant it for good in order to bring about this present result, to pre- serve many people alive. Thus please! Do not be afraid! I will provide for you and your little ones." So he comforted them and spoke kindly to them.

---

2 הִנֵּה is correctly described in the lexicon by Köhler/Baumgartner, 2d edition as a "meist unter-
brechender Aufmerksamkeitserreger [usually a disrupting attention getter]"

Transition

וְהִנֵּה (like וְעַתָּה) appears as a transition signal after an **interruption** when the speech heads for its actual **goal** (d). At the same time, וְעַתָּה and וְהִנֵּה also appear **together** and at the same time, e.g. in 1 Kings 22 (e), serve to apply and to point a just concluded narrative with a particular **focus** to the **situation**. Most of the time, a request follows וְעַתָּה as an opening signal and transition signal (f, → also above, texts b and c).

The introduction formula וְהָיָה (→ § 53.2) only rarely has a macrosyntactical function. Most of the time, it serves to structure smaller units, e.g. two clauses.

שִׁמְעוּ דְבַר־יְהוָה קְצִינֵי סְדֹם	g	Hear the word of YHWH, You rulers of
הַאֲזִינוּ תּוֹרַת אֱלֹהֵינוּ עַם עֲמֹרָה:		Sodom! Give ear to the instruction of our
(Isaiah 1:10)		God, You people of Gomorrah!

The imperative of שמע stands as an appeal for attention and a genre [*Gattung*] marker for the prophetic oath (g—an example for prosaic use → § 48.6, text c).

Speech Transitions

אָז תָּבֹאנָה שְׁתַּיִם נָשִׁים זֹנוֹת אֶל־הַמֶּלֶךְ	h	Then two women who were har-
וַתַּעֲמֹדְנָה לְפָנָיו: וַתֹּאמֶר הָאִשָּׁה הָאַחַת		lots came to the king and stood
בִּי אֲדֹנִי		before him. The one woman said,
אֲנִי וְהָאִשָּׁה הַזֹּאת יֹשְׁבֹת בְּבַיִת אֶחָד וָאֵלֵד		"(Ah, my lord) <u>With permission,</u>
עִמָּהּ בַּבָּיִת:		Majesty, this woman and I live in
(1 Kings 3:16–17)		the same house; and I gave birth
		to a child while she was in the
		house."

וַיִּשְׁלַח שְׁלֹמֹה אֶל־חִירָם לֵאמֹר:	i	Solomon sent word to Hiram,
אַתָּה יָדַעְתָּ אֶת־דָּוִד אָבִי כִּי לֹא יָכֹל לִבְנוֹת		saying,
בַּיִת לְשֵׁם יְהוָה אֱלֹהָיו מִפְּנֵי הַמִּלְחָמָה אֲשֶׁר		"<u>You know (right well)</u> that
סְבָבֻהוּ עַד תֵּת־יְהוָה אֹתָם תַּחַת כַּפּוֹת רַגְלָו:		David my father was unable to
וְעַתָּה הֵנִיחַ יְהוָה אֱלֹהַי לִי מִסָּבִיב אֵין שָׂטָן		build a house for the name of
וְאֵין פֶּגַע רָע:		YHWH his God because of the
וְהִנְנִי אֹמֵר לִבְנוֹת בַּיִת לְשֵׁם יְהוָה אֱלֹהָי		wars which surrounded him, until
כַּאֲשֶׁר דִּבֶּר יְהוָה אֶל־דָּוִד אָבִי ...		YHWH put them under the soles
וְעַתָּה צַוֵּה וְיִכְרְתוּ־לִי אֲרָזִים מִן־הַלְּבָנוֹן		of his feet.
		<u>But now</u> YHWH my God has
		given me rest on every side; there
		is neither adversary nor misfor-
		tune.

(1 Kings 5:16ff.)	(And see, I) <u>Know thus</u> that I intend to build a house for the name of YHWH my God, as YHWH spoke to David my father … (And now) <u>Thus please</u>: Command that they cut for me cedars from Lebanon."

In the category of transition signals also belongs the cliché בִּי אֲדֹנִי, which opens a speech at a place of prominence and indicates the subjugation of the speaker (h).

The nominal clause (CNC), אַתָּה יָדַעְתָּ (i), can also be used as a transition signal when the speaker reaches back to some information about the state of information of the partner.

Incidentally, the section of text from 1 Kings 5 (i) shows again the use of וְהִנֵּה and וְעַתָּה as opening signals. In line 6 (… וְעַתָּה הָנִיחַ) on the other hand, וְעַתָּה still appears to have more of the character of an adverb of time.

54.2 Beginnings of Narratives

There are four types of narrative openings in biblical Hebrew:

וַיֵּלֶךְ אִישׁ מִבֵּית לֵוִי וַיִּקַּח אֶת־בַּת־לֵוִי: וַתַּהַר הָאִשָּׁה וַתֵּלֶד בֵּן … (Exodus 2:1f.)	a	A man from the house of Levi went and he married a daughter of Levi. And the woman conceived and she bore a son …
וּמֹשֶׁה הָיָה רֹעֶה אֶת־צֹאן יִתְרוֹ … וַיִּנְהַג אֶת־הַצֹּאן אַחַר הַמִּדְבָּר וַיָּבֹא אֶל־הַר הָאֱלֹהִים חֹרֵבָה: (Exodus 3:1)	b	(&) Moses was pasturing the flock of his father-in-law … He led the flock to the west side of the wilderness and came to Horeb, the mountain of God.
בָּעֵת הַהִיא חָלָה אֲבִיָּה בֶן־יָרָבְעָם: וַיֹּאמֶר יָרָבְעָם לְאִשְׁתּוֹ… (1 Kings 14:1f.)	c	At that time Abijah the son of Jeroboam became sick. (As at the time [once] Abijah, the son of Jeroboam became sick) Then Jeroboam said to his wife: …
וַיְהִי בָּעֵת הַהִוא וַיֵּרֶד יְהוּדָה מֵאֵת אֶחָיו וַיֵּט עַד־אִישׁ עֲדֻלָּמִי וּשְׁמוֹ חִירָה: (Genesis 38:1)	d	(And it came about) At that time, Judah departed from his brothers and visited a certain Adullamite, whose name was Hirah…

> וַיְהִי מִיָּמִים רַבִּים אַחֲרֵי אֲשֶׁר־הֵנִיחַ e
> יְהוָה לְיִשְׂרָאֵל מִכָּל־אֹיְבֵיהֶם מִסָּבִיב
> וִיהוֹשֻׁעַ זָקֵן בָּא בַּיָּמִים:
> וַיִּקְרָא יְהוֹשֻׁעַ לְכָל־יִשְׂרָאֵל
> (Joshua 23:1f.)
>
> (And it came about) After a long time, after YHWH had given rest to Israel from all their enemies on every side— but Joshua was old and advanced in years—Joshua called for all Israel…

1.   Right into the Middle

1st type: וַיֵּלֶךְ אִישׁ   or: Ø—Narrativ—Narrativ … (a)

The narrative comes directly to the point without introductory remarks. A **change** in the situation of the force of action is a condition, but it is not marked. For the most part there are **indications of place**; never expressions of time. The **first verbs** are frequently verbs of change in place or verbs of communication (as e.g. אמר or דבר).

2.   Background

2nd type: וּמֹשֶׁה הָיָה   or: Waw—{C}NC—Narrativ … (b)[3]

The (simple or compound) nominal clause **marks** the **change** in the situation of the force of action and describes a person or **background relationships**. At the same time, an introductory **waw** is **obligatory**. The main action of the narrative begins with the imperfect consecutive, which is normally first. Expressions of time do not occur.

3.   At the time …

3rd type: בָּעֵת הַהִיא חָלָה אֲבִיָּה   or: expression of time—perfect-X— Narrativ … (c)[4]

An identification of time opens. Then in the verbal clause with a perfect predicate a **first step** is made into the narrative: a **previous action**, which is placed before or placed under the main narrative strand. Then this begins first with an imperfect consecutive.

4.   And it happened …

4th type: וַיְהִי בָּעֵת הַהוּא   or: וַיְהִי—expression of time—{X}—Narrativ … (d)

---

3   Brackets mean that the element is not obligatory.
4   "X" means: "some linguistic sign." To type 3 belongs incidentally also the beginning of Gen 1: בְּרֵאשִׁית בָּרָא אֱלֹהִים … וַיֹּאמֶר אֱלֹהִים.

This is the best-known pattern:[5] "It happened however at the time." Through וַיְהִי and an expression of time that is for the most part very **vague**, the beginning and situation of time are marked. The imperfect consecutive—most of the time the first one—begins the actual narrative. A **change** in the situation of the force of action is obligatory, but it remains unmarked. Indications of place are rare.

Between the narrative-starting signal וַיְהִי and the imperfect consecutive actually beginning the narrative after an expression of time, a {C}NC or perfect-X can still be **inserted** and can introduce the functions of type 2 and type 3 (e). Different complex **introduction-structures** can be formed through combination of the different syntactical **patterns**.

Occasionally, entirely other opening signals also appear, as e.g. אָז in 1Kg 3:16 (→ § 48.5 and § 54.1, text example h) or a *figura etymologica* with the infinitive absolute (→ § 52.5 on Judg 9:8).

The beginnings often mentioned in this context from Job 1:1 (0—CNC—Narrativ) and from Is 6:1 (expression of time—0—Narrativ) are at the time unique and **not typical**.[6]

54.3 Transition Signals in Narratives

וַיְהִי as a Transition Signal

Apart from the beginning of a narrative, וַיְהִי can also appear as a transition signal **inside** a narrative. An example is the episode of Joseph and Potiphar's wife in Gen 39:[7] After a return to chapter 37 and the introduction of the situation of place and situation of person (vv. 1–6),[8] the **entry** into the narrative is marked in v. 7 with וַיְהִי אַחַר הַדְּבָרִים הָאֵלֶּה. At the same time, the wife of Potiphar is introduced as a new person and is tied to the conflict. With וַיְהִי כְּהַיּוֹם הַזֶּה (v. 11), the **high point** of the narrative is announced (v. 12). Then there follows still more cases of וַיְהִי with infinitives, which however do not serve the larger structure of the text, rather present **temporal clauses**, which structure small parts of text-parts: "As she saw," "as he heard," "as I raise my voice," "as his lord hears." Only the next chapter, ch. 40, begins in turn with וַיְהִי אַחַר הַדְּבָרִים הָאֵלֶּה and therefore signals a **new beginning**.

---

5   It is also the most frequent; more than a third of all narratives begin this way.
6   A detailed discussion of the narrative beginning appears in my essay: "Und es begab sich …" in the journal *Biblische Notizen*, 70 (1993): 62–87.
7   It cannot here be quoted in full.
8   The verb form וַיְהִי occurs in the first verse some 6x, however as a simple predicate in clauses about Joseph's life-relationships only once for a subordinate temporal clause.

It appears here that the expressions of time after וַיְהִי are all so vague that the level of structure is higher; the more specific they are, the more narrow is its area of influence.

וְהִנֵּה as a Transition Signal

וְהִנֵּה appears surprisingly **often** as a transition signal in the **narration** context,[9] although it actually has a deictic function (→ § 52.4).

וַיָּסֻרוּ שָׁם לָבוֹא לָלוּן בַּגִּבְעָה וַיָּבֹאוּ וַיֵּשְׁבוּ בִּרְחוֹב הָעִיר וְאֵין אִישׁ מְאַסֵּף־אוֹתָם הַבַּיְתָה לָלוּן: וְהִנֵּה אִישׁ זָקֵן בָּא מִן־מַעֲשֵׂהוּ מִן־הַשָּׂדֶה בָּעֶרֶב (Judges 19:15f.)	a	And they turned aside there in order to enter and lodge in Gibeah, entered, and sat down in the open square of the city. But no one took them into his house to spend the night. Finally an old man was coming out of the field from his work at evening.
וַיְהִי בָעֶרֶב וַיִּקַּח [לָבָן] אֶת־לֵאָה בִתּוֹ וַיָּבֵא אֹתָהּ אֵלָיו וַיָּבֹא אֵלֶיהָ: ... וַיְהִי בַבֹּקֶר וְהִנֵּה־הִיא לֵאָה (Genesis 29:23, 25)	b	In the evening (Laban) took his daughter Leah, and brought her to him; and he went in to her. ... It came about in the morning, however— what must he have seen—yes it was Leah!
וַיִּשָּׂא אַבְרָהָם אֶת־עֵינָיו וַיַּרְא וְהִנֵּה־אַיִל אַחַד נֶאֱחַז בַּסְּבַךְ בְּקַרְנָיו (Genesis 22:13)	c	Abraham (raising his eyes) raised his eyes and looked, (you imagine!) behind him a ram caught in the thicket by his horns.

High Points

As a transition signal, וְהִנֵּה stands before high points and **turning points** of the narrative. It can adopt there almost the function of וַיְהִי (a).

Its originally **deictic** character is suitable to introduce וְהִנֵּה clauses, which contain representations of persons out of the narrative (b, c). Through וְהִנֵּה the hearer/reader is instructed to imagine the following as if he saw it with the **eyes of the person** from the narrative. Accordingly the combination וַיַּרְא וְהִנֵּה frequently occurs. In most cases a nominal clause with a **participle** follows וְהִנֵּה.

---

9   In Genesis and Exodus, e.g., in ca. 75% of all cases.

Dream Narratives

וַיְהִ֕י מִקֵּ֖ץ שְׁנָתַ֣יִם יָמִ֑ים וּפַרְעֹ֣ה חֹלֵ֔ם d וְהִנֵּ֖ה עֹמֵ֥ד עַל־הַיְאֹֽר׃ וְהִנֵּ֣ה מִן־הַיְאֹ֗ר עֹלֹת֙ שֶׁ֣בַע פָּר֔וֹת יְפ֥וֹת מַרְאֶ֖ה וּבְרִיאֹ֣ת בָּשָׂ֑ר וַתִּרְעֶ֖ינָה בָּאָֽחוּ׃ וְהִנֵּ֞ה שֶׁ֧בַע פָּר֣וֹת אֲחֵר֗וֹת עֹל֤וֹת אַחֲרֵיהֶן֙ מִן־הַיְאֹ֔ר רָע֖וֹת מַרְאֶ֑ה ... וַיִּישָׁ֕ן וַיַּחֲלֹ֖ם שֵׁנִֽית וְהִנֵּ֣ה ׀ שֶׁ֣בַע שִׁבֳּלִ֗ים עֹל֛וֹת ... וַיִּיקַ֖ץ פַּרְעֹ֑ה וְהִנֵּ֥ה חֲלֽוֹם׃ (Genesis 41:1ff.)	After two full days that Pharaoh had a dream. (And see) It was him as he was standing by the Nile. (And see) He saw, how from the Nile there came up seven cows, sleek and fat. They grazed in the marsh grass. (And see) He saw further how seven other cows came up after them from the Nile, bad in appearance … Then he fell asleep and dreamed a second time. (And see) And particularly he saw seven ears of grain coming up … Pharaoh awoke, (and see: a dream) and noticed that it was a dream.

The large number of uses of וְהִנֵּה introduces **discourse** features into a narrative. For the narrative of dreams, וְהִנֵּה is for that reason almost **genre-**[*Gattung-*]**typical** (d, → also in § 48.6: Gen 37:5f.).

54.4 Conclusion Signals

Although they are a great deal less common, there are also conclusion signals, in particular in dialogue and in narrative.

Particular **genres** [*Gattungen*] call for elements with them, e.g. נְאֻם יְהוָה "Saying of YHWH" at the end of the words of prophets.[10] Narratives of prophets often end with a hint afterward that all is done just as Yhwh "has spoken" (דבר) it, → below on 1Kg 14:18.

Nominal Clauses

Now and then at the end of narratives or narrative-strands, framing **nominal clauses** appear (→ § 44.2 on Gen 2:4). Frequently the reader learns at the end

---

10 In the Latter Prophets, נְאֻם יהוה also stands very often in the middle of prophetic speeches.

of a narrative that particular conditions continue עַד הַיּוֹם הַזֶּה "up to the present day" (→ § 52.5, text a, on 2Kg 2:22).

וַיִּקְבְּרוּ אֹתוֹ וַיִּסְפְּדוּ־לוֹ כָּל־יִשְׂרָאֵל כִּדְבַר יְהוָה אֲשֶׁר דִּבֶּר בְּיַד־עַבְדּוֹ אֲחִיָּהוּ הַנָּבִיא: וְיֶתֶר דִּבְרֵי יָרָבְעָם ... הֲנָם כְּתוּבִים עַל־סֵפֶר דִּבְרֵי הַיָּמִים לְמַלְכֵי יִשְׂרָאֵל: (1 Kings 14:18f.)	And they buried him and mourned for him—all Israel—according to the word of YHWH, which He spoke through His servant Ahijah, the prophet. The rest of the acts of Jeroboam, however, ... they are yet written in the Book of the Chronicles of the Kings of Israel.

A clause on a **meta-level** can also appear as a conclusion signal. That is: It has been spoken about it outside of a narrative, and what has just or immediately been told is denoted as a "**Geschichte**" (hebr. דְּבָרִים).

However, most of the time, above all in the narrative cycle of Genesis and Exodus and in the books of Samuel and Kings, the end of a narrative is dictated in such a way that a **new one** simply **begins**.

Topical Index

Accents 06.3
Accusative 12.4, 50.1
   adverbial 50.2
   sign of accusative . . . . 11.4, 12.4, 13.4, 44.3 note, 44.4
Adhortative
   → Imperative with He cohortativum
Adjectives 16, 45.4, 46.3
Afformative Conjugation. 24.1, 27
   → also Perfect
Age, Statement of 45.4
Ajin-Ajin
   Nominals. . . . . 20 Note
   Verbs 42
Analysis Features
   nouns. 23
   verb stems 32.4
   weak verb. 43
Anaphoric
   = back-referencing 11.4, 52
Answers. 51.3
Aphaeresis
   = ending of Nun 36.3
   - of Waw 38.2
Apposition 46, 49.1
Aramaized Forms 41.6, 42.7
Article. 12.1, 12.3, 13.1, 15.2, 52.2
   → also Determination 45.2, 47.1, 52.5
Assimilation 12.4, 21.1, 30.3, 31.5, 33.2, 36.1, 36.4, 39.7

Atnách 06.3
Attribute 46.3, 49.1
  prepositional attributes 47.1
  attributive clause 53.4

Background/Foreground 44.2, 48.2, 48.3, 53.1
Basic Form
  → Segolata 18
Basic Stem
  → Qal 25–28
BeGaDKeFaT 01.3, 05.2
Beginnings
  of narratives 54.2
  of speeches 54.1
Binyan/Binyanim → Verb Stems
Budding Narratives 48.7
Bumaf 01.3, 13.1

Case 16.1
  - endings, old 16.3
Causal Clause 53.1, 53.3, 53.4
Causative Stems 29, 32
Chatef Vowels 04.1, 09.1, 09.4, 12.3, 13.1, 15.1
Chiasmus 51.4
Chireq 03.2
  - compaginis 16.3
Cholem 03.2
  - paragogicum 16.3
Citation, Ways of
  - Bible passages 06.3
  - verbs 24.4
Clause 44
  - introducer 13
  - elliptical 44.1, 51.3, 53.5
  - interrogative 51.3
  - position 44, 48, 51.4
  - types 44
  - types in the text 44.2
Cohortative 26.2, 51.4
Comparative (in German) 47.1
Compensatory Lengthening 09.2, 12.1, 12.4, 20, 34.1, 42.9

Concluding Signals 54.4
Conditional Clause 48.3, 53.3, 53.5
Confirmation 51.1, 53.3
Congruence 44.6
   - with numerals 46.3, 47.2
Conjunctions 44.2, 49.3, 53
Connecting Vowels 17.1, 33.2
Consecutive Clause → Result Clause
Consonants 01
   - quiescing → Vowel Letters
Construct Connection 16, 45
   - determination 52.5
   - replacement by "ו" 47.1
   - congruence 44.6
   - with prepositions and clauses 45.5
   - with numbers 47.2
Context 48.5, 48.7, 49.2, 51.4, 52.5
Contraction 02.2
Cursive Script → Written Script 01

Dagesch 05.2
   - forte as analysis feature 23.2, 43.1
   - forte coniunctivum 05.2
   - forte euphonicum 05.2
   - forte falls out . . . . 05.2, 09.2, 36.1 note
   - lene 05.2
Date, Statement of 47.2
Dative 50.3
   - "dativus ethicus" 50.3
Defective/Plene Writing 03.1
Deictic/Deixis
   = referring to the speech situation . . 11.4, 48.3, 48.7, 52.1, 52.4, 52.7, 54.3
Deletion Point 07.3
Demonstrative Pronouns 11.4, 11.5
Determination . . . . 44.3 note
   - → Article 52.5
   - in Construct Connection 45.2
Dialogue 44.2, 48.1, 48.3, 54.1
Distribution
   → Numbers 47.2
Double Questions 51.3, 53.5

Doubled Stems 31
- Hollow Roots 41.7
- Ayin-Ayin Verbs 42.8
Doubling. 05.2
- as analysis feature - verb. 43.1
- in monosyllabic nominals 20
- as characteristic of tense. 29.3, 31.2
- virtual 09.2
Dreams 48.6, 54.3
Dual 16.2, 17.2, 21.4, 23.1, 44.6

Elliptical (clauses) 44.1, 51.3, 53.5
Emphasis. 10, 17.1, 17.2

Feminine
- nouns 16.2, 23.1, 16.2
- for neuter 11.2
- pronouns. 11
- of Segolates 18.2
Figura etymologica 50.4
Final Clause 53.1
Foreground/Background 44.2, 48.2, 48.3

Gender
- of the noun 16.2
- of the verb 24.2
Genitive 45.1, 45.4, 47.2
Gutturals. 01.3, 01.9
- and article 12.1
- in nominals with doubling. 20
- after particles. 12.4, 13.2–4, 15.2
- in Segolates 18.2
- in verbs (strong). 34
-- Ayin-Ayin. 42.9
-- Ayin-Waw/Jod 41.9
-- Lamed-He 39.4
-- Pe-Nun. 36.1

Half Vowels. 02.1
→ also Schwa

He adhortativum . . . . 26.2 note
He cohortativum 26.2, 51.4
He interrogativum 13.3, 15.2, 51.3
He locale 16.3, 18.2, 23.1, 50.2
Helping Vowels 18, 39.3, 39.6
Hifʿil 29, 32
High Point
  - of the narrative 54.3
  - of the speech 54.1
Hireq → Chireq
Hištafʿel 39.6
Hitpaʿel 29, 31.1, 31.5
Hofʿal 29, 32.1, 32.3
Holem → Cholem
Hollow Roots 41
Homogeneous Vowels 03.1

i.C. = in Context 10.5
"If"-Clauses → Conditional Clause
Imperative(s) 26.1, 48.8, 49.2
  - with He cohortativum 26.2
  - weak 36.2, 36.3, 38.1, 38.2, 43.3
Imperfect 25.2, 25.3
  - class 24.1, 26, 31.2, 32.2
  - in speech context 48.3
  - in narrative 48.5
  - at the beginning of a clause 48.3, 51.4
Imperfect Consecutive
  → Narrativ
Infinitive 24.2, 28.1, 48.8
  absolute 28.1, 49.2, 50.4, 51.1
  - construct 28.1, 49.3, 50.5
    -- with suffixes 33.3, 49.3
    -- negated 49.3
Infinitive Verb Forms
  → Nominal Forms 24.2, 28
Intention 51.4
  → also Final Clause
Interrogative Word 51.3
  - particles 51.4, 53.5

Introductory Formulae 53.2
i.P. = in Pause 10.5

Jussive 26.2, 32.2, 39.3, 41.3

Kataphoric
  = forward referencing. 52.2, 52.5–7
Ketib and Qeré 07.1

Lamed
  - Alef 40
  - He. 39
  - Waw-Jod 18.4, 39.1
Laryngial → Guttural
Lengthening of Consonants . . . . 05.2 note
  - of vowels 02.2, 10.5, 24, 41.3, 42.2
Levels of Meaning. 52.2

Main Tenses . . . . 48.1 note
Mappiq. 05.1, 09.4, 34.4, 39.1
Maqqef. 06.2, 10.5
Masculine 11.1–2, 16.2, 24.2
Masora 07.3
Masoretes 03.2
Mater lectionis → Vowel Letters 03.1
Mediae a/e/o
  → Afformative Conjugation 27.3
Mediae geminatae
  → Ayin-Ayin Verbs 42
Mediae gutturalis
  → Verbs, strong with gutturals. 34.2
Metathesis (= transposition) 31.5
Meteg 06.1
Modal Verbs
  - in German translation 48.3, 51.4
  → also Verbs, relative
Modus. 26.2, 51

Narrating/Speaking. 48.1
  discursive narrating 48.6

Narrativ (= imperfect consecutive)...........................25.1, 48.2
  - chains 48.2
  - in discursive context 48.7
Narrative.. 44.5, 48
  beginnings... 54.2
  structure 54.3
  narrative endings 54.4
Negation.........................48.2, 28.8, 49.3, 51.2–4, 53.1, 53.5
Nesiga.. 10.5
Neuter.............................. 11.2, 11.4, 24.2 note
Nif'al...29, 30
  - with suffixes..31.3, note
Nominal Forms (Verb) 24.1, 28, 31.2
Nominal Groups..45–47
Nominal Clause 44
  - subject/predicate 44.3
  - infinitive as subject/predicate...................... 49.3
  - negated 51.2
  - with Waw copulativum 35.1
  - after "wayhi" 53.2
  - compound... 44.1
Nota accusativi → Sign of Accusative
Nota relationis → Schin prefix 13.2
Noun Companions 12
Nouns...16–23
  - analysis features 23
  - end consonant doubled 20, 23.2
  - number and gender 16.2
  - with suffixes..17
  - irregular..21
  - numerals 22
Nouns... (44–52)
  adverbial 50.2
  as subject/predicate 44.2, 49, 50
  as pronoun..52.3, 52.6
Numbers...16, 22
  - distribution ("je") 47.2
  - gender.. 47.2
  - congruence 47.2
  - compound... 47.2

Numerals. 01.1
Nun paragogicum 26.1

Oath Clause
- with "im". 53.5
- with "ki" 53.3
Object
- direct (accusative) 50.1
- remote (dative) 50.3
- pronominal → also Suffix
Object Clause 53.3, 53.4
Ordinal Numbers 22.3, 47.2

Parallel Stems 41.7, 42.8
Parasch 07.3
Particles. 11–15, 51–54
Participle. 28.2, 41.2, 44.3, 49.1, 50.4
- Qal active/passive 28.2
- Doubled Stems and Causative Stems 31.1–2
- with suffixes. 33.3
Passive. 29.4, 50.1, 50.3
- Hollow roots 41.2, 41.5
- Qal . . . . .28.2, 36.4 note
Past. 48
Pašta 06.3
Patach 03.2
- furtivum 03.2, 09.4, 34.4
Pause. 10.5
Pe-
- Alef 35
- Jod. 37
- Nun. 36
- Waw 38
Perfect. 27.2, 27.3
- in discursive context 48.3
- in narrated context 48.2
- with Waw copulativum 48.5
Perfect Class 24.1, 32.2
Perfect Consecutive. 27.4, 44.2, 48.3, 48.5
Performativ 48.3

Person, Change of 48.4
Personal Pronoun 11
Perspective. 48.2
 - back perspective. 48.2
 - forward perspective 48.3, 48.5
Pilel → Polel
Pilpel. . . . . .29.3, note
Place, Statement of 50.2, 54.2
 → also He locale
Plene/Defective Writing 03.1
Pluperfect → Pre-Past Tense
Poʻel, Poʻal, Hitpoʻel 42.8
Polel (or Pilel), Polal, Hitpolel. 41.7
Predicate
 - in nominal clause. 44.3, 49.1
 - in verbal clause 44.5
 - in compound nominal clause. 44.4
 - predicate nominative 49.1
Preformative . . . . 24.1, 25.2, 25.3, 32.1, note
Preformative Conjugation 24.1, 25
 → also Imperfect
Prepositions. 12, 47.1, 50.3
 - with "ʼašer" 53.4
 - with the infinitive 49.5, 50.5
 - after status constructus 45.5
 - instead of status constructus 45.2
 - after "wayhi" 53.4
Present 48.3
 - historic 48.5
Preterite. 25.1, 48.2
Proper Names 45.2
 - determination 44.3, 46.3, 52.5
Primae gutturalis
 → Verbs, strong, with gutturals 34.1
Proclitic. 12.1, 15.1
 - article 12.1
 - prepositions. 12.3, 15.1
 - particles in front of chatef-vowel 09.3
Pronouns. 11
 - adjectival/substantival 11.4, 11.5

- with apposition 46.1
- demonstrative 11.4, 11.5
- as object → suffix
- personal..11.2, 11.5
- as subject/predicate 44.3–5
- indefinite.. 52.6
Pronomilization. 52.3
Pu'al 29, 31.4
Punctuation. 03.2
Pre-Tone Syllable. 10.1
Pre-Tone Vowels 10.1
Pre-Past (pluperfect) .... 48.2 note
Prohibition 51.2, 51.4

Qames.. 03.2
- chatuf .... 03.2, 08.4, 09 note, 34.2 note
Qeré and Ketib 07.1
- perpetuum... 07.2
Qibbus 03.2
Questions 51.3
- with "ha" (He interrogativum)........................ 13.3
- with "im" (אם)..................................... 53.5
- indirect 53.5
- pronouns... 13.4
- rhetorical.......................................51.3, 52.4
- before "we" 53.1
Quiescent consonants → Vowel letters

Radical 24.1
Rafé.. 05.2
Reduction of Vowels 02.2
References in the Text 52
Reflexive 29.3, 33.1
Relative Clause 53.4
- with article 52.5
- German translation for participle................... 49.1
Relative Particle..................................... 53.4
= Schin Prefix...................................... 13.2
Re-Nominalizing....................................... 52.3
→ also Pronominalization

Request 48.3, 51.4
   negative 51.2
   → also Imperative
Result 48.3
   Consecutive Clause 53.1, 53.4
   Narrative Result. 48.2
Root 24.1, 24.4
   - Hollow 41

Schin prefix. 13.2
Schureq. 03.2
Schwa 04
   - compositum 04.1
   - mobile. 04.1
   - quiescens. 04.2
   - mobile or quiescens: difference 04.3
Secondary Stress/Tone. 06.1
Sections in the Biblical Text. 07.3
Seder. 07.3
Segol. 03.2, 18.1
Segolatum 18, 23.1
Semantic
   = "the meaning in question". . . . . 48.1 note
   - levels of the text. 52.2
Seré. 03.2
Sharpening → Doubling. 05.2
Short Form Lamed-He 39.3
Sibilants 31.5
Silluq. 06.3
Singular
   - collective 44.6
   - with numbers 47.2
Sof pasuq. 06.3
Soferim 07.1
Sound Change. 02.2
Speaking/Narrating. 48.1
   discursive narrating 48.6
Speech Posture 48.1
Speech Situation → deictic, Deixis
Square Script. 01

Starting Signals 54
    - in dialogue. 54.1
    - in narrative 54.2
Status absolutus/constructus 16.1, 45.1
Stems of the Verb 24.1, 29
    Analysis Features 32.4
    Meanings. 29.4
    Names 29.3
    Summary. 29.2
Structure Signals 54
Subject/Predicate. 44.3, 44.4
Subordinate Clauses 44.2, 48.2
Substantive → Noun
Suffixes 11.1, 11.3
    - on the noun. 17
    - on the verb 33
    - on particles 12, 14
Superlative (in German) 52.5
Syllables
    - broken open 09.3
    - doubly closed. 08.3, 18
    - sharpened 08.3
    - closed 08.3
    - open 08.2

Temporal Clause 49.3, 53.3
Tense. 24.2, 25.1, 27.1, 48
    primary/secondary Tense 48.1, 48.3
    - in foreign context 48.5
    - transitions 48.4–7
Tense Change 48.4
Tertiae gutturalis
    → Verbs, strong, with gutturals 34.4
Tetragramm. . . . . 07.2 note, 12.3, 12.4
Text Grammar. . . . . 52ff.
Time, Statement of 50.2
    - at the beginning of narrative 54.2
    - in the infinitive with preposition 49.3
    - after "wayhi" 53.2

Tone Syllable. 10.1, 12.3, 13.3
Tone Withdrawal 25.4, 30.3, 37.2, 41.3
Transitions Signals. 54
Transposition = metathesis 31.5

Verb/Verbs. 24–43
   - analysis features of weak verbs 43
   - doubly weak 36.5, 39.7
   - weak 24.3, 35–43
      --Ajin-Waw/Jod 41
      --Ajin-Ajin 42
      --Lamed-Alef 40
      --Lamed-He 39
      --mediae geminatae = Ajin-Ajin 42
      --Pe-Alef. 35
      --Pe-Jod 37
      --Pe-Nun 36
      --Pe-Waw 38
      --two radicals 41–43
   - strong 24–34
   - strong with gutturals 34
   - relative. 50.5
Verbal Clause 44
   - "inverted" . . . . .44.1, note
   - after Waw copulativum 53.1
   - clause structure 44.5
   - negation 53.1
Verbal Nominals 49
Verbatim speech 48
   - introduced with "'ašer" 53.4
   - introduced with "ki" 53.3
Vowel Letters. 03.1
   - and punctuation 03.2
Vowels. 02–04
   - existence 02.1
   - homogeneous 03.1
   - changeable. 10, 17, 23.2
   - change of. 02.2
   - signs 03

Volitive 48.3, 51.4

Waw copulativum 48.5, 53.1
Wish 51.4

YHWH. 07.2

Zaqef. 06.3

Index of Hebrew Letters and Words

א 01.3, 03.1, 03.2, 05.2, 09, 35

אָב 21.1

אבד 29.4, 35

אבה 35, 39.7

אֲדֹנָי 07.2, 12.3, 13.1

אהב 35

אַהֲבָה 28.1

אֹהֶל 18.2

אָוֶן 18.3

אור . . . . 41.8 note

אָז 48.5, 52.3, 54.2

אָח 21.1

אֶחָד 22.1, 47.2, 52.6

אָחוֹת 21.1

אחז 35

אַחֲרֵי 12.2

אֵי, אַיֵּה 14, 51.3, 52.6

אֹיֵב . . . . 41.1 note

אַיִן, אֵין 14, 51.2

אִישׁ 21.2, 45.4, 47.2, 52.3, 52.6

אִישׁ ... אָחִיו 52.6

אִישׁ ... רֵעֵהוּ 52.6

אכל 35

אֶל 51.2, 51.4

אֶל־ 12.5

אֵלֶּה 11.4

אֱלֹהִים 07.2, 12.3, 13.1, 44.6

אֶלֶף 18.2, 22.2, 47.2

אִם 51.3, 51.4, 53.2, 53.5

אֵם 23.2

אמר 35, 28.4, 48.4

אֲנַחְנוּ 11.1

אָנֹכִי   אֲנִי 11.1, 52.4

אֲנָשִׁים 21.2

אסף 35

אסר 34.2

אפה 35

אֶרֶץ 18.2

אִשָּׁה 21.2

אֲשֶׁר 13.2, 44.2, 45.5, 48.2, 48.4, 50.3, 52.5, 53.4

אֵשֶׁת 21.2

אַתְּ . . . . 05.2 note, 11.1

אֵת . . . . accusative 12.4, 44.4, 46.1, 50.1, 50.2

אֵת . . . . preposition 12.4

אַתָּה 11.1, 52.4

אַתָּה יָדַעְתָּ . . . . 44.2 note, 54.1

אַתֶּם 11.1

אַתֵּן 11.1

ב 01.3, 05.2

בְּ 05.2, 12.3, 15.1, 49.3, 53.2

בָּא 41.8

בוא 41.8, 48.8

בוש 41.8

בִּי אֲדֹנִי 54.1

בין 41

בֵּין 12.2

בַּיִת, בֵּית 2.2, 18.3, 21.5

בִּלְתִּי 49.3

בֵּן 21.1, 45.4
בָּנוֹת 21.1
בָּנִים 21.1
בַּעַד 12.2
בַּעַל 45.4
בֹּקֶר 18
ברך 34.3
בֶּרֶךְ 18.2
בַּת 21.1
בָּתִּים 21.5

ג 01.3, 05.2
גדל . . . . 29.4, 33.1 note
גָּוַע . . . . 41.1 note
גַּל 39.3
גלה 39, 43.2, 43.3
גנב . . . . 29.4, 31.4 note
גַּשׁ, גֶּשֶׁת 36.3, 43.3

ד 01.3, 05.2, 31.5
דבר . . . . 31.3 note, 31.5
דָּבָר 10, 16.1, 17, 23.2, 52.3, 52.6
דָּם 10
דַּע, דַּעַת 38.4

ה 01.3, 03.1, 03.2
הַ, הָ, הֶ 13.3, 15.2, 51.3
⊙ הַ (הָ, הֶ) 12.1, 12.3, 15.2
הַגָּל, הֵגֵל 39.3
הִדַּבֵּר 31.5
הָהָר . . . . 12.1 note
הוּא, הִיא 11.1, 11.5, 46.3, 52.3, 52.4
הוּא 07.2
הוֹדוּ 39.7
הַט 39.7

הָיָה 39.6, 44.1, 49.1, 49.3

הַךְ 39.7

הֲלֹא 51.3

הלךְ 25.4, 38, 48.8, 50.4

הלל 29.3

הַלְלוּ־יָהּ 06.1

הַמְדַבְּרִים 06.1

הֵמָּה ,הֵם, הֵנָּה 11.1, 11.5

הֵן ,הִנֵּה 14, 52.4, 54.1

הִנִּיחַ 41.6, 43.1

הִצְטַדֵּק . . . . 31.5 note

הִשְׁתַּחֲוָה 39.6

הִשְׁתַּמֵּר 31.5

ו 01.3, 03.1, 03.2

וְ 13.1, 15.1, 45.3, 48.5, 53.1

וּ . . . . 08.1 note, 13.1

וֶ 13.1, 25.4

וַ 25.4

וְהָיָה 48.3, 53.2, 54.1

וְהִנֵּה 48.6, 54.1, 54.2

וַיְהִי . . . . 49.3, 52.5, 53.2, 54.2, m, 54.3

וַיְהִי־אוֹר 06.1

וַיֵּט ,וַיֵּט 39.7

וַיַּךְ 39.7

וַיַּרְא 04.2, 04.3, 39.6

וַיַּרְא וְהִנֵּה 54.3

וַיִּשְׁתַּחוּ 39.6

וְעַתָּה 48.3, 54.1

ז 31.5

זֶה ,זֹאת 11, 46.3, 48.7, 52.3, 52.4, 52.6

זָקֵן 10, 23.2

זֶרַע 18

ח 01.3, 05.2, 09
חדל 50.5
חוה 39.6
חיה 39.6
חכם 02.2, 04.3, 08.4
חָכְמָה 04.3, 08.4
חלל 50.5
חנה 39.4
חנן 42.9
חֵפֶץ 18.2
חֹק 20
חרה 39.4

ט 31.5
טוב . . . . 41.8 note
טֶרֶם 48.5

י 03.1
יבש 38
ידה 39.7
ידע 38.4
(אַתָּה) יָדַעְתָּ 44.2, 54.1
יהוה 07.2, 12.3, 12.4, 13.1
יִהְיֶה 06.1, 39.6
יוכל 38.6
יֹום 21.5, 47.2, 52.3, 52.4, 52.5, 53.2, 54.3
יֹורֵנִי 39.7
יַט, יֵט 39.7
יטב 02.2, 37
יָדְ 39.7
יכל 27.3
ילד . . . . 38.2, note
ילל . . . . 37 note
יָמִים 21.5

יָמָן . . . . .37 note

יָנַק . . . . .37 note

יָסַף 50.5

יָפֶה 19

יָצָא . . . . 38.6, 40.1 note, 43.2

יָצַת 38.3, 43.1

יָקַץ . . . . .37 note

יָרֵא 38.4, 51.2

יִרְאָה 28.1

יָרַד . . . . 38.2 note

יָרָה 39.7

יְרוּשָׁלַם 07.2

יָרַשׁ 38.4

יִשָּׂא 36.4

יֵשׁ 14

יָשַׁב 02.2, 38, 43.2, 43.3

יָשֵׁן . . . . .37 note

יָשַׁר . . . . .37 note

יָתַר . . . . .38 note

כ 01.3, 05.2

כְּ 05.2, 12.3, 15.1, 49.3, 53.2

כָּבֵד 25.3, 26.2, 28.1

כָּבֵד 02.2

כִּבֶּס . . . . 31.3 note

כֹּה 52.6

כִּי 44.2, 48.2, 51.1, 53.2, 53.3, 53.4

כֵּן 52.3

כְּלִי 21.5

כֵּלִים 21.5

כִּלְכֵּל . . . . 29.3 note

כִּפֶּר . . . . 31.3 note

כָּתַב 24.4, 25.4, 26.2, 27.4

לְ 12.3, 15.1, 45.3, 47.1, 47.2, 49.3, 50.3, 50.5

לֹא 44.2, 51.2, 51.3, 51.4, 53.5

לֵאמֹר 35.2, 52.6
לֵבָב 10, 20
לָבֵשׁ 29.4
לוֹ 51.4
לחם . . . . 33.1 note
לֶחֶם 18.2
לֵךְ, לֶכֶת 38.1, 43.3, 48.8
לָמָה 51.3
לְמַעַן 12.2
לקח 36.4

מ 01.3
מֵאָה 22.2, 47.2
מַה, מֶה 13.4, 51.3, 52.6
מהר 50.5
מות 41.8
מֶוֶת מות 02.2, 18.3
מִי 13.4, 51.3, 52.6
מִי יִתֵּן 51.4
מַיִם 21.4
מֶלֶךְ . . . . 05.2 note, 18
מַלְכָּה 18.2
מַלְכוּת 16.2
מַמְלָכָה 16.2
מִן, מ, מֶ 12.4, 12.6, 15.1, 47.1, 49.3, 50.3
מָסֹרָה . . . . 03.2, note
מצא 40
מִקְנֶה 19
מֵת 41.8

־נָא 51.4
נבא 36.5
נֶגֶד 12.2, 18.2
נגש 36, 43.3
נגע 36
נֶדֶר 18.2

נוּחַ 41.6, 41.9

נחל . . . . 33.1 note, 34.3

נחם 36.1

נטה 39.7

נכה 39.7

נִסְמָךְ . . . . 16.1 note

נַעַר 18.2

נפל 36, 43.1

נִפְרָד . . . . 16.1 note

נֶפֶשׁ 52.6

נקה 39.7

נשׂא 36.4, 36.5

נָשִׁים 21.2

נתן 36.4, 43.3

נָתַתְּ . . . . 05.2 note, 36.4

נָתַתְּ 36.4

ס 07.3, 31.5

סַב, סֹב 42.3, 43.3

סבב 42, 43

סְבִיבוֹת 12.2

סוּס 16.2, 17

סְמִיכוּת . . . . 16.1 note

סֵפֶר 18

ע 01.3, 05.2, 09

עבד 34.2

עַד 12.5

עוֹד 41.9

עוֹד 14

עַיִן 18.3

עִיר 21.5

עַל 12.5

עַם 20

עִם 12.4

עָרִים 21.5

עשׂה 39.4, 39.5

עֶשֶׂר עֶשְׂרֵה 22.1

עַשְׁתֵּי 22.1

עֵת 20

עַתָּה 52.4, 54.1

פ 01.3, 05.2, 07.3

פֶּה, פִּי 21.3

פֹּה 52.4

פַּח 20

פֶּן 51.4

פעל 24.3, 29.3

פְּרִי 18.4

צ 31.5, 38.3

צֵא, צֵאת 38.4, 43.1

צדק 31.5

צְדָקָה 17

קבר 29

קָדָשִׁים 18.2

קום 41, 43, 48.8

קַח, קַחַת 36.4, 43.3

קָטֹן 02.2

קלל 42.5

קָם 23.2, 41.2

קרא 40.1

קרה 40.1

ר 01.3, 05.2, 09

ראה 39.6, 43.2, 54.3

רֹאשׁ רָאשִׁים 02.2, 21.5

רְבִיעִי 22.3

רַע 20.2

רָעֶה 52.6

רעע 42.9

רֵשׁ ,רֶשֶׁת 39.4, 43.3

שׂ 03.2, 31.5

שָׂא ,שְׂאֵת 36.4, 36.5

שָׂדֶה 19

שֶׂה 21.3

שָׂפָה 16.2, 17.2

שַׂר 20.2

שׁ 03.2, 31.5

שֶׁ◌ 13.2, 53.4

שֵׁב ,שֶׁבֶת 38.1, 38.2, 43.3

שְׁבִית 16.2

שׁוב 50.5

שׁחה . . . . 39 note

שׁכם 50.5

שׁלח 16.2, 34.4

שׁלך 29.4

שָׁם 52.3

שֵׁם 10, 16, 17

שָׁמַיִם 21.4

שָׁמַע 54.1

שׁמר 29.4, 31.5

שָׁנָה 47

שפט 33.3

שָׁרָשִׁים 18.2

שְׁתַּיִם . . . . 04.3 note, 08.1 note, 22.1

ת 01.3, 05.2, 31.5

תֹּהוּ 18.4

תַּחַת 12.2

תמם 41.7

תֵּן 36.4, 43.3

תֵּת 36.4, 43.3

Index of Scripture Passages

Genesis

1:1	50.1a
1:1ff.	44.1
1:2	44.3a
1:2	49.1a
1:3	51.4a
1:4	50.3f
1:10	53.3g
1:24	16.3
1:31	46.3h
2:4	44.2, 54.4
2:18	49.3h
3:14	53.3h
3:19	44.3b
3:22	54.1b
4:2	46.1d
4:9	13.3
4:9	51.3a
4:17	49.1e
6:10	47.2d
8:3	50.4h
8:7	50.4g
8:10	50.5d
10:12	46.3d
11:29	44.6b
11:29	53.1a
12:1	50.3d
12:1f.	53.1g
12:3	49.1h
12:4	45.4g

12:11. . . . . 53.4e
12:11ff. 53.2a
12:14. . . . . 49.3b
12:16. . . . . 44.6d
13:1ff. 52.5b
13:2. . . . . 53.4c
13:16. . . . . 52.6b
13:16. . . . . 53.5b
14:19. . . . . 45.3e
15:3. . . . . 54.1a
17:5. . . . . .50.1f
17:17. . . . . 13.3
18:1f. 49.1b
18:1ff. 48.2a
18:2ff. 51.4e
18:5. . . . . .53.4f
18:15. . . . . 53.3b
18:20. . . . . 45.4a
18:20. . . . . 51.1
19:1. . . . . 47.2a
19:2. . . . . 53.3c
20:1ff. 52.3b
20:6. . . . . 44.5b
20:8. . . . . .46.3f
20:16. . . . . .47.2j
21:6. . . . . 50.5a
21:26. . . . . 51.2a
21:27. . . . . 50.3a
22:1. . . . . 53.2b
22:2. . . . . 47.2c
22:13. . . . . 54.3c
23:1. . . . . 47.2h
23:6. . . . . 49.3c
24:3. . . . . .45.3f
24:15ff. 50.5e
24:34. . . . . 44.3c
24:55. . . . . 51.4c
24:54ff. 48.4
25:34. . . . . 44.5a
26:9. . . . . 53.3a

26:31f. 52.4a
27:2f. 54.1c
27:20. . . . . 50.5b
29:5. . . . . 13.3
29:5f. 51.3e
29:23ff. 54.3b
30:29. . . . . 44.2c
32:6. . . . . 50.3b
32:10. . . . . 44.3d
32:12. . . . . 51.2g
37:5ff. 48.6c
37:16f. 52.4c
37:19. . . . . .45.4f
37:26. . . . . .53.3f
37:33. . . . . .50.4f
38:1. . . . . 54.2d
38:17. . . . . 53.5g
39 . . . . 54.3
39:9. . . . . 53.4d
41:1ff. 54.3d
42:9–14. . . . . 44.2b
42:15. . . . . .53.5i
42:30. . . . . .49.1f
43:31ff. 48.5a
44:16. . . . . 31:5 (note)
44:30ff. 48.3d
47:9. . . . . 45.3c
47:20ff. 48.5g
49:31. . . . . 44.5d
50:19ff. 54.1f

Exodus
2:1f. 54.2a
2:13f. 51.3h
3:1. . . . . 54.2b
3:3. . . . . 46.3g
4:10. . . . . 51.2d
7:11. . . . . 46.1b
11:5. . . . . 49.1d
13:7. . . . . 50.2d

18:25f. 48.5b
20:13ff. 51.4k
21:2. .... 53.3k
22:6. .... 52.6e
23:22. .... 41.1 (note)
24:18. .... 47.2i
31:6. ....45.4j
32:7. .... 48.8e

Leviticus
2:1f. 48.3f
19:1ff. 51.4j
19:3. .... 52.6c

Numbers
2:16. .... 47.2g
3:14. .... 45.4c
6:23f. 50.4b
13:3. .... 45.3b
13:17f. 51.3c
13:18. .... 13.3
14:2. ....51.4f
20:14ff. 54.1d
20:29. .... 41.1 (note)
23:19. .... 53.1h
34:2. .... 46.1a
35:19. .... 49.3g

Deuteronomy
2:25. .... 50.5c
2:35. .... 45.4b
4:40. ....53.4j
6:4ff. 48.3g
6:20ff. 48.7b
11:7. .... 46.3e
19:4f. 51.2e
26:1f. 53.2d
27:16. ....44.3f
28:67. .... 51.4g

Joshua

1:2. . . . . 46.1c
1:16ff. 48.3a
2:1. . . . . 53.1d
3:12. . . . . 47.2k
4:21f. 53.4k
5:13. . . . . .53.5f
7:22. . . . . 50.2c
23:1f. 54.2e
24:15. . . . . 50.1g
24:15. . . . . .51.4i

Judges

1:1. . . . . 48.3c
1:26. . . . . 50.2a
4:21. . . . . 52.5e
5:10. . . . . 45.5b
6:13. . . . . 13.2
6:14. . . . . .46.3i
7:4. . . . . 52.4b
9:5. . . . . 45.3a
9:8. . . . . 52.5c
12:5. . . . . 13.3, 51.3f
17:1ff. 52.2a, 52.3a, 52.7
18:26. . . . . 47.1c
19:15f. 54.3a

1 Samuel

2:4. . . . . 44.6e
3:7. . . . . 48.5e
3:17. . . . . 53.5h
10:3. . . . . 44.2a
10:25. . . . . 52.5d
11:1f. 52.6f
14:1. . . . . .52.5f
15:20. . . . . .53.4m
16:2. . . . . 48.3e
16:10. . . . . 47.2b
17:14. . . . . 53.1b

17:14. . . . . 52.5g
17:46f. 44.6a
18:15. . . . . .53.4l
19:11. . . . . .49.3f
20:2. . . . . 52.6d
21:15f. 51.3d
23:5. . . . . 17.2 (note)
24:12. . . . . .49.3j
24:21. . . . . 50.4c
25:1. . . . . 50.1d
26:15. . . . . 51.3g
31:12f. 50.1e

2 Samuel
3:24. . . . . 52.4d
6:1. . . . . 35.2 (note)
10:7. . . . . 46.2a
12:5. . . . . 53.3e
12:28. . . . . 51.4h
13:4. . . . . 44.4c
16:5. . . . . .50.4i
16:8. . . . . 45.4e
19:5. . . . . 50.2b
23:22. . . . . .47.2f

1 Kings
1:2. . . . . 46.2b
3:12. . . . . .53.4i
3:16. . . . . 48.5c
3:16f. 54.1h
3:18. . . . . 51.2c
3:19. . . . . 53.4h
5:10. . . . . .45.4d, 47.1d
5:16ff. 54.1i
8:23f. 48.7a
11:6. . . . . 47.1a
11:17. . . . . 53.1c
11:25. . . . . 53.4b
13:20. . . . . 53.2c
14:1f. 54.2c

14:18f. 54.4
14:19. . . . . 45.3d
18:31f. 50.1h
21:19. . . . . 45.5c
22:21ff. 54.1e

2 Kings
1:2. . . . . 51.3b, 53.5e
2:18ff. 52.5a, 54.5
3:26. . . . . 44.6c
4:9. . . . . 46.3c
6:14. . . . . 50.1b
7:6. . . . . 49.3a
13:14. . . . . 48.5d

Isaiah
1:2f. 44.2d
1:10. . . . . 54.1g
1:17. . . . . 50.4a
3:1. . . . . 44.2e
6:1ff. 48.6b
6:11. . . . . .51.2f
6:8f. 48.8a
7:8. . . . . 50.3e
9:2. . . . . 45.5a
9:5. . . . . 44.5c
11:9. . . . . 50.1c
11:10. . . . . 53.2e
14:12. . . . . 33.1 (note)
16:5. . . . . 48.8b
40:1f. 48.8d
43:4. . . . . 53.4g
43:25. . . . . 44.4b
66:1f. 52.4e

Jeremiah
1:16. . . . . 53.4a
2:1f. 48.8c
7:1f. 48.3h
10:10. . . . . 44.3e

19:1..49.2a
19:15...49.3d
23:17...50.4e
23:33ff..52.6a
36:27...49.3e

Ezekiel
2:6...51.2b

Hosea
1:2...45.5d
4:1f..49.2b
11:1..53.3j

Jonah
1:3ff...48.2b
1:13..48.2c
4:5...48.5f

Zechariah
7:1...47.2l

Psalms
3:1...47.1b
5:12..49.1g
6:3...53.3i
8:2ff...52.2b
11:4..44.4a
60:13...53.1e
81:9..53.5d
95:3–5..44.2f
104:20..51.4b
104:29..35.2 (note)
109:3...33.1 (note)
109:..49.3i
116:26..48.3b
127:1...49.1c
132:2..13.2
149:1ff...51.4d

Job
9:15. . . . . 53.5c
37:2. . . . . 50.4d
31:18. . . . . 33.1 (note)

Proverbs
6:23f. 45.4h
9:12. . . . . 53.5a
14:20. . . . . 50.3c
24:14. . . . . .53.1f

Qoheleth
4:10. . . . . 13.2

Ruth
1:10. . . . . 53.3d
4:9. . . . . 41.4 (note)

Nehemiah
9:13. . . . . .45.4i

1 Chronicles
25:5. . . . . 47.2e
25:14f. 48.6a

STUDIES IN BIBLICAL HEBREW

Dennis R. Magary
General Editor

Studies in Biblical Hebrew is a series of monographs designed to promote and publish topical research into the Hebrew of the Old Testament. The focus of the series is specifically the corpus of the Hebrew Bible, since the composition and compilation of these writings continue to generate major interest worldwide for reasons historical and academic, as well as religious. The series is devoted to fresh philological, syntactical, and linguistic study of the language of the Hebrew canon, with the subsidiary aim of displaying the contribution of such study to informed and accurate exegesis. Research into the broader evidence of the period, including inscriptional materials, is welcome, provided the results are cast in terms of their particular bearing upon Biblical (classical) Hebrew.

For additional information about this series or for the submission of manuscripts, please contact:

Peter Lang Publishing
Acquisitions Department
29 Broadway, 18th floor
New York, NY 10006

To order other books in this series, please contact our Customer Service Department:

800-770-LANG (within the U.S.)
212-647-7706 (outside the U.S.)
212-647-7707 FAX

Or browse online by series at:

www.peterlang.com